Interactions 2

READING

Pamela Hartmann

Elaine Kirn

Lawrence J. Zwier
Contributor, Focus on Testing

Pamela Hartmann
Reading Strand Leader

McGraw
Hill

Interactions 2 Reading, Silver Edition

ISBN 13: 978-0-07-340635-0 (Student Book)
ISBN 10: 0-07-340635-X
  2 3 4 5 6 7 8 9 10 VNH 11 10 09 08

ISBN 13: 978-0-07-333197-3 (Student Book with Audio Highlights)
ISBN 10: 0-07-333197-X
1 2 3 4 5 6 7 8 9 10 VNH 11 10 09 08 07 06

Editorial director: Erik Gundersen
Series editor: Valerie Kelemen
Developmental editor: Terre Passero
Production manager: Juanita Thompson
Production coordinator: Vanessa Nuttry
Cover designer: Robin Locke Monda
Interior designer: Nesbitt Graphics, Inc.
Artist: Kay McCabe
Photo researcher: Photoquick Research
Maps: Mapping Specialists LTD

The credits section for this book begins on page 248 and is considered an extension of the copyright page.

Cover photo: Bob Krist/Corbis

McGraw-Hill

www.esl-elt.mcgraw-hill.com

The McGraw·Hill Companies

A Special Thank You

The Interactions/Mosaic Silver Edition team wishes to thank our extended team: teachers, students, administrators, and teacher trainers, all of whom contributed invaluably to the making of this edition.

Macarena Aguilar, **North Harris College**, Houston, Texas ■ Mohamad Al-Alam, **Imam Mohammad University**, Riyadh, Saudi Arabia ■ Faisal M. Al Mohanna Abaalkhail, **King Saud University**, Riyadh, Saudi Arabia; Amal Al-Toaimy, **Women's College, Prince Sultan University**, Riyadh, Saudi Arabia ■ Douglas Arroliga, **Ave Maria University**, Managua, Nicaragua ■ Fairlie Atkinson, **Sungkyunkwan University**, Seoul, Korea ■ Jose R. Bahamonde, **Miami-Dade Community College**, Miami, Florida ■ John Ball, **Universidad de las Americas**, Mexico City, Mexico ■ Steven Bell, **Universidad la Salle**, Mexico City, Mexico ■ Damian Benstead, **Sungkyunkwan University**, Seoul, Korea ■ Paul Cameron, **National Chengchi University**, Taipei, Taiwan R.O.C. ■ Sun Chang, **Soongsil University**, Seoul, Korea ■ Grace Chao, **Soochow University**, Taipei, Taiwan R.O.C. ■ Chien Ping Chen, **Hua Fan University**, Taipei, Taiwan R.O.C. ■ Selma Chen, **Chihlee Institute of Technology**, Taipei, Taiwan R.O.C. ■ Sylvia Chiu, **Soochow University**, Taipei, Taiwan R.O.C. ■ Mary Colonna, **Columbia University**, New York, New York ■ Lee Culver, **Miami-Dade Community College,** Miami, Florida ■ Joy Durighello, **City College of San Francisco**, San Francisco, California ■ Isabel Del Valle, **ULATINA**, San Jose, Costa Rica ■ Linda Emerson, **Sogang University**, Seoul, Korea ■ Esther Entin, **Miami-Dade Community College**, Miami, Florida ■ Glenn Farrier, **Gakushuin Women's College**, Tokyo, Japan ■ Su Wei Feng, Taipei, Taiwan R.O.C. ■ Judith Garcia, **Miami-Dade Community College**, Miami, Florida ■ Maxine Gillway, **United Arab Emirates University**, Al Ain, United Arab Emirates ■ Colin Gullberg, **Soochow University**, Taipei, Taiwan R.O.C. ■ Natasha Haugnes, **Academy of Art University**, San Francisco, California ■ Barbara Hockman, **City College of San Francisco**, San Francisco, California ■ Jinyoung Hong, **Sogang University**, Seoul, Korea ■ Sherry Hsieh, **Christ's College**, Taipei, Taiwan R.O.C. ■ Yu-shen Hsu, **Soochow University**, Taipei, Taiwan R.O.C. ■ Cheung Kai-Chong, **Shih-Shin University**, Taipei, Taiwan R.O.C. ■ Leslie Kanberg, **City College of San Francisco**, San Francisco, California ■ Gregory Keech, **City College of San Francisco**, San Francisco, California ■ Susan Kelly, **Sogang University**, Seoul, Korea ■ Myoungsuk Kim, **Soongsil University**, Seoul, Korea ■ Youngsuk Kim, **Soongsil University**, Seoul, Korea ■ Roy Langdon, **Sungkyunkwan University**, Seoul, Korea ■ Rocio Lara, **University of Costa Rica**, San Jose, Costa Rica ■ Insung Lee, **Soongsil University**, Seoul, Korea ■ Andy Leung, **National Tsing Hua University**, Taipei, Taiwan R.O.C. ■ Elisa Li Chan, **University of Costa Rica**, San Jose, Costa Rica ■ Elizabeth Lorenzo, **Universidad Internacional de las Americas**, San Jose, Costa Rica ■ Cheryl Magnant, **Sungkyunkwan University**, Seoul, Korea ■ Narciso Maldonado Iuit, **Escuela Tecnica Electricista**, Mexico City, Mexico ■ Shaun Manning, **Hankuk University of Foreign Studies**, Seoul, Korea ■ Yoshiko Matsubayashi, **Tokyo International University**, Saitama, Japan ■ Scott Miles, **Sogang University**, Seoul, Korea ■ William Mooney, **Chinese Culture University**, Taipei, Taiwan R.O.C. ■ Jeff Moore, **Sungkyunkwan University**, Seoul, Korea ■ Mavelin de Moreno, **Lehnsen Roosevelt School**, Guatemala City, Guatemala ■ Ahmed Motala, **University of Sharjah**, Sharjah, United Arab Emirates ■ Carlos Navarro, **University of Costa Rica**, San Jose, Costa Rica ■ Dan Neal, **Chih Chien University**, Taipei, Taiwan R.O.C. ■ Margarita Novo, **University of Costa Rica**, San Jose, Costa Rica ■ Karen O'Neill, **San Jose State University**, San Jose, California ■ Linda O'Roke, **City College of San Francisco**, San Francisco, California ■ Martha Padilla, **Colegio de Bachilleres de Sinaloa,** Culiacan, Mexico ■ Allen Quesada, **University of Costa Rica**, San Jose, Costa Rica ■ Jim Rogge, **Broward Community College**, Ft. Lauderdale, Florida ■ Marge Ryder, **City College of San Francisco**, San Francisco, California ■ Gerardo Salas, **University of Costa Rica**, San Jose, Costa Rica ■ Shigeo Sato, **Tamagawa University**, Tokyo, Japan ■ Lynn Schneider, **City College of San Francisco**, San Francisco, California ■ Devan Scoble, **Sungkyunkwan University**, Seoul, Korea ■ Maryjane Scott, **Soongsil University**, Seoul, Korea ■ Ghaida Shaban, **Makassed Philanthropic School**, Beirut, Lebanon ■ Maha Shalok, **Makassed Philanthropic School**, Beirut, Lebanon ■ John Shannon, **University of Sharjah**, Sharjah, United Arab Emirates ■ Elsa Sheng, **National Technology College of Taipei**, Taipei, Taiwan R.O.C. ■ Ye-Wei Sheng, **National Taipei College of Business**, Taipei, Taiwan R.O.C. ■ Emilia Sobaja, **University of Costa Rica**, San Jose, Costa Rica ■ You-Souk Yoon, **Sungkyunkwan University**, Seoul, Korea ■ Shanda Stromfield, **San Jose State University**, San Jose, California ■ Richard Swingle, **Kansai Gaidai College**, Osaka, Japan ■ Carol Sung, **Christ's College**, Taipei, Taiwan R.O.C. ■ Jeng-Yih Tim Hsu, **National Kaohsiung First University of Science and Technology**, Kaohsiung, Taiwan R.O.C. ■ Shinichiro Torikai, **Rikkyo University**, Tokyo, Japan ■ Sungsoon Wang, **Sogang University**, Seoul, Korea ■ Kathleen Wolf, **City College of San Francisco**, San Francisco, California ■ Sean Wray, **Waseda University International**, Tokyo, Japan ■ Belinda Yanda, **Academy of Art University**, San Francisco, California ■ Su Huei Yang, **National Taipei College of Business**, Taipei, Taiwan R.O.C. ■ Tzu Yun Yu, **Chungyu Institute of Technology**, Taipei, Taiwan R.O.C.

Author Acknowledgements

This edition is dedicated to Beatrice Hartmann,
an inspiration and buoy.

— Pamela Hartmann

Table of Contents

Introducing Interactions/Mosaic Silver Edition

NEW to the Silver Edition:

- **World's most popular and comprehensive academic skills series**—thoroughly updated for today's global learners
- **Full-color design** showcases compelling instructional photos to strengthen the educational experience
- **Enhanced focus on vocabulary building, test taking, and critical thinking skills** promotes academic achievement
- **New strategies and activities for the TOEFL® iBT** build invaluable test taking skills
- **New "Best Practices" approach** promotes excellence in language teaching

NEW to Interactions 2 Reading:

- **All new content:** Chapter 10 Ceremonies
- **Enhanced design**—featuring larger type and 50% more instructional photos—ensures effective classroom usage
- **Transparent chapter structure**—with consistent part headings, activity labeling, and clear guidance—strengthens the academic experience:
  Part 1: Reading Skills and Strategies
  Part 2: Reading Skills and Strategies
  Part 3: Building Vocabulary and Study Skills
  Part 4: Focus on Testing
- **Dynamic vocabulary acquisition program**—systematic vocabulary introduction and practice ensures students will interact meaningfully with each target word at least four times.
- **New focus on vocabulary from the Academic Word List** offers additional practice with words students are most likely to encounter in academic texts.
- **Line numbering and paragraph lettering** in reading passages allows students and teachers to easily find the information referred to in activities.
- **Expanded audio program** includes all reading selections, vocabulary words, and selected listening activities to accelerate reading fluency.
- **New *Vocabulary index*** equips student and instructors with chapter-by-chapter lists of target words.

---

* TOEFL is a registered trademark of Educational Testing Service (ETS). This publication is not endorsed or approved by ETS.

Interactions/Mosaic
Best Practices

Our Interactions/Mosaic Silver Edition team has produced an edition that focuses on Best Practices, principles that contribute to excellent language teaching and learning. Our team of writers, editors, and teacher consultants has identified the following six interconnected Best Practices:

Making Use of Academic Content

Materials and tasks based on academic content and experiences give learning real purpose. Students explore real world issues, discuss academic topics, and study content-based and thematic materials.

Organizing Information

Students learn to organize thoughts and notes through a variety of graphic organizers that accommodate diverse learning and thinking styles.

Scaffolding Instruction

A scaffold is a physical structure that facilitates construction of a building. Similarly, scaffolding instruction is a tool used to facilitate language learning in the form of predictable and flexible tasks. Some examples include oral or written modeling by the teacher or students, placing information in a larger framework, and reinterpretation.

Activating Prior Knowledge

Students can better understand new spoken or written material when they connect to the content. Activating prior knowledge allows students to tap into what they already know, building on this knowledge, and stirring a curiosity for more knowledge.

Interacting with Others

Activities that promote human interaction in pair work, small group work, and whole class activities present opportunities for real world contact and real world use of language.

Cultivating Critical Thinking

Strategies for critical thinking are taught explicitly. Students learn tools that promote critical thinking skills crucial to success in the academic world.

Highlights of Interactions 2 Reading Silver Edition

Full-color design showcases compelling instructional photos to strengthen the educational experience.

Interacting with Others
Questions and topical quotes stimulate interest, activate prior knowledge, and launch the topic of the unit.

Chapter

10

Ceremonies

Connecting to the Topic

1 What do you think these people are celebrating? Why?

2 Name ten adjectives to describe this photo.

3 What are some of your favorite ceremonies or celebrations? Describe one of them.

In This Chapter

When did you last go to a wedding? What was it like? The first reading selection explores universal rituals called "rites of passage." Weddings are just one type of rite of passage. Funerals and graduations are other types. In Part 2, you will read about and discuss modern variations on traditional rituals. There are unique ways that cultures all around the world are celebrating and marking rites of passage. You will be able to discuss some of your favorite ceremonies. Part 3 includes activities to help you develop and build your vocabulary. The final part of this chapter focuses on comprehension of a reading selection that deals with a rite of passage that many teenagers anticipate—driving.

❝ When humans participate in ceremony, they enter a sacred space. Everything outside of that space shrivels in importance. Time takes on a different dimension. **❞**

—Sun Bear
Medicine Chief of the Bear Tribe Medicine Society (1929–1992)

Activating Prior Knowledge
Prereading activities place the reading in context and allow the student to read actively. ●

Making Use of Academic Content
Magazine articles, textbook passages, essays, and website articles explore stimulating topics of interest to today's students. ●

Part 1 Reading Skills and Strategies

Global Trade

Before You Read

1 Previewing the Topic In small groups, discuss these questions.

1. Look at all of the things around the room. What countries are the products from? (Include the clothing that you're wearing.)
2. What might be some reasons for the economic success of some cities (such as Dubai) and countries (such as Singapore)?
3. What might be some reasons for economic failure in other countries?
4. How can geography help or hurt a country's economy?

2 Previewing Vocabulary Read the words and phrases below. Listen to the pronunciation of each word. Put a check mark (✓) next to the words you know. For the words that you don't know, *don't* use a dictionary.

Nouns	Verbs	Idioms and Expressions
❑ benefits	❑ obstacle	❑ contribute	❑ goes without
❑ consumers	❑ priority	❑ created	saying
❑ fuel	❑ protectionist policies	❑ reduce	❑ in turn
❑ gap	(policy)		
❑ goods	❑ soil	**Adjectives**	
❑ harbor	❑ standards	❑ economic	
❑ infotech (information	❑ subsidy	❑ global	
technology)	❑ tide	❑ landlocked	
❑ infrastructure		❑ startling	
❑ nutrients		❑ tropical	

3 Previewing Look over the reading on pages 119–121. Discuss these questions.

1. What is the topic of the whole reading? (Look at the title of the reading.)
2. What are the five subtopics? (Look at the headings of each paragraph.)
3. Which workers in the photos probably have the highest yearly income?

Read

4 Reading the Article As you read the following selection, think about the answer to this question: *What seems to be the key to a country's economic success?*

Read the selection. Do not use a dictionary. Then do the exercises that follow the reading.

Global Trade

A For the first time in history, almost the entire world is now sharing the same economic system. Communism began to fall in the late 1980s, and since then, capitalism has spread to most corners of the world. The basis of a "pure" capitalist economy is free trade, also called "open trade." There are **benefits** of open trade for both rich and poor countries. For developed countries such as Japan and England, free trade brings with it more competition, which **in turn** brings advantages such as lower prices and more choices of products for **consumers**. For developing countries, open trade means that people have access to essential **goods** such as food, clothing, and **fuel** (for transportation and heat). An open economic system can be a key to improving the lives of people in both poor and rich countries because it can **reduce** poverty and improve living conditions.

▲ Boats and ships in Hong Kong harbor ▲ Factory workers in India

"Leaking Boats"

B This is apparently very good news. Optimists often say that "the rising **tide** lifts all boats." What do they mean by this? Imagine a **harbor** filled with boats—some small ones, some medium-sized, and some huge ships. As the ocean tide comes in every twelve hours, the water rises and literally lifts all boats—both large and small. In economics, this expression means that in good economic times, poor countries benefit as much as rich countries do. However, pessimists point out that many of the "small boats" seem to be "leaking"—have holes in them—and so are going down instead of up. In other words, the **gap** between rich and poor—the economic difference between them—is wider than it was in the past. The contrast can be **startling**. A former U.S. president, Jimmy Carter, once put it this way: "Globalization, as defined by rich people, . . . is a very nice thing. . . . You are

Scaffolding Instruction
Instruction and practice with reading skills helps students increase their reading fluency.

Cultivating Critical Thinking
Enhanced focus on critical thinking skills promotes academic achievement.

---

7 Finding the Main Idea Read the sentences below and select the one main idea of the whole reading selection.

- (A) Workaholism can lead to serious problems, but it can also create a happy life.
- (B) Job hopping is a new trend that causes stress but can also lead people into good work experiences if they learn new job skills.
- (C) It is important for people to be flexible in this changing world of work and to continue their education because they may need to change jobs several times in their lifetime.
- (D) The world economy, globalization, and technology are causing many changes in the way people work today.
- (E) In the workplace today, new technology is making it possible for people to work in different locations, even from home.

8 Comprehension Check: Finding Important Details Which statements are true about work today, according to the reading? Check (✓) them.

1. _____ People probably need to be prepared to change jobs several times in their lifetimes.
2. _____ Decreasing manufacturing jobs and increasing use of outsourcing are leading to less job security today than in the past.
3. _____ Lack of job security is always a bad thing.
4. _____ People who can change to fit a new situation are usually happier than people who can't.
5. _____ Many people find a sense of self through their work.
6. _____ People in some professions move from job to job more often than people in other professions.
7. _____ Technology is making work life better for everyone.
8. _____ Telecommuters don't need to drive to the office every day.
9. _____ All workaholics have problems with stress.
10. _____ The most successful people are workaholics.

9 Checking Vocabulary Find a word or expression in the reading for each definition below.

1. people who give advice about professions and careers = _____
2. the feeling that a worker will never lose his or her job = _____
3. the movement of jobs to places with lower salaries = _____
4. changing from one job to another = _____
5. disadvantage = _____

Critical Thinking: Recognizing Cause and Effect
In Chapters 1, 2, and 3 you saw three types of graphic organizers. Another use of a graphic organizer is to show causes (or reasons) effects (or results). This graphic organizer shows the relationship between different actions such as why something happens or the result of an action.

10 Critical Thinking: Recognizing Cause and Effect Paragraph B presents several causes and effects. Look back at Paragraph B and find information to complete this graphic organizer.

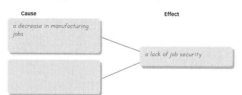

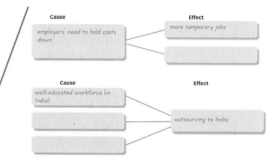

Organizing Information
Graphic organizers provide tools for organizing information and ideas.

Part 3 — Building Vocabulary and Study Skills

1 Focusing on Words from the Academic Word List Fill in the blanks with words from the Academic Word List in the box. When you finish, turn back to page 75, Paragraph B, and check your answers.

areas	economy	jobs	traditionally
benefits	enormous	labor	varies
computer	job	secure	
creating	job security	temporary	

The situation ___*varies*___ from country to country, but in today's ___2___, there is generally less job security worldwide. Even in Japan, where people ___3___ had a very ___4___ job for life, there is now no promise of a lifetime ___5___ with the same company. One reason for the lack of ___6___ is the worldwide decrease in manufacturing ___7___. Another reason is employers' need to hold down costs. This has resulted in two ___8___ changes for the workforce. First, employers are ___9___ more and more ___10___ jobs because they don't need to pay health insurance or other ___11___ to employees in these positions, as they would to people in permanent posts. Second, more and more companies are outsourcing. In other words, they are closing offices and factories and sending work to other ___12___ of the country or to other countries where ___13___ is cheaper. This happens with factory work and ___14___ programming. Also, the call center industry is on the move—mostly to India.

8 Searching the Internet Search the Internet for one of the topics below. Explore one website and find something that interests you. Share this with a small group.

Choose from these topics:

- tours of the Silk Road
- the meaning of tattooing or scarification among tribal peoples
- *mehndi* designs in different cultures
- the latest fashions in "body art" these days

Part 4 — Focus on Testing

TOEFL® iBT

QUESTIONS ABOUT BASIC COMPREHENSION
In the Focus on Testing section of Chapter 1, the three types of reading questions on the TOEFL® Internet-Based Test (iBT) are listed. One type is the *basic comprehension question*, which focuses on the understanding of facts, what facts mean, and how language ties one fact to others. You must understand not only words and phrases but entire groups of sentences. You must also be able to find main ideas and recognize how they are supported in the reading.

Vocabulary questions make up 20 to 25 percent of all TOEFL® iBT reading questions. These are considered *basic comprehension questions*. To answer them, you have to understand the context, not just the words themselves.

1 Practice Read again the Focus on Testing reading selection in Chapter 7, "As English Spreads, Speakers Morph It into World Tongue," on pages 164–165. Answer the basic-comprehension questions below. You may refer to the reading as often as you want. Try to answer all five questions in five minutes or less.

1. Which pair names groups that, according to the article, both dislike the spread of "Englishes" around the world?
   - Ⓐ purists and multiculturalists
   - Ⓑ native speakers and nonnative speakers
   - Ⓒ businesspersons and linguists
   - Ⓓ linguists and multiculturalists

2. According to the article, which of the following statements would Tom McArthur, editor of the *Oxford Companion to the English Language*, agree with?
   - Ⓐ People invent too many new words.
   - Ⓑ Hybrid Englishes are not really English.
   - Ⓒ The spread of English is unstoppable.
   - Ⓓ The British should stop the degradation of English.

Scope and Sequence

Chapter	Reading Selections	Reading Skills and Strategies
1 Education and Student Life pg. 2	*Education: A Reflection of Society* *Campus Life is Changing*	Previewing the topic and vocabulary Identifying the topic and main idea Skimming for the topic and main idea Predicting content of a reading
2 City Life pg. 22	*A City That's Doing Something Right* *Sick-Building Syndrome*	Previewing the topic and vocabulary Identifying the main idea Identifying supporting details Predicting content of a reading Skimming for the topic and the main ideas Scanning
3 Business and Money pg. 46	*Banking on Poor Women* *Consumerism and the Human Brain*	Previewing the topic and vocabulary Identifying the main idea and details Understanding conclusions Skimming for the topic and the main ideas
4 Jobs and Professions pg. 70	*Changing Career Trends* *Looking for Work in the 21st Century*	Previewing the topic and vocabulary Getting meaning from context Previewing a reading Identifying the main idea Identifying important details Skimming for the topic and the main ideas

Critical Thinking Skills	Vocabulary Building	Language Skills	Focus on Testing
Interpreting a photograph Relating a reading passage to a broader world view Summarizing a paragraph Organizing information using a T-chart	Getting meaning from context: punctuation, other sentences, logic Practicing new vocabulary Identifying words and phrases that work together Using prepositions Focusing on the Academic Word List	Understanding pronoun reference Discussing student life in different countries Writing a paragraph	Focusing on question types TOEFL® iBT
Organizing details using a graphic organizer Making inferences Summarizing a paragraph Understanding contrast	Getting meaning from context: examples, opposites, & *in other words* Understanding the meaning of italics in readings Focusing on the Academic Word List Understanding and looking up parts of speech in a dictionary	Understanding pronoun reference Interviewing students about city life Discussing some problems and solutions in big cities Writing a paragraph	Getting meaning from context
Identifying problems and solutions Organizing ideas using a graphic organizer Comparing and contrasting Making inferences Understanding irony Analyzing advertisements Summarizing a paragraph	Getting meaning from context (*e.g.* and *i.e.*) Using parts of speech to understand vocabulary Using suffixes to identify parts of speech Recognizing synonyms Focusing on the Academic Word List	Understanding pronoun reference Discussing social problems and solutions Analyzing advertisements Writing a paragraph	Focusing on implications and inferences TOEFL® iBT
Identifying cause and effect Organizing cause and effect using a graphic organizer Summarizing a paragraph Understanding proverbs and quotations	Using the prefix *over-* Focusing on the Academic Word List Understanding adjective and noun phrases Understanding and creating compound words	Understanding pronoun reference Discussing proverbs and quotations Identifying challenges and changes within today's work world Writing a paragraph	Increasing reading speed

Critical Thinking Skills	Vocabulary Building	Language Skills	Focus on Testing
Organizing details using a graphic organizer Expressing and supporting an opinion Studying for exams: organizing information Summarizing a paragraph	Focusing on the Academic Word List Analyzing suffixes and prefixes Understanding dictionary entries: words with single and multiple meanings	Expressing opinions Discussing fads and trends Writing a paragraph	Focusing on vocabulary questions TOEFL® iBT
Understanding the literal and figurative meanings of words Organizing information using an outline Summarizing in writing Identifying inferences	Focusing on the Academic Word List Understanding idioms Focusing on expressions and idioms Using participles as adjectives	Stating and explaining opinions Writing a paragraph	Identifying inferences
Categorizing Interpreting a photograph Identifying details and analyzing material using graphic organizers Identifying inferences Distinguishing facts from assumptions Summarizing a paragraph	Understanding homophones Focusing on the Academic Word List Working with prefixes and suffixes Understanding words in phrases Learning new vocabulary: making a vocabulary log	Discussing the nature/ nurture question Writing a paragraph	Focusing on comprehension questions about details
Organizing information using an outline Identifying and making inferences Summarizing a paragraph	Recognizing words with similar meanings Understanding general and specific words Understanding connotations Focusing on the Academic Word List	Discussing ideas on art and beauty Writing a paragraph	Focusing on basic comprehension questions TOEFL® iBT

Critical Thinking Skills	Vocabulary Building	Language Skills	Focus on Testing
Analyzing diagrams and photographs Distinguishing facts from assumptions Synthesizing and applying information from a reading Categorizing Making inferences Summarizing a paragraph	Matching words with similar meanings Putting words into categories Analyzing word roots and affixes Focusing on the Academic Word List	Expressing opinions based on facts Identifying similarities and differences among family members Writing a paragraph	Getting meaning from context TOEFL® iBT
Making inferences Comparing and contrasting Using a graphic organizer to organize and analyze information Distinguishing facts from opinions Summarizing a paragraph	Determining categories Analyzing word roots and affixes Focusing on the Academic Word List	Applying information in the reading to personal situation Conducting a survey on traditional and nontraditional weddings Writing a paragraph	Identifying main idea patterns TOEFL® iBT

1

Education and Student Life

In This Chapter

What can we learn about a culture from its educational system? In the first reading, you will read about four countries and have a chance to compare positive and negative aspects of those countries' educational systems. You will also discuss your own educational life. In Part 2, you will read about how the student population has changed in the United States and how this, as well as technology and studies about learning styles, have changed classes and campuses. In Part 3, you will learn strategies to help build your vocabulary and develop good study skills. Finally, Part 4 focuses on improving your understanding of question types on a reading test.

❝ If you are planning for a year, sow rice; if you are planning for a decade, plant trees; if you are planning for a lifetime, educate people. ❞

—Chinese proverb

Connecting to the Topic

1 What do you see in the photo?

2 What do you think the students are talking about?

3 What do you think is important at an educational institution? Name ten things.

Education: A Reflection of Society

Before You Read

1 **Previewing the Topic** Look at the photos and discuss the questions.

1. Where is each scene taking place? What is happening?

2. What might be similar about education in these countries? Make guesses.

3. What might be different about education in these countries? Make guesses.

4. In your opinion, what are important cultural values in each of these countries?

▲ Primary school students in Mexico

▲ High school students in Japan

▲ A university student in England

▲ High school science students in the United States

2 **Previewing Vocabulary** Read the words and phrases below. Listen to the pronunciation. Put a check mark (✓) next to the words that you know. For the words that you don't know, *don't* use a dictionary. Try to understand them from the reading. You'll work with some of these words in the activities.

Nouns

- ❑ aspects
- ❑ constitution
- ❑ contrasts
- ❑ discipline
- ❑ indigenous people
- ❑ native people
- ❑ primary school
- ❑ secondary school

- ❑ statistic
- ❑ status
- ❑ tuition
- ❑ values

Verbs

- ❑ achieve
- ❑ afford
- ❑ determines
- ❑ reflects
- ❑ value

- ❑ identical
- ❑ isolated
- ❑ rural
- ❑ universal
- ❑ vocational

Adjectives

- ❑ compulsory
- ❑ egalitarian
- ❑ entire

Idioms

- ❑ on the one hand
- ❑ on the other hand

Strategy

Getting Meaning from Context

When you read, you do not need to look up the meanings of all new words in a dictionary. You can often guess the meanings of many new words from the context—the other words in the sentence and the other sentences in the paragraph. Here are three types of clues that will help you guess new words.

1. **Punctuation**: Sometimes a sentence gives a definition of a new vocabulary item or information about it. This information may be in parentheses ( ), after a dash (—), or after a comma (,).

   Example

   There is a **drawback**, a disadvantage, to that idea.

   (*Drawback* means *disadvantage*.)

2. **Another Sentence**: Sometimes a clue to the meaning of a new vocabulary item is in another sentence or sentence part.

   Example

   A school system in one country is not **identical** to the system in any other country. It cannot be exactly the same because each culture is different.

   (In the second sentence, you see the meaning of *identical—exactly the same*.)

3. **Logic**: Sometimes simple logic helps you to guess a new word.

   Example

   The educational system is a mirror that **reflects** the culture.

   (You probably know the word *mirror*, so you can guess that *reflects* means *shows*.)

3 **Getting Meaning from Context** This exercise will help you with vocabulary that you will find in the first reading selection. Read the sentences. Figure out the meanings of the underlined words from the context and write them on the lines.

1. <u>On the one hand</u>, there are many advantages to this system. <u>On the other hand</u>, there are also several drawbacks.

   on the one hand = _____*from one point of view*_____

   on the other hand = _____

2. In a number of countries, education is both <u>compulsory</u>—required—and <u>universal</u>, available to everyone, at least in <u>primary school</u> (elementary school).

   compulsory = _____

   universal = _____

   primary school = _____

3. There are many more schools in cities than in <u>rural</u> areas.

   rural = _____

4. Public schools are all both free and <u>egalitarian</u>; all students are considered equal and learn the same material.

   egalitarian = _____

5. College students need great <u>discipline</u>; in order to make time for their studies, they need the self-control to give up hobbies, sports, and social life.

   discipline = _____

6. Results on these exams affect the <u>entire</u> family because there is high <u>status</u>, or social position, for a whole family in which children have high test scores.

   entire = _____

   status = _____

7. Students themselves decide if they want college-preparatory or vocational classes in high school; no national exam <u>determines</u> this for them.

   determines = _____

Read

4 **Reading an Article** As you read the following selection, think about the answer to this question: *What can we learn about a culture from its educational system?* Read the selection. Do not use a dictionary. Then do the exercises that follow the reading.

Education: A Reflection of Society

A   Visit schools anywhere in the world, and you will probably notice a number of similarities. There are students, teachers, books, blackboards, and exams everywhere. However, a school system in one country is not **identical** to the system in any other country. It cannot be exactly the same because each culture is different. The educational system is a mirror that   5
reflects the culture. Look at the school system, and you will see the social structure and the **values** of its culture.

Mexico

B   In Mexico, the educational system reflects some of the country's many **contrasts**. **On the one hand**, it is believed that the nation can **achieve** equality of rights for everyone *through education*. The basis of the Mexican   10
educational system is the country's **constitution**, which was written in 1917. It requires education to be free, **compulsory**, and **universal**. It also states that education should support national unity and lead to social, economic, and cultural improvement of the people. At lower levels, this means that there is emphasis on the country's rich cultural history. Children   15
write historical essays, participate in activities for national holidays, and read about national heroes—especially **native people** (Indians). However, it is often difficult to provide education in **rural** areas, where many of the **indigenous people** live. People in these areas are poor and **isolated** geographically. There aren't enough schools, and rural teachers must be   20
able to teach all six grades of primary school. Also, traditions among some indigenous people do not typically include school attendance.

Japan

C   The Japanese **value** education highly. One **statistic** reflects this: the Japanese place such importance on education that 88 percent of all students complete not only **primary school** but also high school. Public schools are   25
all both free and egalitarian; all students are considered equal and learn the same material. For social reasons, it's important for a student to receive a university degree—and a degree from "the right university." To reach this goal, students have to go through "examination hell." There are difficult exams for entrance to all universities, to many of the better primary and   30
secondary schools, and even to some *kindergartens*! Japanese students need great **discipline**; in order to make time for their studies, they need the self-control to give up hobbies, sports, and social life. Results of these exams affect the **entire** family because there is high **status**, or social position, for the whole family when the children have high test scores.   35

Britain

D   In the United Kingdom (Britain), the educational system reflects the class system. All state schools—primary, secondary, and university—are free, and the first nine years are **egalitarian**; all students learn the same material. At age eleven, students take an important national exam. After this, they attend one of three possible secondary schools: college preparatory, **vocational** (for job training), or comprehensive (with both groups of students). However, 6 percent of British students attend expensive private schools. These are students from upper-class families. Half of the students at Oxford and Cambridge universities come from such expensive secondary schools. It might seem that anyone can **afford** to go to a university because all universities are free, but only 1 percent of the lower class goes to university. Because graduates from good universities get the best jobs, it is clear that success is largely a result of one's social class.

The United States

E   Education in the United States is available to everyone, but not all schools are equal. Public primary and secondary schools are free for everyone; there is no **tuition**. Almost 80 percent of all Americans are high school graduates. Students themselves decide if they want college-preparatory or vocational classes in high school; no national exam **determines** this. Higher education is not free, but it is available to almost anyone, and about 60 percent of all high school graduates attend college or university. Older people have the opportunity to attend college, too, because Americans believe that "you're never too old to learn." **On the other hand**, there are also problems in U.S. schools. In many secondary schools, there are problems with lack of discipline and with drugs and crime. In addition, public schools receive their money from local taxes, so schools in poor areas receive less money. As a result, they don't have enough good teachers or laboratory equipment, and the buildings are often not in good condition. Clearly, U.S. education reflects both the best and the worst of the society.

Conclusion

F   It is clear that each educational system is a reflection of the larger culture—both positive and negative **aspects** of its economy, values, and social structure. Look at a country's schools, and you will learn about the society in which they exist.

Strategy

Identifying the Main Idea

A reading passage may include many ideas, but there is only one main idea. This is the most important idea, or point, of the reading. It is the main point, thought, or opinion that the author has about the topic. It is an "umbrella" that includes all of the more specific ideas and details. The main idea is usually stated in the introduction. Often, it is repeated in the conclusion.

5 **Identifying the Main Idea** Find one sentence in Paragraph A that seems to be the main idea of the entire reading passage. Then find another sentence in Paragraph F that seems to mean about the same. Write them here.

From Paragraph A: _____

_____

From Paragraph F: _____

_____

6 **Understanding Reading Structure** Paragraphs divide reading material into topics, or subjects. One paragraph is usually about one topic. Match the paragraphs from the reading on pages 6–8 with their topics below. Write the letters of the paragraphs on the lines.

1. __F__ Conclusion: Education as a reflection of society

2. _____ A country that places a lot of importance on education and makes students take difficult exams

3. _____ A country that offers education to everyone but also has problems in its schools

4. _____ A country where equality and national unity are important

5. _____ A country where social class is very important

6. _____ Introduction: Education as a mirror of a culture

7 **Checking Your Vocabulary** Check your understanding of vocabulary from the reading selection. Read the definitions below and write words and expressions that fit these definitions. The letters in parentheses refer to paragraphs in the reading.

1. a paper containing the laws that a country is based on (B) = *constitution*

2. Indians (B) = _____

3. far away from towns or cities (B) = _____

4. a school for job training (D) = _____

5. to have enough money for something (D) = _____

6. fees (money) for education (E) = _____

7. sides, parts, characteristics (F) = _____

Strategy

Organizing Information: Using a *T-Chart*
Readings often present both positive and negative aspects of something (such as an educational system). Sometimes, these are easy to find because the writer uses the words *advantages* and *disadvantages*, but frequently these words don't appear. Instead, you need to look for other words and expressions that show opposite viewpoints, such as *on the one hand, on the other hand, but,* and *however.*

One way to organize this information is in a graphic organizer. One effective graphic organizer to show positive and negative aspects is a T-chart (called a T-chart because it is shaped like the letter *T*).

You can work with a T-chart in the next activity.

8 **Organizing Information: Using a T-Chart** In the T-chart on page 11, write the four countries from the reading on the left. Work in groups of four and have each student choose one country. Fill out the positive and negative aspects of that country's educational system. When you finish, share your information with the students in your group and complete the chart with their information.

	Positive Aspects	Negative Aspects
1. *Mexico*		
2.		
3.		
4.		

Cultural Note

Education in North America and Asia

In a Western society, such as the United States or Canada, that has many national, religious, and cultural differences, people highly value **individualism**—the differences among people—and independent thinking. Students do not often memorize information. Instead, they find answers themselves, and they express their ideas in class discussion. At an early age, students learn to form their own ideas and opinions.

In most Asian societies, by contrast, the people have the same language, history, and culture. Perhaps for this reason, the educational system in much of Asia reflects society's belief in **group goals and traditions** rather than individualism. Children in China, Japan, and Korea often work together and help one another on assignments. In the classroom, the teaching methods are often very formal. The teacher lectures, and the students listen. There is not much discussion. Instead, the students recite rules or information that they have memorized. There are advantages and disadvantages to both systems.

9 **Discussing the Reading** In small groups, talk about your answers to these questions about a country that you know well.

1. Are there both private schools and public schools? Is public education free, or do students need to pay tuition?

2. Do most students go to secondary school? Do most students complete high school? Do many students go to college or university?

3. Are there different types of high schools (for example, college-preparatory or vocational)?

4. What are some advantages of the educational system? Disadvantages?

Campus Life is Changing

Before You Read

Strategy

Skimming for the Topic and Main Idea

You can skim a reading to identify the topic and the main idea. To skim, read the title and any subheadings, look at any photos and diagrams, read the first two and the last two sentences of each paragraph, read quickly, and don't read every word.

The topic of a paragraph is what the paragraph is about. This is a noun or noun phrase. The main idea of a paragraph is what the writer wants to say about the topic—giving information and/or his or her opinion about the topic. Sometimes, a sentence or two includes the main idea of the paragraph. This is often the first or second sentence in the paragraph. The other sentences give details about the main idea.

Example

Statistics reflect recent changes in the U.S. college population. One change these days is that there are fewer foreign students than several years ago but that more U.S. students are studying abroad. There are over half a million foreign students in colleges and universities in the United States (down 5–6 percent). The leading country of origin is India, followed by China, Korea, Japan, Canada, Taiwan, Mexico, Turkey, and Thailand. Meanwhile, there are 175,000 U.S. students who are studying abroad (up 8.5 percent). American students typically spend much less time abroad than foreign students do in the United States. In fact, 92 percent of all U.S. students who go abroad spend only one semester there.

Topic: _the U.S. college population_

Main idea: _There are fewer foreign students in the United States these days but more U.S. students abroad._

> **Hint**
>
> Remember that the **topic** is just a word or noun phrase—a few words. It is not a sentence. The **main idea** is in a sentence or two and can be found at the beginning, middle, or end of a paragraph.

Read

1 Skimming for the Topic and the Main Idea Read the following paragraphs quickly. Do not use a dictionary, and don't worry about the details. When you finish, write the topic and main idea of each paragraph. You can copy the main idea directly from the sentence (or sentences), or use your own words to restate it.

Campus Life is Changing

A   For many years in the United States, most undergraduate students (in their first four years of college) were 18 to 22 years old. They attended college full-time, lived in a dormitory on campus, and expected many "extras" from their colleges, not just classes. But things began to change in the 1970s and are very different now. Today, these "traditional" students are 5 less than one-quarter (1/4) of all college students. These days the nontraditional students are the majority; they are different from traditional undergraduates in several ways. They are older. Many attend college part-time because they have families and jobs. Most live off campus, not in dorms. These nontraditional students don't want the extras that colleges 10 usually offer. They aren't interested in the sports, entertainment, religious groups, and museums that are part of most U.S. colleges. They want mainly good-quality classes, day or night, at a low cost. They also hope for easy parking, access to information technology, and polite service. Both time and money are important to them. 15

Topic: _____

Main idea: _____

_____

B   Psychological tests reflect different learning styles in this new student population, too. Each person has a certain learning style, and about 60 percent of the new students these days prefer the *sensing* style. This means

that they are very practical. They prefer a practice-to-theory method of learning, which 20 is experience first and ideas after that. They often have difficulty with reading and writing and are unsure of themselves. Most of these students are attending college because they want to have a good job and 25 make a lot of money.

▲ A college lecture class

Topic: _____

Main idea: _____

_____

C   In contrast, other students (but not as many) prefer the *intuitive* learning style. These students love ideas. They prefer a theory-to-practice method of learning and enjoy independent, creative thinking. These "intuitives" are not very practical. They are attending college because they   30
want to create unique works of art or study philosophy or someday help in the field of science.

Topic: _____

Main idea: _____

_____

D   There is a drawback for the students who prefer the sensing style of learning. A majority of college professors prefer the intuitive learning style. These teachers value independent thinking and creative ideas. Students in   35
the sensing group are at a disadvantage because their way of thinking doesn't match their teachers'.

Topic: _____

Main idea: _____

_____

E   Politically, too, students these days are different from students in the past. In the 1960s and 1970s, many students demonstrated against the government and hoped to make big changes in society. In the 1980s, most   40
students were interested only in their studies and future jobs. Today, students seem to be a combination of the two: they want to make good money when they graduate, but they're also interested in helping society. Many students today are volunteering in the community. They are working to help people, without payment. For example, they tutor (teach privately)   45
children in trouble, or they work with organizations for homeless people. In these ways, they hope to make changes in society.

Topic: _____

Main idea: _____

_____

F   On all college campuses, student life is very different from what it used to be because of technology—specifically, the Internet. At most colleges, all entering first-year students receive an email address. Dormitory rooms offer high-speed Internet access. Computer systems are available to everyone in computer labs, the library, and student centers. Application for classes and registration are usually now possible online. Most schools offer entire courses online. Many professors still have "office hours," when students can come to talk with them about class work or ask for help. But increasingly, students can contact professors 24 hours a day, thanks to email. In many classes, students complete assignments and even take exams online. Perhaps most important for both students and professors, research is now easier and faster because of the new technology.

Topic: _____

Main idea: _____

_____

After You Read

UNDERSTANDING PRONOUN REFERENCE

As you know, pronouns take the place of nouns. When you read, it's important to understand the meanings of pronouns, to know which noun a pronoun refers to. To find the noun that a pronoun refers to, look back in the sentence or in the sentences that come before the pronoun.

Example

Over 100,000 international students attend graduate school. Most of them are studying business and management.

2 **Understanding Pronoun Reference** Look back at the reading selection "Campus Life is Changing" to find the meanings of the following pronouns. What does each pronoun refer to?

1. they (Paragraph A, line 2) *most undergraduate students*

2. they (Paragraph A, line 8) _____

3. them (Paragraph A, line 15) _____

4. their (Paragraph D, line 37) _____

5. their (Paragraph E, line 41) _____

6. them (Paragraph F, line 55) _____

 3 Discussing the Reading Discuss these questions. Think about a country that you know well.

1. In that country, are there foreign students in colleges and universities? If so, where do they come from? Are there many?

2. In that country, are students today different from students in the past? If so, how are they different?

3. How has technology changed campus life in that country?

Responding in Writing

Strategy

Summarizing

In academic classes, the most common type of writing is *summary*. A summary is written in the student's own words. It includes the main idea and important details of another piece of writing (a paragraph, section, article, chapter, or book). It does not include less important details. Students who summarize well can prove to the instructor that they truly understand the reading material.

4 Summarizing Choose one country from the reading in Part 1, pages 6–8. Write a summary of its educational system, according to the paragraph about that country. Because a summary is shorter than the original, try to write only two to four sentences. Follow these steps.

- Read the paragraph and make sure that you understand it well.
- Identify the topic, main idea, and important details.
- Put the original paragraph aside as you write.
- Write the summary in your own words, including the important details.
- Include a balance of positive and negative aspects.
- Do not include less important details.

When you finish writing, compare your summary with those of other students who summarized the same paragraph. Did you have the same main idea? Did you choose the same details?

5 Writing Your Own Ideas Choose one of the topics below to write a paragraph about. Write your own thoughts. Try to use vocabulary from this chapter.

- the educational system in your country
- comparing and contrasting education in your country now and in the past
- your own learning style

What's the main idea of your paragraph? _____

_____

UNDERSTANDING "POLITICALLY CORRECT" LANGUAGE

Politically correct (or PC) language is a term used to describe language that is regarded as "correct" because it tries not to offend people. It is an attempt to use language that shows respect for different people, cultures, physical characteristics, and lifestyles. This term and this language is commonly heard and discussed in the United States—on college campuses, at work, and in social settings. Many people attempt to use this language as a sign of respect, but some feel that they have to be too careful and that "things have gone too far." What do you think?

6 **Identifying Politically Correct Words and Phrases** Below are some words and phrases that people traditionally used in the past and the politically correct words that many people use now. Why do you think some people prefer politically correct words? Which PC words seem good to you? Do any seem strange?

Words and Phrases	Politically Correct Words and Phrases
blind	visually challenged
disabled, handicapped	differently abled
fat people	people of size
mankind	humanity
Orientals	Asians
policeman	police officer
remedial classes	basic classes
Third World countries	developing countries

 7 **Beyond the Text: Interviewing** Interview five people. Ask them their opinions about positive and negative aspects of the educational system in their country. Take notes on their answers. When you finish, report your findings to the class.

Part 3 Building Vocabulary and Study Skills

THE ACADEMIC WORD LIST

There is a list of words that college students should know because these words occur frequently in academic English. This is called the "Academic Word List." In Part 3 of each chapter of this book, there is an activity to help you focus on these words. (See page 18 for the first Focusing on Words from the Academic Word List Activity.) Also, in the Self-Assessment Log at the end of each chapter these words have an asterisk (*) next to them. (See page 21 for the first Self-Assessment Log.) For more information on Averil Coxhead's Academic Word List, see www.vuw.ac.nz/lals/research/awl.

---

1 **Focusing on Words from the Academic Word List** In this exercise, fill in the blanks with words from the Academic Word List in the box. When you finish, turn back to page 11 and check your answers.

assignments	culture	lectures
contrast	goals	methods
cultural	individualism	traditions

Education in North America and Asia

In a Western society, such as the United States or Canada, that has many national, religious, and _____*cultural*_____ differences, people

1

highly value _____—the differences among people—and

2

independent thinking. Students do not often memorize information. Instead, they find answers themselves, and they express their ideas in class discussion. At an early age, students learn to form their own ideas and opinions.

In most Asian societies, by _____, the people have the

3

same language, history, and _____. Perhaps for this

4

reason, the educational system in much of Asia reflects society's belief in

group _____ and _____ rather than

5 6

individualism. Children in China, Japan, and Korea often work together

and help one another on _____. In the classroom, the

7

teaching _____ are often very formal. The teacher

8

_____, and the students listen. There is not much

9

discussion. Instead, the students recite rules or information that they

have memorized.

2 **Recognizing Word Meanings** Match the words with their meanings. Write the letters on the lines, as in the example.

1. _h_ determine   **a.** unusual

2. _____ afford   **b.** disadvantage

3. _____ reflect   **c.** side, part, or characteristic

4. _____ nontraditional   **d.** developing new ideas

5. _____ drawback   **e.** fact in the form of a number

6. _____ statistic   **f.** control

7. _____ discipline   **g.** whole

8. _____ aspect   **h̸.** decide on

9. _____ involves   **i.** have enough money for

10. _____ tuition   **j.** show

11. _____ entire   **k.** fees (money) for school

12. _____ creative   **l.** includes

3 **Words in Phrases** As you read, it's important to begin noticing words that often go together. Go back to the paragraphs on pages 13–15. Find words to complete the following phrases and write them in the blanks. Most are prepositions, but two are verbs.

Paragraph A

1. lived _____ _in_ _____ a dormitory _____ _on_ _____ campus

2. many _____ college part-time (verb)

3. access _____ information technology

Paragraph D

4. are _____ a disadvantage

Paragraph E

5. tutor children _____ trouble

Paragraph F

6. life is different because _____ technology

7. are available _____ everyone

8. students _____ exams (verb)

4 **Searching the Internet** Do an Internet search on colleges and universities. Use a search engine such as Google. Find a college or university that does the following things:

- has an interesting virtual (online) tour: _____

- offers classes in horseback riding: _____

- allows students to spend one year studying abroad: _____

- offers classes in many African languages (such as Amharic, Yoruba, Swahili, and Zulu): _____

- has an art museum: _____

- (*your choice*): _____

Write down the names and locations of the colleges. Compare your findings with those of another student.

Part 4 | Focus on Testing

READING QUESTION TYPES

There are three types of multiple-choice questions in the reading section of the TOEFL® (Test of English as a Foreign Language™) Internet-Based Test (iBT): (1) information questions, (2) basic comprehension questions, and (3) "reading to learn" questions.

1. Most *information* questions can be answered by scanning for a certain keyword or number. The answer involves finding a specific point of information.

2. *Basic comprehension* questions test the reader's skill at understanding the vocabulary, grammar, and basic organization of the passage. The answer often involves understanding the interrelationship of several sentences or paragraphs.

3. *Reading to learn* questions test the reader's ability to understand the main ideas of a reading, implied ideas, the author's attitudes, relations among groups of facts in the reading, and so on.

1 **Practice** Look again at the reading "Education: A Reflection of Society" on pages 6–8. Answer the following questions (similar to those on the TOEFL® iBT). The question type is in parentheses after the question.

1. According to the passage, what happened in 1917? (information question)
   - (A) Mexico's constitution was written.
   - (B) Mexico achieved equality of rights for everyone.
   - (C) Mexico made education free.
   - (D) Education in Mexico supported national unity.

2. Which of the following is closest in meaning to *determines*, as it is used in Paragraph E? (basic comprehension question)
   - (A) limits
   - (B) finishes
   - (C) decides
   - (D) provides

3. What can be inferred (guessed) about Japanese universities from Paragraph C? (reading to learn question)
   - (A) They are free and egalitarian.
   - (B) They offer degrees in many disciplines.
   - (C) Students there take too many examinations.
   - (D) Some universities have better reputations than others do.

Self-Assessment Log

Read the lists below. Check (✓) the strategies and vocabulary that you learned in this chapter. Look through the chapter or ask your instructor about the strategies and words that you do not understand.

Reading and Vocabulary-Building Strategies

- ❑ Previewing vocabulary
- ❑ Getting meaning from context
- ❑ Identifying the main idea
- ❑ Understanding reading structure
- ❑ Organizing information: using a t-chart
- ❑ Skimming for the topic and main idea
- ❑ Understanding pronoun reference

Target Vocabulary

Nouns
- ❑ aspects*
- ❑ assignments*
- ❑ constitution*
- ❑ contrasts*
- ❑ culture*
- ❑ discipline
- ❑ goals*
- ❑ indigenous people
- ❑ individualism*

- ❑ methods*
- ❑ native people
- ❑ primary* school
- ❑ secondary school
- ❑ statistic*
- ❑ status*
- ❑ traditions*
- ❑ tuition
- ❑ values

Verbs
- ❑ afford
- ❑ determines
- ❑ involves*
- ❑ lectures*
- ❑ reflects

Adjectives
- ❑ compulsory
- ❑ creative*
- ❑ cultural*
- ❑ egalitarian
- ❑ entire
- ❑ rural
- ❑ universal
- ❑ vocational

Idioms
- ❑ on the one hand
- ❑ on the other hand

* These words are from the Academic Word List. For more information on this list, see www.vuw.ac.nz/lals/research/awl.

2

City Life

In This Chapter

What do you think about big cities? In this chapter, you will read about some challenges that big cities face. In Part 1, you will read about how one city in particular found some creative ways to deal with garbage collection, transportation, social issues, and other urban problems. A common problem that big cities face is air pollution, but as you will learn in Part 2, pollution is not limited to the outdoors. There is also indoor pollution. Many things cause pollution in office buildings, schools, and homes. You will learn about and discuss things that we can do to address this problem. Then Parts 3 and 4 introduce a variety of strategies and activities to help build vocabulary, study skills, and test-taking skills.

❝ When you look at a city, it's like reading the hopes, aspirations, and pride of everyone who built it. **❞**

—Hugh Newell Jacobsen
U.S. Architect (1929–)

Connecting to the Topic

1. What do you see in the photo? What do you think the people there are doing?

2. What are five advantages of living in a big city? What are five disadvantages?

3. Do you like living in a big or a small city? Do you like visiting a big or small city? Explain your answers.

A City That's Doing Something Right

Before You Read

1 **Previewing the Topic** Look at the photos and discuss the questions.

1. In what cities or countries do you think the photos were taken? What is it like there?

2. What adjectives can you think of to describe each photo? Make a list.

▲ Photo A

▲ Photo B

2 **Thinking Ahead** The first reading discusses some common problems in big cities and the solutions that one city has found. Before you read, think about the good and bad things about the city that you come from or the city that you live in now. Interview at least four students. Complete the chart below.

Student's Name and City	What are the three worst problems in your city?	What are the three best features of your city?

3 **Previewing Vocabulary** Read the words and phrases below. Listen to the pronunciation. Put a check mark (✓) next to the words that you know. For the words that you don't know, *don't* use a dictionary. Try to understand them from the reading. You'll work with some of these words in the activities.

Nouns
- ❑ agricultural operation
- ❑ crops
- ❑ developing countries
- ❑ difficulties (difficulty)
- ❑ gridlock
- ❑ mass transit
- ❑ pedestrian zone
- ❑ pollution
- ❑ priorities
- ❑ produce
- ❑ recycling plant
- ❑ trash
- ❑ urban dwellers

Verbs
- ❑ commute
- ❑ crowd
- ❑ cultivate
- ❑ predict
- ❑ solve
- ❑ worsening

Adjectives
- ❑ affluent
- ❑ creative

Adverb
- ❑ efficiently

Strategy

Getting Meaning from Context

You do not need to look up the meanings of new words if you can guess them from the context. Here are three more types of clues that will help you guess new words.

1. The words *for example, for instance, such as*, and *among them* introduce examples that may help you. (Sometimes examples appear without these words, in parentheses, or between dashes.)

   Example

   Context: Almost four billion people will be living in cities in **developing countries** such as India and Nigeria.

   Meaning: You can guess that developing countries are not rich.

2. Sometimes another word or words in another sentence or sentence part has the opposite meaning from a new vocabulary item.

   Example

   Context: In some cities, instead of **worsening**, urban life is actually getting much better.

   Meaning: You see that *worsening* is the opposite of *getting better*.

3. A definition or explanation follows the connecting words *that is* or *in other words*.

   Example

   Context: The downtown shopping area is now a **pedestrian zone**—in other words, an area for walkers only, no cars.

   Meaning: A *pedestrian zone* is an area for walkers only.

4 Getting Meaning from Context This activity will help you with vocabulary in the first reading selection. Figure out the meanings of the underlined words and write them on the lines. Use punctuation, logic, examples, opposites, and connecting words to help you.

1. People who study population growth <u>predict</u> a nightmare by the year 2025: the global population will be more than 8 billion, and almost 4 billion of these people will be living in cities in developing countries such as India and Nigeria.

   predict = _____*say in advance that something will happen*_____

2. People spend hours in <u>gridlock</u>—that is, traffic so horrible that it simply doesn't move—when they <u>commute</u> daily from their homes to their work and back.

   gridlock = _____

   commute = _____

3. It might not be a surprise to find that life in <u>affluent</u> cities is improving, but what about cities that aren't rich?

   affluent = _____

4. Under his leadership, city planners established <u>priorities</u>—in other words, a list of what was most important.

   priorities = _____

5. In neighborhoods that garbage trucks can't reach, people bring bags of <u>trash</u> to special centers.

   trash = _____

6. They exchange the trash for fresh <u>produce</u>—such as potatoes or oranges—or for bus tickets.

   produce = _____

7. At a <u>recycling plant</u>, workers separate glass bottles, plastic, and cans from other trash.

   recycling plant = _____

8. Curitiba needed a <u>mass-transit</u> system but couldn't afford an expensive subway. City planners began, instead, with an unusual system of buses.

   mass-transit = _____

9. There is an <u>agricultural operation</u> just outside Curitiba that looks like other farms but actually helps to solve a social problem, in addition to growing <u>crops</u>.

   agricultural operation = _____

   crops = _____

10. They <u>cultivate</u> medicinal plants and then process them into herbal teas.

    cultivate = _____

11. Curitiba provides the city people with twenty-two million square meters of parks and green areas; this is more than three times the amount that the World Health Organization recommends for <u>urban dwellers</u>.

urban dwellers = _____

Read

5 **Reading an Article** As you read the following selection, think about the answer to this question: *What is the city Curitiba, Brazil doing right?* Then do the exercises that follow the reading.

A City That's Doing Something Right

A   There's good news and bad news about life in modern cities—first, the bad. People who study population growth **predict** a nightmare by the year 2025: the global population will be more than eight billion, and almost four billion of these people will be living in cities in **developing countries** such as India and Nigeria. Population growth is already causing 5 unbelievable overcrowding. Due to this overcrowding, many cities have problems with air **pollution**, disease, and crime. People spend hours in **gridlock**—that is, traffic so horrible that it simply doesn't move—when they **commute** daily from their homes to their work and back. There isn't enough water, transportation, or housing. Many people don't have access to health 10 services or jobs. Now the good news: in *some* cities, instead of **worsening**, urban life is actually getting much better.

A City and Its Mayor

B   It might not be a surprise to find that life in **affluent** cities is improving. But what about cities that *aren't* rich? The city of Curitiba, Brazil, proves that it's possible for even a city in a developing country to offer a good life 15 to its residents. The former mayor of Curitiba for 25 years, Jaime Lerner is an architect and a very practical person. Under his leadership, the city planners established a list of **priorities**—in other words, a list of what was most important to work on. They decided to focus on the environment and on the quality of life. With an average income of only about $2,000 per person 20 per year, Curitiba has the same problems as many cities. However, it also has some **creative** solutions.

Garbage Collection

C   One creative solution is the method of garbage collection—*Cambio Verde*, or Green Exchange. This does far more than clean the streets of **trash**. In neighborhoods that garbage trucks can't reach, poor people bring bags of trash to special centers. At these centers, they exchange the trash for fresh **produce** such as potatoes and oranges. They receive one kilo of produce for every four kilos of trash that they bring in. At a **recycling plant**, workers separate glass bottles, plastic, and cans from other trash. *Two-thirds* of Curitiba's garbage is recycled, which is good for the environment. And the plant gives jobs to the poorest people, which improves their lives.

Transportation

D   Due to careful planning, Curitiba does not have the same traffic problems that most cities have. The statistics are surprising. The population has grown fast, to over two million people, but traffic has actually *decreased* 30 percent. Curitiba needed a **mass-transit** system but couldn't afford an expensive subway. City planners began, instead, with an unusual system of buses in the center lanes of five wide major streets. At each bus stop, there is a forty-foot-long glass tube. Passengers pay *before* they enter the tube. Then they get on the bus "subway style"—through wide doors. This allows people to get on and off the bus quickly and **efficiently**. People don't **crowd**

▲ Passengers exit efficiently through the tube in Curitiba, Brazil.

onto the bus; loading and unloading takes only 30 seconds. This makes commuting more pleasant and also helps to **solve** the problem of air pollution.

A Creative Social Program

E   There is an **agricultural operation** just outside Curitiba that looks like other farms but actually helps to solve a social problem, in addition to growing **crops**. At *Fazenda da Solidaridade* (Solidarity Farm), the workers are not experienced farmers. Instead, they are drug addicts and alcoholics who volunteer to spend up to nine months in a program called *Verde Saude* (Green Health). The program helps them in two ways. First, it gives them jobs. They **cultivate** medicinal plants and then process them into herbal teas, syrups, and other products that are sold in health food stores. Second, it helps them to get off drugs and alcohol and to turn their lives around. In exchange for their labor, they receive counseling, medical care, and job training.

The Environment

F   To make the environment both cleaner and more beautiful, Curitiba encourages green space. It has low taxes for companies that have green areas, so several hundred major industries such as Pepsi and Volvo have offices in the city— being willing to incorporate green space in their plants in order to take advantage of the city's low tax rate. Bringing natural beauty into the city is a priority. For this reason, Curitiba gave 1.5 million young trees to neighborhoods to plant and take care of. And the downtown shopping area is now a **pedestrian zone**—in other words, for walkers only, no cars—and is lined with gardens. Curitiba provides the city people with 22 million square meters of parks and green areas—more than three times the amount that the World Health Organization recommends for **urban dwellers**.

▲ "There is little in the architecture of a city that is more beautifully designed than a tree," says Jaime Lerner.

A Symbol of the Possible

G   Clearly, overcrowding in big cities worldwide is the cause of serious problems. However, the example of Curitiba provides hope that careful planning and creative thinking can lead to solutions to many of them. Curitiba is truly, as Lewis Mumford once said of cities in general, a "symbol of the possible."

After You Read

IDENTIFYING THE MAIN IDEA

As you read in Chapter 1, usually one or two sentences in an essay or article state the main idea of the whole passage (the "umbrella" idea). You can usually find the main idea near the beginning of an essay.

6 Identifying the Main Idea In the article that you just read, the main idea is in Paragraph B. Write the main idea below. Then find another sentence in the conclusion, Paragraph G, which seems to mean about the same. Write that sentence on page 30.

From Paragraph B: _____

From Paragraph G: _____

_____

7 **Identifying Supporting Details** Complete this graphic organizer with information from Paragraphs C, D, and E to answer the questions. Follow the examples.

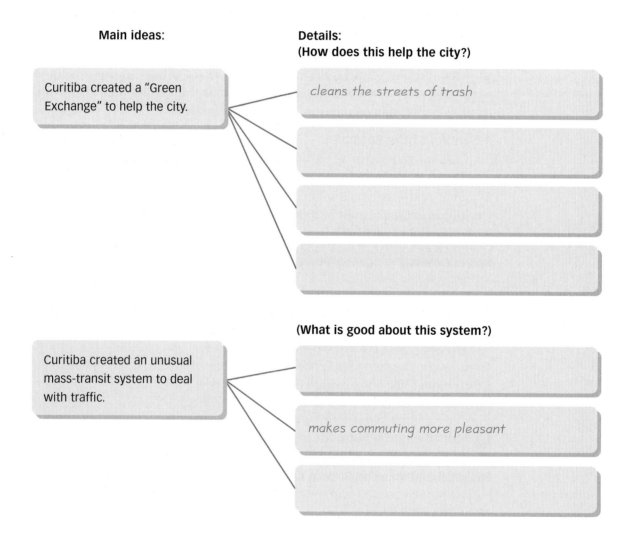

Main ideas:

Curitiba created a "Green Exchange" to help the city.

Details:
(How does this help the city?)

cleans the streets of trash

Curitiba created an unusual mass-transit system to deal with traffic.

(What is good about this system?)

makes commuting more pleasant

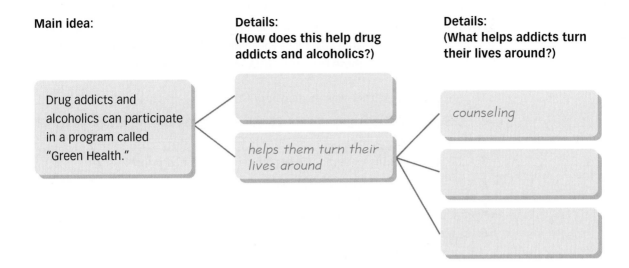

Main idea:	Details: (How does this help drug addicts and alcoholics?)	Details: (What helps addicts turn their lives around?)

Drug addicts and alcoholics can participate in a program called "Green Health."

helps them turn their lives around

counseling

UNDERSTANDING ITALICS

Writers use *italics* (slanted letters) for several reasons. Here are two:

1. Writers use italics for emphasis. The italics indicate that the word is important.

   Example Overcrowding is a *huge* problem in that city.

2. Italics indicate a foreign word in an English sentence.

   Example In open areas in Seoul, *kaenari* blooms everywhere in the spring.

---

8 **Understanding Italics** Find the words in italics in the reading on pages 27–29. Which are used for emphasis? Circle them. Read these sentences aloud, placing emphasis on the words in italics. Which words indicate a foreign word or term? Underline them.

UNDERSTANDING CONTRAST

Sometimes writers use contrast to express an idea. In other words, they begin with the opposite of the point that they want to make.

---

 9 **Understanding Contrast** The reading selection "A City That's Doing Something Right" can be divided into two parts. What is the first part? What is the second part? How do these parts show contrast? Discuss your answers with one classmate.

Strategy

Critical Thinking: Making Inferences

Writers usually state information clearly. However, they also often **imply** information. In other words, they just suggest an idea without actually stating it. It is important for students to be able to make **inferences**—that is, to "read between the lines" and understand information that is not clearly stated.

10 **Making Inferences** Below is information from the reading. Which information is stated in the reading? Write *S* on those lines. Which information is implied but not clearly stated? Write *I* on those lines. Look back at Paragraphs B, C, and D to decide.

1. ___S___ Jaime Lerner was the mayor of Curitiba.

2. _____ Jaime Lerner wanted the people of Curitiba to have a better quality of life.

3. _____ Under his leadership, city planners established priorities.

4. _____ Jaime Lerner was an architect.

5. _____ He was a creative thinker.

6. _____ Poor people receive fresh food when they bring bags of garbage to special centers.

7. _____ The food they receive (in exchange for trash) is good for the health.

8. _____ Curitiba's mass-transit system consists of a system of buses.

9. _____ Subways are more expensive than buses.

10. _____ Subway-style doors allow passengers to get on and off the bus efficiently.

11 **Discussing the Reading** Talk about your answers to these questions.

1. What is the population of the major cities in your country? Is overcrowding a problem?

2. What are some problems in your city?

3. What kind of mass transit is available in your city? Is it clean and efficient?

4. Does your city have a recycling program? If so, tell your group about it. How does it work?

5. Are there homeless people in your city? If so, is there a program to help them?

6. What programs are there to protect the environment in your city?

Part 2 Reading Skills and Strategies

Sick-Building Syndrome

Before You Read

1 **Making Predictions** The next reading discusses a problem in big cities—indoor air pollution. Before you read, think about the causes of air pollution, both outdoors (outside) and indoors (inside buildings). Brainstorm as many causes as you can think of and write them in the chart on page 33. Look at the picture for help.

Causes of Outdoor Air Pollution	Causes of Indoor Air Pollution

▲ How many pollutants can you find?

Reading Tip

As you learned in Chapter 1, a paragraph usually tells about one topic and gives a **main idea** or point about that topic. Often there is one sentence that tells the **main idea** of the paragraph.

Read

2 Skimming for Main Ideas Skim the next article. Do not use a dictionary, and don't worry about the details. When you finish each paragraph, write the topic and main idea of that paragraph. You can copy the main idea directly from the sentence (or sentences) or use your own words to restate the main idea.

Sick-Building Syndrome

A   Elizabeth Steinberg was a healthy 16-year-old student on the tennis team at St. Charles High School, west of Chicago, Illinois. But then she started to have strange health problems. The same thing happened to dozens of teachers and students at the school. They went to doctors for treatment of a number of symptoms such as sore throats, tiredness, headaches, and respiratory (breathing) difficulties. Doctors treated respiratory infections with antibiotics, but the condition didn't seem to improve, except—mysteriously—on weekends and over vacations, when the symptoms disappeared. Experts came to investigate and find the cause. They discovered that St. Charles High, like thousands of other schools and office buildings nationwide, is a "sick building"—in other words, a building that creates its own indoor air pollution.

Topic: _____

Main idea: _____

_____

B   People have worried about smog for many years, and the government has spent billions of dollars to try to clean up the air of big cities. But now we find that there is no escape from unhealthy air. Recent studies have shown that air inside many homes, office buildings, and schools is full of pollutants: chemicals, mold, bacteria, smoke, and gases. These pollutants are causing a group of unpleasant and dangerous symptoms that experts call "sick-building syndrome." First discovered in 1982, sick-building syndrome most often includes symptoms similar to those of the flu (watering eyes, headaches, and so on) and respiratory infections such as tonsillitis, bronchitis, and pneumonia.

Topic: _____

Main idea: _____

_____

C   Although most common in office buildings and schools, the indoor pollution that causes sick-building syndrome can also occur in houses. Imagine a typical home. The people who live there burn oil, wood, or gas for cooking and heating. They might smoke cigarettes, pipes, or cigars. They use chemicals for cleaning. They use products made of particleboard, which is an inexpensive kind of board made of very small pieces of wood held together with a chemical. They use products such as computers, fax machines, and copiers that are made of plastic. These products give off chemicals that we can't see, but we do breathe them in. In some homes, carbon monoxide from cars in the garage can enter the house. And in many areas, the ground under the building might send a dangerous gas called radon into the home. The people in the house are breathing in a "chemical soup."

Topic: _____

Main idea: _____

_____

D   Then what causes sick-building syndrome in an office building or school, where people don't smoke or burn oil, wood, or gas? Experts have discovered several sources of sick-building syndrome; among these are mold and bacteria, synthetic products, and lack of ventilation—or the movement of fresh air into and out of the building. In many buildings, rain has leaked in and caused water damage to walls and carpets. This allows mold and bacteria to grow. Air conditioning systems are another place where mold and bacteria can grow. Synthetic (that is, man-made) products such as paint, carpeting, and furniture can be found in all offices and schools. These products release toxic (poisonous) chemicals into the air. Perhaps the most common cause of sick-building syndrome, however, is lack of ventilation. Most modern office buildings are tightly sealed; in other words, the windows don't open, so fresh air doesn't enter the building. In a building with mold, bacteria, or toxic chemicals, lack of ventilation makes the situation more serious.

Topic: _____

Main idea: _____

_____

E   There are several solutions to the problem of sick-building syndrome; the most important of these is cleaning the building. First, of course, experts must determine the specific cause in any one building. Then workers probably need to take out carpets, wallpaper, and ceiling tiles in order to remove mold and bacteria. Also, they need to clean out the air conditioning system and completely rebuild the system of ventilation. They should remove synthetic products and bring in natural products, instead, if they are available.

Topic: _____

Main idea: _____

_____

F   All of this sounds difficult and expensive. But there is another possible solution that is simple and inexpensive. NASA (the National Aeronautics and Space Administration) was trying to find ways to clean the air in space stations. One scientist with NASA discovered that *houseplants* actually remove pollutants from the air. Certain plants seem to do this better than others. Spider plants, for example, appear to do the best job. Even defoliated plants (without leaves) worked well! In another study, scientists found that the chemical interaction among soil, roots, and leaves works to remove pollutants. 70

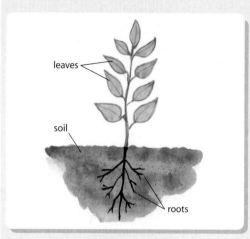

▲ Plants help clean the air.

Topic: _____

Main idea: _____

_____

G   This seems like a good solution, but we don't know enough yet. There are many questions. For instance, which pollutants can plants remove? Which can't they remove? How many plants are necessary to clean the air in a room—one or two or a whole *forest* of plants? When we are able to answer these questions, we might find that plants offer an important pollution-control system for the 21st century. 75

Topic: _____

Main idea: _____

_____

After You Read

3 **Checking Your Answers** Compare your answers from Activity 2 with the answers of another student. Are they the same? Are they the same but perhaps in different words? Give reasons for your answers. It's okay if one of you wants to change an answer after listening to your partner's ideas!

4 Understanding Pronoun Reference Look back at the reading selection "Sick-Building Syndrome" to find the meanings of the following pronouns. What does each pronoun refer to?

1. they (Paragraph A, line 4) _____

2. they (Paragraph C, line 26, twice) _____

3. them (Paragraph C, line 31) _____

4. these (Paragraph D, line 37) _____

5. these (Paragraph E, line 50) _____

6. they (Paragraph E, line 53) _____

7. they (Paragraph G, line 73) _____

5 Discussing the Reading Talk about your answers to these questions.

1. Is there a problem with smog in your city? When is it the worst? What are the causes?

2. Have you ever experienced sick-building syndrome? If so, what were your symptoms?

3. How many possible pollutants can you find in your home and classroom? Make a list.

4. In your home country, do people usually have houseplants? Why or why not?

5. In your opinion, why wasn't sick-building syndrome a problem in the past?

Responding in Writing

6 Summarizing Choose one of the following paragraphs from the reading in Part 1, page 28, to summarize.

- Garbage Collection (Paragraph C)
- Transportation (Paragraph D)
- A Creative Social Program (Paragraph E)

Because a summary is shorter than the original, try to write only three or four sentences. To write this summary, follow these steps:

- Make sure that you understand the paragraph well.
- Identify the topic, the main idea, and important details.
- Choose two or three important details.
- Do not include less important details.

In order to summarize this in your own words, *don't look at the original paragraph as you write.* When you finish writing, compare your summary with those of other students who summarized the same paragraph. Is your main idea the same? Did you choose the same details?

7 **Writing Your Own Ideas** Choose one of the topics below to write a paragraph about. Write your own thoughts. Try to use vocabulary from this chapter.

- something you like (or don't like) about living in a city
- improving city life
- what you have learned about sick-building syndrome

What's the main idea of your paragraph? _____

Talk it Over

8 **Interviewing** Interview as many people as you can. Ask them the two questions below and take notes on their answers. Then compare your findings with those of other students.

1. Do you think that city life in the future will be better or worse than it is today? Give two reasons that explain why.

2. How will city life be different in the future from what it is today? Make predictions.

Part 3 Building Vocabulary and Study Skills

1 **Focusing on Words from the Academic Word List** Fill in the blanks with words from the Academic Word List in the box. When you finish, turn back to page 27 and check your answers.

access	established	income	residents
creative	focus	method	transportation
environment	global	predict	under

A City That's Doing Something Right

There's good news and bad news about life in modern cities—first, the bad. People who study population growth _____ a nightmare by the year 2025: the _____ population will be more than eight billion, and almost four billion of these people will be living in cities in developing countries such as India and Nigeria. Population growth is already causing unbelievable overcrowding. Due to this overcrowding, many cities have problems with air pollution, disease, and crime. People spend hours in gridlock—that is, traffic so horrible that it simply doesn't move—when they commute daily from their homes to their work and back. There isn't enough water, _____, or housing. Many people don't have _____ to health services or jobs. Now the good news: in *some* cities, instead of worsening, urban life is actually getting much better.

A City and Its Mayor

It might not be a surprise to find that life in affluent cities is improving. But what about cities that *aren't* rich? The city of Curitiba, Brazil, proves that it's possible for even a city in a developing country to offer a good life to its _____. The former mayor of Curitiba for 25 years, Jaime Lerner is an architect and a very practical person. _____ his leadership, the city planners _____ a list of priorities— in other words, a list of what was most important to work on. They decided to _____ on the _____ and on the quality of life. With an average _____ of only about $2,000 per person per year, Curitiba has the same problems as many cities. However, it also has some _____ solutions.

Strategy

Scanning

You can scan a reading to find information quickly. Follow these steps to scan:

- Know the information that you want to find, or the question you want answered.
- Look for that information.
- Move your eyes quickly across the words until the information that you want "jumps out" at you.
- Don't read every word.

You will practice scanning throughout the book when you look for specific information and details.

Language Similarities: False Cognates

Some words in English might sound similar to words in your language. These are called cognates. Usually, cognates help your English vocabulary. However, sometimes the meaning is completely different. This can cause you problems! Words in two languages with a similar sound but a different meaning are called **false cognates**. Do not try to translate them. Here are some examples.

- *Actualmente* (in Spanish) means "presently, now," so Spanish-speaking students think that *actually* (in English) means the same thing. But it doesn't. In English, actually means "really, truly" or "although this seems strange."

  Example The population has grown, but traffic has **actually** decreased 30 percent.

- *Manshon* (in Korean and Japanese) means "an expensive apartment building." However, in English, *mansion* means "a large expensive single-family house."

  Example If I win the lottery, I'll buy a **mansion** in Beverly Hills.

- *Magazi* (in Greek) means "store, shop." However, in English, a *magazine* is something to read.

  Example I read an interesting article yesterday in a news **magazine**.

- *Lunatik* (in Russian) means "a sleepwalker—a person who walks in his or her sleep." However, in English, *lunatic* means "a crazy person."

  Example Everyone thought he was a **lunatic** when he decided to quit school one month before graduation.

Are there any false cognates that give trouble to people who speak your language? If so, share them with the class.

Understanding Parts of Speech

To figure out the meaning of a new word from the context, you may find it helpful to know its part of speech; that is, is the word a noun, a verb, an adjective, or an adverb? Many words are related to one another; they have the same stem (base word) but different endings for different parts of speech.

Example

Cities around the **globe** need to find solutions to similar problems, so city planners sometimes meet at a **global** conference. (*Globe* is a noun. *Global* is an adjective; it describes the noun *conference*.)

2 **Understanding Parts of Speech** Read the words below. Write the missing noun, verb, adjective, or adverb in the blank white boxes. Then listen and check your answers. (The shaded boxes indicate that no word exists for that part of speech.)

	Noun	Verb	Adjective	Adverb
1.	beauty, beautification	beautify	*beautiful*	beautifully
2.	creation		creative	creatively
3.	crowd		crowded	
4.	difference		different	differently
5.			difficult	
6.	efficiency		efficient	
7.	pollution, pollutant	pollute		
8.		predict	predictable	predictably
9.	safety	save		safely
10.		solve	solvable	
11.		worsen	worse	

Next, complete each sentence below with words from the preceding chart. Use the correct form of the base word and write the part of speech in the parentheses after each blank—(*n.*) for noun, (*v.*) for verb, (*adj.*) for adjective, and (*adv.*) for adverb.

1. solve

They are trying to find a _____solution_____ (*n.*) to the problem of

overcrowding, but this is a difficult problem to _____solve_____ (*v.*).

2. pollute

Most people know about air _____ (   ) in big cities, but

they're just beginning to learn about the many _____ (   )

that we have inside buildings.

3. crowd

There are _____ (   ) of people everywhere; the mass-transit

system is especially _____ (   ).

4. save

The city is not _____ (   ) because of crime. People can't

leave their homes _____ (   ) at night, and the police can't

provide for their _____ (   ).

5. beautify

Many people bring plants into their homes because the plants are

_____ (   ). However, it's possible that these plants not only

_____ (   ) the environment but also clean the air.

6. predict, worsen

Some people _____ ( ) that urban life will get _____

( ); according to their _____ ( ), conditions will

_____ ( ) every year.

7. differ

The causes of indoor air pollution _____ ( ) from area to

area. One reason for the _____ ( ) is that people heat their

homes _____ ( ). People in some areas burn wood for

heat; in other areas, they use something _____ ( ).

8. efficient

The mass-transit system in our city is not very _____ ( ),

so we need to replace it with one that runs more _____ ( ).

LOOKING UP PARTS OF SPEECH

You learned in Chapter 1 that you don't need to look up every new word in a dictionary because you can often guess the meaning from the context. Sometimes, however, you cannot figure out the meaning and need to use a dictionary. Also, you may want to use a dictionary for other purposes. For instance, you might want to find out the part of speech of a word or to learn related words. A dictionary will tell you the parts of speech a word can be, usually with these abbreviations:

n. = noun	adj. = adjective	prep. = preposition
v. = verb	adv. = adverb	conj. = conjunction

The abbreviation appears before the meanings of the word with that part of speech. The dictionary entry below shows that the word *access* can be a noun (with two meanings) or a verb (with one meaning). A related adjective is *accessible*.

> **ac·cess**[1] /ˈæksɛs/ *n.* [U] **1** the right to enter a place, use something, see someone, etc.: *Anyone with* **access to** *the Internet can visit our website.* | *Do you* **have access to** *a car?* **2** the way you enter a building or get to a place, or how easy this is: *The only* **access to** *the building is through the parking lot.* | *The law requires businesses to improve* **access for** *disabled customers.*
> →**gain access** at GAIN
> **access**[2] *v.* [T] to find and use information, especially on a computer: *I couldn't access the file.*
> **ac·ces·si·ble** /əkˈsɛsəbəl/ *adj.* **1** easy to reach or get into [≠ **inaccessible**]: *The park is not* **accessible by** *road.* **2** easy to obtain or use: *A college education wasn't* **accessible to** *women until the 1920s.* **3** easy to understand and enjoy: *I thought his last book was more accessible.*
> —**accessibility** /əkˌsɛsəˈbɪləti/ *n.* [U]

---

3 **Looking Up Parts of Speech** If possible, everyone in the class should use the same kind of dictionary for the following activity. Work quickly. The first student with the correct answers is the winner.

Find these words in your dictionary. Write the part of speech on the lines before each word. (See page 42 for abbreviations.). Some words, in different contexts, can be more than one part of speech.

1. _adj._ terrible
2. _____ discipline
3. _____ value
4. _____ original
5. _____ pleasant

6. _____ water
7. _____ expert
8. _____ commute
9. _____ farm
10. _____ smog

11. _____ produce
12. _____ actually
13. _____ mystery
14. _____ individual
15. _____ trash

4 **Searching the Internet** Do an Internet search for English-language newspapers in one of the countries below (or choose any other country in which English is not the native language). Use a search engine.

Armenia	Egypt	Mexico	Senegal
Brazil	Greece	Russia	Taiwan
Costa Rica	Japan	Saudi Arabia	Thailand

What is happening in the capital city of that country today? Find an article online about this. Discuss your findings with another student.

Part 4 Focus on Testing

GETTING MEANING OF VOCABULARY FROM CONTEXT

Some standardized exams test how well you can guess the meaning of a new word or phrase from the context. Often on such tests, one or more answers may be very close in meaning, but not correct. Another answer might have the correct part of speech, but the wrong meaning. Another might simply be wrong; perhaps it is the opposite of the correct answer or has the wrong part of speech. Always keep in mind that there is only one correct answer.

1 **Practice** Guess the meanings of the underlined words from the reading selection "Sick-Building Syndrome" on pages 34–36. Choose the correct answers.

1. They went to doctors for treatment of a number of <u>symptoms</u> such as tiredness, headaches, <u>sore</u> throats, and respiratory problems.

   symptoms:
   - (A) syndromes
   - (B) pains in the head
   - (C) signs of a sickness
   - (D) kinds of medicine
   - (E) kinds of tiredness

   sore:
   - (A) well
   - (B) painful
   - (C) difficult
   - (D) problem
   - (E) in the throat

2. These pollutants are causing a group of unpleasant and dangerous symptoms that experts call "sick-building <u>syndrome</u>."
   - (A) polluted
   - (B) problem with a large building
   - (C) symptom
   - (D) combination of symptoms
   - (E) danger

3. In many buildings, rain has <u>leaked in</u> and caused water damage to walls and carpets.
   - (A) escaped
   - (B) entered the ventilation system
   - (C) come in accidentally
   - (D) worsened
   - (E) rained

4. The air was full of <u>pollutants</u>: chemicals, mold, bacteria, smoke, and gases.
   - (A) pollution
   - (B) chemicals
   - (C) smog inside a building
   - (D) things that pollute
   - (E) gases

Self-Assessment Log

Read the lists below. Check (✓) the strategies and vocabulary that you learned in this chapter. Look through the chapter or ask your instructor about the strategies and words that you do not understand.

Reading and Vocabulary-Building Strategies

❏ Getting meaning from context
❏ Recognizing the main idea
❏ Recognizing supporting details
❏ Understanding italics
❏ Making inferences
❏ Skimming for main ideas
❏ Understanding parts of speech
❏ Looking up parts of speech

Target Vocabulary

Nouns

❏ access*
❏ agricultural operation
❏ crops
❏ developing countries
❏ environment*
❏ gridlock
❏ income*
❏ mass transit
❏ method*
❏ pollution
❏ priorities
❏ produce
❏ recycling plant

❏ residents*
❏ transportation*
❏ trash
❏ urban dwellers

Verbs

❏ commute
❏ crowd
❏ cultivate
❏ established*
❏ focus*
❏ predict*
❏ solve
❏ worsening

Adjectives

❏ affluent
❏ creative*
❏ global*

Adverb

❏ efficiently

Preposition

❏ under*

* These words are from the Academic Word List. For more information on this list, see www.vuw.ac.nz/lals/research/awl.

Business and Money

This chapter looks at business and money, or we could say, *the business of money.* The first reading selection in this chapter discusses organizations that are helping people escape from poverty. It looks at different types of loans and reports what women and men do with such loans. In Part 2, the reading selection explores the question "Why do we buy things?" It explores the relationship between advertising and psychology by looking at consumerism and the human brain. What kind of advertising makes you want to buy something? Part 3 focuses on suffixes and parts of speech to help build vocabulary. In Part 4, you will analyze the difference between an *implication* and an *inference*, which is an important distinction that will help you with tests.

> ❝ Prosperity is a way of living and thinking, and not just money or things. Poverty is a way of living and thinking, and not just a lack of money or things. ❞
>
> —Eric Butterworth
> Scholar, author of *Spiritual Economics* (1916–2003)

Connecting to the Topic

1. What do you think this shopper is buying?

2. Why do people shop? Name ten reasons.

3. What do you like about shopping? What do you dislike?

Banking on Poor Women

Before You Read

1 **Previewing the Topic** Look at the photos and discuss the questions.

1. Compare the social or economic classes of the people in the photos below. What are some words to describe their economic situations?

2. What might people be doing in the photo of the bank? Think of as many verbs as you can for activities that usually take place in a bank.

3. What is necessary in order to get a business loan (to borrow money) from a bank?

▲ Selling produce in a market in Ecuador

▲ Women weaving in the Philippines

▲ Banking in the United Arab Emirates

4. Is it possible for people to move up in their economic class? (If so, how can they do it?) Is there more possibility of this in some countries than in others?

5. Brainstorm the problems of very poor people. Then brainstorm possible solutions to these problems. Write your ideas in the chart below.

Problems	Possible Solutions

2 Thinking Ahead Read these quotations. Can you state them in other words? Which one(s) do you like or agree with? Why? Discuss them with a group.

> "From borrowing one gets poorer and from work one gets richer."
> —Isaac Bashevis Singer, Yiddish novelist (1904–1991)

> "A bank is a place where they lend you an umbrella in fair weather and ask for it back when it begins to rain."
> —Robert Frost, American poet (1874–1963)

3 Previewing Vocabulary Read the words and phrases below. Listen to the pronunciation of each word. Put a check mark (✓) next to the words you know. For the words that you don't know, *don't* use a dictionary. Try to understand them from the reading. You'll work with some of these words in the activities.

Nouns
- ❏ capacity
- ❏ character
- ❏ collateral
- ❏ eradication
- ❏ fund
- ❏ grants
- ❏ literacy
- ❏ microlending
- ❏ poverty
- ❏ requirement

Verbs
- ❏ funding
- ❏ lift
- ❏ plow
- ❏ took (take) the initiative

Adjectives
- ❏ anonymous
- ❏ subsidiary
- ❏ worthless

Expressions
- ❏ social ills
- ❏ peer pressure

Getting Meaning from Context: Understanding *e.g.* and *i.e.*

Sometimes certain abbreviations (shortened forms of words) help you understand a new word or phrase. Here are two.

e.g. = for example

i.e. = that is; in other words

4 Getting Meaning from Context Read the sentences below. Use a felt-tip pen (yellow, green, etc.) to highlight the words that give clues to the meaning of the underlined word(s). Then answer the questions.

1. This is a group of <u>entrepreneurs</u>—i.e., people who own and run their own small businesses.

What are entrepreneurs?

_____

2. Instead of collateral, there is <u>peer pressure</u>; i.e., group members make sure that each person pays back his or her loan.

What happens when there is peer pressure?

_____

3. The Global Fund for Women helps find solutions to <u>social ills</u>—e.g., violence and lack of education.

What are examples of social ills?

_____

Recognizing Similar Meanings but Different Parts of Speech

Sometimes the context has an explanation of the new word, but in order to think of a synonym, you need to change the part of speech.

Example

For many people, there seems to be no escape from **poverty**; in other words, they are **poor**, and they have no hope that this will change.

In this example, you see that *poverty* is close in meaning to *poor*, but the two words have different parts of speech. *Poverty* is a noun, and *poor* is an adjective. (*Poverty* is "poorness" or the condition of being poor.)

5 Recognizing Synonyms Highlight the words below that mean the same or almost the same as the underlined words. Then write your answers to the questions that follow.

> If this woman wants to borrow money, she must show that she (1) is honest (has <u>character</u>), (2) is able to run her business (has <u>capacity</u>), and (3) owns a house or land or something valuable.

1. What part of speech is *character*? _____

2. What does *character* mean? (Write the noun form.) _____

3. What part of speech is *capacity*? _____

4. What does *capacity* mean? (Write the noun form.) _____

Strategy

Using Parts of Speech to Understand Vocabulary

Sometimes the context does not give a clear definition or example of a new word. You can't be sure about the exact meaning, but you can still make an intelligent guess and not waste time by going to the dictionary. First, figure out the part of speech of the new word. Then imagine in your mind what other word might be logical in that place.

Example

> Everyone in the group must **approve** the loan of every other group member, or Grameen Bank won't lend the money.

Part of speech: verb
Possible meanings: agree to; say OK about; sign

Some of your guesses might be wrong, but that's not a problem. If you see the word again in a different context, the meaning will become clearer.

6 Using Parts of Speech to Understand Vocabulary Make guesses about the underlined words below. Don't worry about being right or wrong. Just try to be logical. When you finish, compare your answers with a partner's.

1. A poor woman has an idea to <u>lift</u> her and her family out of poverty.

Part of speech: _____

Possible meanings: _____

2. The primary goal of Grameen Bank and other, similar programs is the <u>eradication</u> of poverty.

Part of speech: _____

Possible meanings: _____

3. As poverty has decreased, there have been some surprising secondary effects of microlending programs. Perhaps the main <u>subsidiary</u> effect has been a change in the social status of women.

Part of speech: _____

Possible meanings: _____

4. She began the Global Fund for Women. This <u>fund</u> has given $37 million to over 2,500 women's groups. It gives <u>grants</u>, not loans. The money is given, not lent.

fund

Part of speech: _____

Possible meanings: _____

grants

Part of speech: _____

Possible meanings: _____

5. With careful planning and cooperation, most people use the money well and then <u>plow</u> both money and knowledge back into their communities.

Part of speech: _____

Possible meanings: _____

Read

7 **Reading an Article** As you read the following selection, think about the answer to this question: *How can banks help poor women to change their lives?* Then do the activities that follow the reading.

Banking on Poor Women

A   For many people, there seems to be no escape from **poverty**; in other words, they are poor, and they have no hope that this will ever change. In addition, they have the social problems of poverty—among them, low social status, violence, poor health, and lack of education.

B   Imagine this situation: a poor woman has an idea for a small business to 5
lift herself and her family out of poverty. She needs a little money to begin
this business. She goes to a bank to borrow the money, and the banker
interviews her. At this bank, as at most banks, the borrower must meet three
necessary conditions: character, capacity, and collateral. That is, if this
woman wants to borrow money from the bank, she must show that she (1) 10
is honest (has character), (2) is able to run her business (has capacity), and
(3) owns a house, land, or something valuable (has collateral) for the bank
to take if she can't pay back the money. So what happens to the woman?
The bank won't lend her the money because she doesn't have any collateral.
In such a situation, there seems to be no way for the woman to break the 15
cycle of poverty and the problems that are associated with it.

Microlending

C   One possible solution these days is microlending. This is a system of
special banks and programs that are loaning money to "the poorest of the
poor." The idea began in Bangladesh, with a man named Mohammad
Yunus, who founded Grameen Bank. The bank lends small amounts of 20
money to people who want to go into business. These are people who
could never receive a loan from a "regular" bank. To receive a loan through
Grameen Bank, people still must have character and capacity, but
collateral is not necessary any longer. There is a different requirement:
each borrower must join a "borrowing group." This small group meets 25
regularly, follows a list of rules from the bank, and offers advice and
support to members. Instead of collateral, there is peer pressure; i.e.,
group members make sure that each person pays back his or her loan. They
want to keep their "good name" and continue doing business with the bank.

What Works, What Doesn't

D   Grameen Bank has had many successes and only a few failures. In a 30
developing country such as Bangladesh, a person can buy a cow or a
sewing machine and begin a small business with only $20 to $50. Today,
there are 3.7 million borrowers in 46,000 villages in Bangladesh. The bank
makes over $33 million in loans in a typical month, and the repayment rate
is an amazing 98%. At first, the bank lent half of the money to men and half 35
to women. Unfortunately, most of the Bangladeshi men spent the money
on themselves, not the business. Now, 94 percent of the borrowers are women.
In Bangladesh—and other countries that started similar microlending
programs—the bankers soon learned that urban programs were not as
successful as rural ones. Borrowers in cities did not always repay the loans. 40
Because of the importance of peer pressure, microlending is more effective
in small villages, where everyone knows and depends on everyone else,
than in urban areas (where it's possible to be anonymous—unknown).

Subsidiary Effect

E   The primary goal of this and other similar programs is the **eradication** of poverty. However, as poverty has decreased, there have been some surprising secondary effects of microlending programs. Perhaps the main **subsidiary** effect has been a change in the **social** status of women. Traditionally, in some societies people thought of women as **worthless**. But when a woman has **access** to money and is able to demonstrate her capacity for business, she often receives more respect than before from the male members of her family and from the entire village.

Global Fund for Women

F   In any country, women are the poorest of the poor. They produce more than half of the world's food, but they own just one percent of the world's land. They are 51 percent of the world's population, but very, very little money goes to programs to help them. In the late 1980s, Anne Firth Murray **took the initiative** and began the Global Fund for Women. Unlike microlending programs, this **fund** gives **grants**, not loans. The money is *given*, not *lent*. Another difference is that unlike Grameen Bank, which helps people begin businesses, the

▲ Woman at work in Nigeria

direct focus of the Global Fund for Women is to help find solutions to **social ills**—e.g., violence against women, lack of health care, and lack of education. Since 1987, the fund has given $37 million to over 2,500 women's groups in 160 countries. For instance, the fund has helped the Petersburg Center for Women in St. Petersburg, Russia. This center cares for women who are the victims of violence and abuse from family members. In Kenya, the Global Fund supports a program that gives health care and education to women with AIDS. In a village in southern India, it is **funding** a woman who has started a **literacy** program to teach poor women to read.

Breaking the Cycle

G   Grameen Bank and the Global Fund for Women may use different methods, but they have the same goal—the eradication of poverty. They also have a lesson for banks around the world: it's good business to give a chance to the poor. With careful planning, education, and cooperation, most people use the money well and then **plow** the money and knowledge back into their communities. There is hope that they can begin to break the cycle of poverty for themselves, their families, and society.

Strategy

Organizing Ideas Using a Venn Diagram

One way to show similarities and differences between two things is with a graphic organizer called a Venn diagram. This diagram has two connecting circles. In the center is anything that is true of *both* things. On the right and left are the differences between them.

Bananas   **Bananas and Oranges**   **Oranges**

- yellow color
- long, curved shape

- fruit
- sweet

- orange color
- circular shape

8 **Organizing Ideas Using a Venn Diagram** What is the goal of both Grameen Bank and the Global Fund for Women? How do they differ in the way they work? Fill in this graphic organizer with information about Grameen Bank and the Global Fund for Women to show that they share the same goal but work in different ways.

Grameen Bank   **Common Goals**   **Global Fund for Women**

How does it work?   How does it work?

9 **Checking Comprehension: Identifying Details** On a piece of paper, write your answers to these questions.

1. What is necessary in order to borrow from Grameen Bank? What *isn't* necessary?

2. Why does Grameen Bank lend mostly to women? Why does it not lend to people in urban areas?

3. What is a subsidiary effect of microlending programs?

4. What are some social ills that are often associated with poverty?

10 Critical Thinking: Making Inferences Read the excerpt below from Paragraph E. Answer this question: *What might be some specific ways in which a woman with her own business "receives more respect"?* In other words, make inferences about how this changes her life.

> Traditionally, in some societies, people thought of women as worthless. But when a woman has access to money and is able to demonstrate her capacity for business, she often receives more respect than before from the male members of her family and from the entire village.

11 Discussing the Reading Talk about your answers to the questions below.

1. In a country that you know well, what kind of collateral do banks require before they loan money to someone?

2. Do people sometimes join a cooperative group to borrow money in that country? If so, what are these groups called? How do they work?

3. What are some social problems in that country? What are people doing to solve them?

12 Talk It Over: Understanding Irony *Irony* describes a situation that has the opposite result from what you might expect. Usually, this result is negative or bad. The following cartoon is ironic. What idea is the cartoonist expressing? Do you agree?

Consumerism and the Human Brain

Before You Read

Strategy

Previewing the Topic
It always helps to have ideas or questions in mind before you read. The more you think about and know about a topic before reading, the more you will understand the reading. The reading passage will confirm some of your ideas (tell you they are right), answer some of your questions, and correct some of your mistaken ideas.

1 **Previewing the Topic** Talk about your answers to the questions below.

1. Who are consumers? What do they do?

2. What are some reasons that people choose one brand of a product instead of a similar brand of the same product?

3. How does advertising influence people?

4. Look at the photo. Why might someone want to buy an SUV after seeing this?

▲ This could be yours!

Read

2 **Identifying the Topic and Main Idea** Read these paragraphs. Do not use a dictionary and don't worry about the details. When you finish, write the topic and main idea of each paragraph. You can copy the main idea directly from the sentence (or sentences), or use your own words to restate the main idea.

Consumerism and
the Human Brain

A   We are all consumers. We all buy and use products and services; that is, we consume. The word comes from the Latin *consumere*, which means "to use up, to waste or destroy." Most of us don't think of ourselves as wasteful or destructive, but the world economy is based on consumerism. Today, people worldwide have greater access than ever before to a huge variety of 5 products and, often, to dozens of brands of the same product. What makes us decide to buy Brand A instead of Brand B, when the two items are really identical? Why do we buy things that we don't actually need? The answer lies in marketing—the advertising and selling of products. Successful marketers use their knowledge of psychology and, increasingly, of recent 10 studies of the human brain, to persuade us to consume more and more.

Topic: _____

Main idea: _____

_____

B   A good understanding of human weakness is essential if a company wants to sell a product. One way that advertisers persuade us to buy a product is by targeting our dissatisfaction with ourselves, our fears. Consider for a moment a typical fear—fear of being offensive to other people. 15 Advertisers persuade us, for example, that if we don't buy their mouthwash, we'll have bad breath and offend other people. Dentists tell us that mouthwash is actually unnecessary; they explain that we need only simple dental hygiene—regular, correct use of a soft toothbrush and of dental floss. But we continue to spend money on mouthwash, breath freshener, and 20 breath mints. Our fear of offending people outweighs our dentists' logic.

Topic: _____

Main idea: _____

_____

C   In a similar way, advertisers also take advantage of our need for a good self-image, our desire to appear attractive, successful, and even exciting. Take the example of the Marlboro cowboy. For years, this famous image has appeared everywhere, in even the smallest rural villages. Many men 25 see it and think that's the kind of person they would like to be—strong, handsome, and adventurous—a person with an exciting life. Although it's irrational—impossible to explain reasonably—they buy the cigarettes because they want to be like the Marlboro man. It's common knowledge that the original model for these advertisements was a man addicted to 30 smoking who died of lung cancer. However, this brand of cigarette remains very popular. Another example is the recent popularity in the United States 35 of SUVs—sport utility vehicles. These vehicles are more expensive than most cars. They use more gas and create more pollution than most cars. 40 They take up more space than most cars. But TV commercials show them climbing rocky mountain roads and crossing rivers, which seems exciting to 45 many people. Most people who buy an SUV never get out of the city. They spend their morning commute in gridlock, not driving up and down mountains. Although it may seem irrational, advertisers persuade them that SUV owners are people with an exciting life.

▲ Is it worth it to have an SUV in the city?

Topic: _____

Main idea: _____

_____

▲ Why is this person choosing one sneaker instead of another?

D   With so many different (but 50 almost identical) brands of the same product, what causes us to choose one brand instead of another? According to Dr. Alan Hirsch, our sense of smell 55 actually influences our opinion of a product and our decision to buy it. A scientist at the Smell and Taste Treatment and Research Foundation in 60 Chicago, Hirsch ran a careful, well-organized study. There were two identical rooms with an identical pair of Nike sneakers in each room. There was only one difference: he sprayed one of the rooms with a scent of flowers. Volunteers entered each room and answered questions about the sneakers. The result was that 84 percent of the people preferred the sneakers in the room with the floral smell even though they were exactly the same as the ones in the other room! 65

Topic: _____

Main idea: _____

_____

E   There is also the effect of self-fulfilling prophecies. A self-fulfilling prophecy is a situation in which people cause a prediction to come true. 70 (For example, a teacher tells a class that they are especially intelligent, and that semester the class does especially well on exams.) In marketing, a successful advertisement persuades consumers that a product works well; their belief causes them to use the product in such a way that it does work well. For example, the ads for Brand X of a diet pill say, "Take this pill, and 75 you will lose weight because you won't be hungry." So people buy Brand X. Because they believe it will cause weight loss, they begin to eat less. They establish a new habit of eating less. The result? They lose weight. Is this because of the pill or because they are eating less?

Topic: _____

Main idea: _____

_____

F   Most of us like to think that we are reasonable, independent thinkers. 80 We like to believe that we have a good reason for our choices. We don't want to buy products because of some strange compulsion—some irrational desire that we can't control. The truth is, however, that with their increasing knowledge of what goes on in the human brain, marketers might have more power over us than we realize. 85

Topic: _____

Main idea: _____

_____

After You Read

3 **Identifying the Topic and Main Idea** After you write the topic and main idea of each paragraph above, compare your answers with those of another student. Are your answers the same? Are they the same but perhaps in different words? Give reasons for your answers. You can change an answer after listening to your partner's ideas.

4 **Understanding Pronoun Reference** Look back at the reading selection on pages 58–60 to find the meanings of the following pronouns. What does each pronoun refer to?

1. their (Paragraph A, line 10) _____

2. they (Paragraph B, line 18) _____

3. they (Paragraph C, line 28) _____

4. it (Paragraph D, line 58) _____

5. he (Paragraph D, line 64) _____

6. their (Paragraph E, line 74) _____

Cultural Note

Fighting Consumerism in Japan

In Japan, as in many other countries, advertising influences people to buy more and more. However, the Seikatsu Club is fighting against this. The Seikatsu Club is a **consumers'** cooperative group with over 259,000 members who don't like to call themselves **"consumers."** They are working to reduce the influence of marketing in their lives. They hold meetings at which they discuss the actual ingredients, value, and cost of various products. They do not buy any products (such as synthetic detergents) that harm the environment. They do not buy any food products that contain harmful or inessential chemicals. Most important, they are working to educate people to think for themselves. Are there organizations or movements similar to this in other countries?

5 **Discussing the Reading** Talk about your own buying habits. Follow these steps.

Step 1: Working alone, write a list of ten products that you buy regularly.
Step 2: Think about your answers to these questions:

- Do you always buy the same brand of each product?
- If so, can you give a reason for your choice?
- Does advertising influence your choice of products?

Step 3: In a group, share your list and answers.

6 **Summarizing** Choose one of the following paragraphs from the reading in Part 2, pages 58–60, to summarize.

- Paragraph B
- Paragraph C
- Paragraph D

Because a summary is shorter than the original, try to write only three or four sentences. To write this summary, follow these steps:

- Make sure that you understand the paragraph well.
- Identify the main idea.
- Choose two or three important details.
- Do not include less important details.

In order to summarize this in your own words, *don't look at the original paragraph as you write*. When you finish writing, compare your summary with those of other students who summarized the same paragraph.

7 Responding in Writing Choose one of the topics below to write a paragraph about. Write your own thoughts. Try to use vocabulary from this chapter.

- your opinion about microlending
- your opinion about the Global Fund for Women
- your opinion about the Seikatsu Club
- something that you have learned about advertising

What's the main idea of your paragraph? _____

_____

Talk it Over

8 **Discussing Advertisements** In small groups, choose one of the following products: toothpaste, cars, laundry detergent, or cigarettes. Look through magazines for advertisements on your product. Bring as many ads as you can to your group. Together, study them. What kind of psychology is the advertiser using? (Fear? Desire for a good self-image? Self-fulfilling prophecy?)

Part 3 Building Vocabulary and Study Skills

1 **Recognizing Word Meanings** Match the words with their meanings. Write the letters on the lines.

1. _____ literacy   **a.** being poor

2. _____ poverty   **b.** necessity

3. _____ requirement   **c.** not valuable

4. _____ anonymous   **d.** ability to read

5. _____ worthless   **e.** unknown

2 **Focusing on Words from the Academic Word List** Fill in the blanks with words from the Academic Word List in the box. When you finish, turn back to page 58 and check your answers. This activity continues on page 64.

access	consumers	identical	logic
consume (used 2 times)	economy	items	targeting

Consumerism and the Human Brain

A   We are all _____. We all buy and use products and
$_1$

services; that is, we _____. The word comes from the Latin
$_2$

consumere, which means "to use up, to waste or destroy." Most of us

don't think of ourselves as wasteful or destructive, but the world

_____ is based on consumerism. Today, people worldwide
$_3$

have greater _____ than ever before to a huge variety of
$_4$

products, and, often, to dozens of brands of the same product. What

makes us decide to buy Brand A instead of Brand B, when the two

_____ are really _____? Why do we buy
$_5$ $_6$

things that we don't actually need? The answer lies in marketing—the

advertising and selling of products. Successful marketers use their knowledge

of psychology, and, increasingly, of recent studies of the human brain, to

persuade us to _____ more and more.
$_7$

B   A good understanding of human weakness is essential if a company wants

to sell a product. One way that advertisers persuade us to buy a product is

by _____ our dissatisfaction with ourselves, our fears.
$_8$

Consider for a moment a typical fear—fear of being offensive to other people. Advertisers persuade us, for example, that if we don't buy their mouthwash, we'll have bad breath and offend other people. Dentists tell us that mouthwash is actually unnecessary; they explain that we need only simple dental hygiene—regular, correct use of a soft toothbrush and of dental floss. But we continue to spend money on mouthwash, breath freshener, and breath mints. Our fear of offending people outweighs our dentists' _____.

9

UNDERSTANDING PARTS OF SPEECH: SUFFIXES

Remember that in order to guess the meaning of a new word from the context, you might find it helpful to know its part of speech. Sometimes you can tell the part of speech from the suffix (the word ending). Here are some common suffixes, listed by the parts of speech that they usually indicate.

Nouns		**Adjectives**	
-er/-or	-ee	-ive	-ful
-ist	-(i)ty	-able/-ible	-ant/-ent
-sion/-tion	-ance/-ence	-(u)al	-ous
-ment	-ure	-ic(al)	-ar(y)
-acy		-ate	

3 **Understanding Parts of Speech: Suffixes** Are the following words nouns or adjectives? The suffixes will tell you. On the lines, write *n.* or *adj.* as in the examples.

1. _adj._ compulsive
2. _n._ spender
3. _____ successful
4. _____ marketer
5. _____ psychologist
6. _____ literacy
7. _____ identical
8. _____ violent
9. _____ influence
10. _____ information
11. _____ offensive

12. _____ influence
13. _____ compulsion
14. _____ violence
15. _____ computer
16. _____ pressure
17. _____ society
18. _____ addition
19. _____ expensive
20. _____ different
21. _____ poverty
22. _____ requirement

23. _____ pleasure
24. _____ enormous
25. _____ scientist
26. _____ basic
27. _____ failure
28. _____ special
29. _____ consumer
30. _____ public
31. _____ floral
32. _____ logical
33. _____ culture

4 Understanding Parts of Speech: Changing the Suffix Complete each sentence with a word related to the underlined word. Then look back at the list of suffixes to check your answers. The first one is done as an example.

1. _Marketers_ _____ use their knowledge of psychology to <u>market</u> their products. They hope that _____ will buy their goods, <u>consume</u> them, and soon feel the need to buy more.

2. That _____ TV commercial was _____ to many people. They were <u>offended</u> by its <u>violence</u> and didn't see the need for it.

3. Advertising is a kind of _____ that has a strong _____ on consumers; it should not only <u>influence</u> people to buy products, but also <u>inform</u> them.

4. This organization has been _____ in solving some serious <u>social</u> problems in that _____. Their <u>success</u> is due to hard work and the cooperation of many people.

Strategy

Paying Attention to Phrases

In recent years, linguists (experts on language) have been emphasizing the importance of learning new words in *phrases* instead of individually. Learning phrases instead of single words will help you to know how to use each new word as you learn it.

Certain words belong together in phrases. For example, a *noun phrase* can include adjectives and other words before or after the noun. A *verb phrase* may include noun objects or adverbs. A *prepositional phrase* begins with a preposition. An *infinitive phrase* begins with an infinitive and includes an object after the verb. Examples include the following:

Noun Phrases
greater access
access to information

Verb Phrases
spend money
educate people to spend wisely

Prepositional Phrases
in a similar way
with exciting lives

Infinitive Phrases
to save money
to buy Brand X

When you read, it is important to begin to notice words in phrases. Look just before and just after a word to see if it is part of a phrase. For example, if the word is a verb, is it followed by an object or by a preposition? If it is followed by a preposition, which one?

5 Paying Attention to Phrases Read the following paragraph from Part 1. Notice the underlined phrases. (There are more phrases than the ones underlined, but don't worry about those.) When you finish reading, decide what type of phrase each one is: *noun, verb, prepositional,* or *infinitive.* Write your answers in your notebook.

For many people, there seems to be no escape from poverty; in other words, they are poor, and they have no hope that this will ever change. In addition, they have the social problems of poverty. Imagine this situation: a poor woman has an idea for a small business to lift herself and her family out of poverty. She needs a little money to begin this business. She goes to a bank to borrow the money, and the banker interviews her. At this bank, as at most banks, the borrower must meet three necessary conditions: character, capacity, and collateral. That is, if this woman wants to borrow money from the bank, she must show that she (1) is honest (has character), (2) is able to run her business (has capacity), and (3) owns a house, land, or something valuable (has collateral) for the bank to take if she can't pay back the money. So what happens to the woman? The bank won't lend her the money because she doesn't have any collateral. In such a situation, there seems to be no way for the woman to break the cycle of poverty.

6 Noticing Words in Phrases Fill in the blanks with words that complete the phrases. If you need help (or to check your answers), you can scan each paragraph that follows the set of phrases. These paragraphs are from the reading in Part 2, "Consumerism and the Human Brain."

1. persuade us _____ buy a product

2. dissatisfaction _____ ourselves

3. fear of being offensive _____ other people

4. _____ hygiene

5. _____ floss

6. our fear _____ offending people

A   A good understanding of human weakness is essential if a company wants to sell a product. One way that advertisers persuade us to buy a product is by targeting our dissatisfaction with ourselves, our fears. Consider for a moment a typical fear—fear of being offensive to other people. Advertisers persuade us, for example, that if we don't buy their mouthwash, we'll have bad breath and offend other people. Dentists tell us that mouthwash is actually unnecessary; they explain that we need only simple dental hygiene—regular, correct use of a soft toothbrush and of dental floss. But we continue to spend money on mouthwash, breath freshener, and breath mints. Our fear of offending people outweighs our dentists' logic.

7. _____ a similar way

8. _____ advantage _____ our need for a good self-image

9. _____ knowledge

10. addicted _____ smoking

11. died _____ lung cancer

B   In a similar way, advertisers also take advantage of our need for a good self-image, our desire to appear attractive, successful, and even exciting. Take the example of the Marlboro cowboy. For years, this famous image has appeared everywhere, in even the smallest rural villages. Many men see it and think that's the kind of person they would like to be—strong, handsome, and adventurous—a person with an exciting life. Although it's irrational—impossible to explain reasonably—they buy the cigarettes because they want to be like the Marlboro man. It's common knowledge that the original model for these advertisements was a man addicted to smoking who died of lung cancer. However, this brand of cigarette remains very popular.

12. sport _____ vehicle

13. take _____ more space

14. get _____ _____ the city

C   Another example is the recent popularity in the United States of SUVs—sport utility vehicles. These vehicles are more expensive than most cars. They use more gas and create more pollution than most cars. They take up more space than most cars. But TV commercials show them climbing rocky mountain roads and crossing rivers, which seems exciting to many people. Most people who buy an SUV never get out of the city. They spend their morning commute in gridlock, not driving up and down mountains. Although it may seem irrational, advertisers persuade them that SUV owners are people with an exciting life.

 7 **Searching the Internet** Do an Internet search on the home page of one of the organizations in the chart on page 68. Find the answer to your question, write it in the chart, and share it with two other students.

Organization	Question	Answer
Grameen Bank	What types of businesses do Grameen borrowers have?	
Global Fund for Women	What is one program that the Global Fund is currently supporting?	
Seikatsu Club	What are some of the club's principles on safety, health, and the environment?	

Part 4 Focus on Testing

IMPLICATIONS AND INFERENCES

In this chapter and others, you have learned about implications and inferences. In the Focus on Testing section in Chapter 1, you also saw an example of how an inference question on the TOEFL® Internet-Based Test might be worded: *What can be inferred about Japanese universities from Paragraph C?*

After every passage in the reading section of the TOEFL® iBT, there will be at least one question about inferences or implications. Here is a summary of the differences between *imply* and *infer*.

About the verb *imply*:

- It means "communicate a meaning without directly saying it."

- Its subject is a person or thing that can communicate meanings. For example, "I implied that . . . "; "The author implies that . . . "; "Paragraph 4 implies that . . . "

About the verb *infer*:

- It means "understand a meaning even though it is not stated directly."

- Its subject must be a human or group of humans. For example, "I inferred that . . . "; "readers might infer that . . . "; "The police inferred that . . . "

1 **Practice** Look again at the reading "Consumerism and the Human Brain" on pages 58–60. Read it, then read the statements below and put a checkmark (✓) next to any statement that is both true according to the reading and grammatically correct. (Three sentences use *imply* and *infer* incorrectly—don't check those; underline them.) Write *false* next to the sentences that are false.

1. _____ Paragraph A implies that people are more wasteful than they think they are.

2. _____ Paragraph A infers that successful marketers are in favor of more consumption.

3. _____ We can infer from Paragraph B that good tooth care stops bad breath.

4. _____ In Paragraph C, the author implies that SUV owners live an exciting life.

5. _____ In Paragraph C, the author infers that SUV owners do not use their vehicles for exciting trips.

6. _____ Dr. Hirsh's research implies that a product could sell better if it smells better.

7. _____ Paragraph E implies that diet pills really do reduce a person's weight.

8. _____ Paragraph E implies that people believe diet pills work better than they actually do.

9. _____ The author implies throughout the reading that advertisers try to manipulate consumers' thoughts.

10. _____ Most readers will imply that this article takes a negative view of advertisers.

Self-Assessment Log

Read the lists below. Check (✔) the strategies and vocabulary that you learned in this chapter. Look through the chapter or ask your instructor about the strategies and words that you do not understand.

Reading and Vocabulary-Building Strategies

❑ Getting meaning from context: understanding *e.g.* and *i.e.*

❑ Recognizing synonyms

❑ Using parts of speech to understand vocabulary

❑ Organizing ideas: using a Venn diagram

❑ Understanding irony

❑ Skimming for the topic and main idea

❑ Understanding pronoun reference

❑ Understanding parts of speech: suffixes

❑ Paying attention to phrases

Target Vocabulary

Nouns

❑ access*
❑ capacity*
❑ character
❑ common knowledge
❑ consumer*
❑ dental floss
❑ dental hygiene
❑ dissatisfaction with (something)
❑ economy*
❑ eradication
❑ fear of (something)
❑ fund*

❑ grants*
❑ items*
❑ logic*
❑ marketers
❑ microlending
❑ poverty
❑ requirement*
❑ sport utility vehicle
❑ success
❑ violence

Verbs

❑ consume*
❑ died of (something)
❑ funding*
❑ influence
❑ inform
❑ lift
❑ offend
❑ persuade (someone) to (do something)
❑ plow
❑ take advantage of (something)
❑ targeting*

Adjectives

❑ addicted to (something)
❑ anonymous
❑ identical*
❑ social
❑ subsidiary*
❑ worthless

Expressions

❑ in a similar way
❑ peer pressure
❑ social ills
❑ take up space

* These words are from the Academic Word List. For more information on this list, see www.vuw.ac.nz/lals/research/awl.

Jobs and Professions

The world of work is changing, due in part to globalization and technology. Some of these changes include job security, job hopping, telecommuting, and workaholism. You will read about and discuss these issues in Part 1. The next reading is about how people are finding jobs these days. How do you look for work? Do you look online? In a newspaper? Is your interview in person, on the phone, or by video? There is a variety of creative options to the type of work we can do and the ways in which we find work. Part 3 provides opportunities to build vocabulary and study skills. Last, Part 4 focuses on strategies to help you read faster.

❝ Every job is a self-portrait of the person who does it. ❞

—Unknown

Connecting to the Topic

1 What business do you think these people are involved in?

2 What do you think they are discussing? Think of one sentence that each person might say.

3 Does this look like a company you would like to work for? Why or why not?

Changing Career Trends

1 Previewing the Topic Look at the photos and discuss the questions.

1. Where are the people in each photo? What are they doing?

2. What are five advantages of working from home? What are five disadvantages?

3. Can you think of some ways in which work has changed in the past 20 to 50 years?

4. Are the situations in the photos similar to work situations around the world?

▲ Working in cubicles

▲ Working from home

2 Previewing Vocabulary Read the words and phrases below. Listen to the pronunciation of each word. Put a check mark (✓) next to the words you know. For the words that you don't know, *don't* use a dictionary. Try to understand them from the reading. You'll work with some of these words in the activities.

Nouns

❏ career counselors	❏ manufacturing jobs
❏ cell phones	❏ outsourcing
❏ construction	❏ pleasure
❏ drawback	❏ posts
❏ globalization	❏ self-confidence
❏ identity	❏ stress
❏ job hopping	❏ telecommuting
❏ job security	❏ workaholism
❏ livelihood	❏ workforce

Verbs

❏ distract	❏ passionate
❏ keep up with	❏ rigid
❏ overwork	❏ secure
❏ upgrade	❏ temporary
❏ varies (vary)	❏ worldwide

Adjectives

❏ flexible
❏ leisure

Expression

❏ on the move

3 Getting Meaning from Context Use both specific clues in these sentences and your own logic to determine the meanings of the underlined words and expressions. Then write your guess about the meaning. Compare your answers with those of a partner.

1. Twenty years ago, in many countries, people could choose their <u>livelihood</u>, but they couldn't usually choose to change from one profession to another.

   _____

2. Many people with temporary jobs would prefer more permanent <u>posts</u>.

   _____

3. Even in Japan, where people traditionally had a very <u>secure</u> job for life, there is now no promise of a lifetime job with the same company.

   _____

4. When they lose their job, they also lose their <u>self-confidence</u>, or belief in their own ability.

   _____

5. They usually need to <u>upgrade</u> their skills to find a new, better job.

   _____

6. Because technology changes fast, workers need continuing education if they want to <u>keep up with</u> the field.

   _____

7. In many professions, <u>telecommuting</u> is now possible. People can work at home for some—or all—of the week and communicate by computer, telephone, and fax.

   _____

8. It's difficult for some people to focus on work when they are at home. The refrigerator, TV, and their children often <u>distract</u> them.

   _____

9. There is an advantage to technology: customers and clients have access to businesspeople at any time and anywhere. However, there is also a <u>drawback</u>: many businesspeople don't want to be available day and night.

   _____

10. Many people don't have time for their family, friends, or <u>leisure</u> activities such as hobbies, sports, or movies.

   _____

11. There are advantages and disadvantages to <u>globalization</u>, and we are all affected by it.

   _____

12. Some people are <u>flexible</u> and can adjust well to change, but others are more <u>rigid</u>.

flexible: _____

rigid: _____

13. Many people in society suffer from <u>alcoholism</u>, an addiction to alcohol. <u>Workaholism</u> is another common problem in the 21st century.

_____

4 **Comparing Answers** Compare your answers in the previous activity with those of other students. Were your answers similar? Now, go back to the vocabulary chart in Activity 2. Can you check any more words?

> ## Strategy
>
> **Previewing a Reading**
> It helps to preview a chapter or passage before you read it so you can get an idea of what the article is about. In other words, look it over quickly to see what you can expect. Specifically, look at
> - headings (the "titles" of the paragraphs), which indicate main topics
> - pictures
> - charts, figures, or diagrams

5 **Previewing a Reading** Look over the reading on pages 75–77, "Changing Career Trends." Answer the questions below.

1. What is the main topic? (Look at the title.) What are the five subtopics? (Look at the headings in bold)

2. What do the pictures tell you about the article?

3. Write at least two questions you have about the topic after previewing the article.

Read

6 **Reading an Article** As you read the following selection, think about the answer to this question: *What are some ways in which work is changing?* Read the selection. Do not use a dictionary. Then do the exercises that follow the reading.

Changing Career Trends

A   **A** hundred years ago in most of the world, people didn't have much choice about the work that they would do, where they would do it, or how they would do it. If their parents were farmers, they became farmers. The society—and tradition—determined their profession. Twenty years ago in many countries, people could choose their **livelihood**. They also had the certainty of a job for life, but they usually couldn't choose to change from one employer to another or from one profession to another. Today, this is not always the case. **Career counselors** tell us that the world of work is already changing fast and will change dramatically in the next 25 years.   10

Job Security

B   The situation **varies** from country to country, but in today's economy, there is generally less job security **worldwide**. Even in Japan, where people traditionally had a very **secure** job for life, there is now no promise of a lifetime job with the same company.   15 One reason for the lack of **job security** is the worldwide decrease in **manufacturing jobs**. Another reason is employers' need to hold down costs. This has resulted in two   20 enormous changes for the **workforce**. First, employers are creating more and more **temporary** jobs because they don't need to pay health insurance or other benefits to employees in these positions, as they would to people in permanent **posts**. Second, more and more companies are   25 **outsourcing**. In other words, they are closing offices and factories and sending work to other areas of the country or to other countries where labor   30 is cheaper. This happens with factory work and computer programming. Also, the call center industry is **on the move** —mostly to India. Increasingly,   35 when customers in Canada, the United States, England,

Decrease in Manufacturing Jobs, 1995–2002	
Brazil	↓20%
China	↓15%
Japan	↓16%
U.S.A.	↓11%
worldwide	↓11%

▲ A busy call center in India

and Australia call a company to order a product or ask for help with their computer, they actually speak with someone in India, although they might not know it. India is popular with companies because there is a well educated workforce, salaries are much lower than in other countries, and educated people are already fluent in English. New call center employees in India spend months in training. They learn to use the *accent* of their customers—Australian or American, for example.

The Effect of Insecurity

C   On the surface, it may seem that lack of job security is something undesirable. Indeed, pessimists point out that it is certainly a cause of **stress**. Many people find an **identity**—a sense of self—through their work. When they lose their job (or are afraid of losing it), they also lose their **self-confidence**, or belief in their own ability. This causes worry and depression. In Japan, for example, the daily newspaper *Asahi* reports a sudden rise in the number of businessmen who need psychological help for their clinical depression. However, this decrease in job security

▲ Japanese workers have far less job security than in the past.

may not necessarily be something bad. It is true that these days, workers must be more **flexible**—able to change to fit new situations. But optimists claim that flexible people are essentially happier, more creative, and more energetic than people who are **rigid**.

Job Hopping

D   Jumping from job to job (or "**job hopping**") has always been more common in some professions, such as building **construction**, and not very common in other professions like medicine and teaching. Today, job hopping is increasingly common in many fields because of **globalization**, technology, and a movement from manufacturing to services in developed countries. For example, people with factory jobs in industrial nations lose their jobs when factories move to countries where the pay is lower. The workers then need to **upgrade** their skills to find a new job. This is stressful, but the new job is usually better than the old one. Because technology changes fast, workers need continuing education if they want to **keep up with** the field. Clearly, technology provides both challenges and opportunities.

Telecommuting

E   In many ways, technology is changing the way people work. There are advantages and disadvantages to this. In some professions, for instance, **telecommuting** is now possible. People can work ₈₀ at home for some—or all— of the week and communicate by computer, telephone, and fax. An advantage of this is that it saves them from the stress of ₈₅ commuting to the workplace. It also allows them to plan their own time. On the other hand, it is difficult for some people to focus on work when they ₉₀ are at home. The refrigerator, TV, and their children often **distract** them. Telecommuters

▲ Do cell phones make life easier or more stressful?

must have enormous discipline and organizational skills. Technology is changing the way people work in another way—in the use of **cell** ₉₅ **phones**. There is an advantage: customers and clients have access to businesspeople at any time, anywhere. However, there is also a **drawback**: many businesspeople don't *want* to be available day and night. They prefer to have a break from their work life.

Workaholism

F   In the 21st century, **workaholism** will continue to be a fact of life for ₁₀₀ many workers. Workaholics are as addicted to their work as other people are to drugs or alcohol. This sounds like a problem, but it isn't always. Some people **overwork** but don't enjoy their work. They don't have time for their family, friends, or **leisure** activities such as hobbies, sports, and movies. These people become tired, angry, and depressed. The tension and ₁₀₅ stress often cause physical symptoms such as headaches. However, other people love their work and receive great **pleasure** from it. These people appear to be overworking but are actually very happy. Psychologists tell us that the most successful people in the changing world of work are flexible, creative, disciplined, and **passionate** about their work. But they are also ₁₁₀ people who make time for relaxing activities and for other people. They enjoy their work and enjoy time away from it, too.

7 **Finding the Main Idea** Read the sentences below and select the one main idea of the whole reading selection.

(A) Workaholism can lead to serious problems, but it can also create a happy life.

(B) Job hopping is a new trend that causes stress but can also lead people into good work experiences if they learn new job skills.

(C) It is important for people to be flexible in this changing world of work and to continue their education because they may need to change jobs several times in their lifetime.

(D) The world economy, globalization, and technology are causing many changes in the way people work today.

(E) In the workplace today, new technology is making it possible for people to work in different locations, even from home.

8 **Comprehension Check: Finding Important Details** Which statements are true about work today, according to the reading? Check (✓) them.

1. _____ People probably need to be prepared to change jobs several times in their lifetimes.

2. _____ Decreasing manufacturing jobs and increasing use of outsourcing are leading to less job security today than in the past.

3. _____ Lack of job security is always a bad thing.

4. _____ People who can change to fit a new situation are usually happier than people who can't.

5. _____ Many people find a sense of self through their work.

6. _____ People in some professions move from job to job more often than people in other professions.

7. _____ Technology is making work life better for everyone.

8. _____ Telecommuters don't need to drive to the office every day.

9. _____ All workaholics have problems with stress.

10. _____ The most successful people are workaholics.

9 **Checking Vocabulary** Find a word or expression in the reading for each definition below.

1. people who give advice about professions and careers = _____

2. the feeling that a worker will never lose his or her job = _____

3. the movement of jobs to places with lower salaries = _____

4. changing from one job to another = _____

5. disadvantage = _____

Critical Thinking: Recognizing Cause and Effect
In Chapters 1, 2, and 3 you saw three types of graphic organizers. Another use of
a graphic organizer is to show causes (or reasons) and effects (or results). This
graphic organizer shows the relationship between different actions such as why
something happens or the result of an action.

10 Critical Thinking: Recognizing Cause and Effect Paragraph B presents
several causes and effects. Look back at Paragraph B and find information to complete
this graphic organizer.

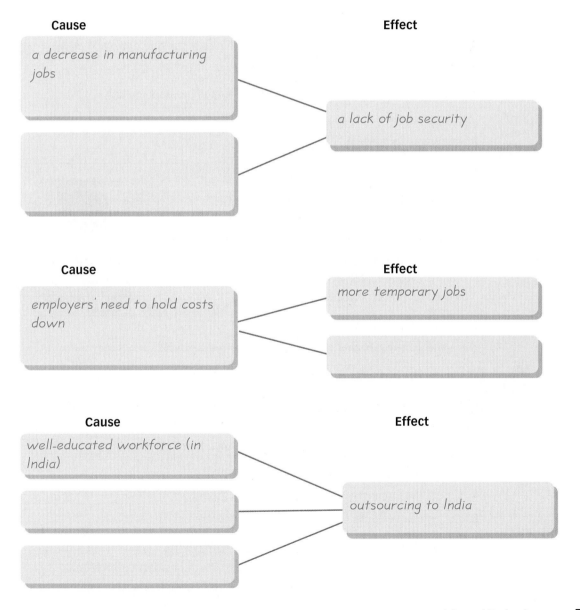

Cause

a decrease in manufacturing jobs

Effect

a lack of job security

Cause

employers' need to hold costs down

Effect

more temporary jobs

Cause

well-educated workforce (in India)

Effect

outsourcing to India

USING THE PREFIX *OVER-*

The prefix *over-* can appear as part of a noun, verb, or adjective. In some words, it indicates that there is too much of something or that someone is doing too much of a certain action.

> **Example** Some people **overwork** and don't enjoy their work.
> *overwork* (verb) = work too much

11 **Using the Prefix *Over-*** Read the definitions below. Write the words being defined. They begin with *over*. Then compare your answers with another student's.

1. do something too much (verb) = <u>*overdo*</u>

2. a place with too many people or things; a crowded place (adjective) =

   _____

3. give an estimate that is too high (verb) = _____

4. left unpaid, undone, or unreturned too long, past the due date (adjective) =

   _____

5. too many people in an area; a population that is too high (noun) =

   _____

Cultural Note

What Do You Call It?
In various countries, people have different terms for a portable telephone. In some countries, this is a **cell phone**. In other countries, it's a **hand phone** or a **mobile phone**. What do people call it in countries you are familiar with? Do you have one? How often do you use it?

▲ "Hello?"

12 **Discussing the Reading** Talk about your answers to these questions about a country that you know well.

1. Is it difficult for people to find jobs there? Why or why not?

2. Do most people have job security, or is there a lot of job hopping?

3. Is it possible for people to change professions?

4. How is the employment situation different from what it was 20 years ago?

5. Are companies outsourcing work *to* that country or *from* it?

6. Is telecommuting common? If so, in what professions?

7. Do people talk about workaholism? If so, do they consider it a problem?

8. How has technology changed the way in which people live and work?

Looking for Work in the 21st Century

1 **Thinking Ahead** Discuss your answers to these questions.

1. Where do people usually find out about job openings? Make a list of the places.

2. How do people prepare for a career? What steps do they need to take?

2 **Skimming for the Topic and the Main Idea** Read these paragraphs quickly. Don't worry about the details. When you finish, write the topic and main idea of each paragraph.

Looking for Work in the 21st Century

A   Not very long ago, when people needed to find a job, there were several possible steps. They might begin with a look through the classified ads in the newspaper. They could go to the personnel office at various companies and fill out an application, or they could go to an employment agency. They could even find out about a job opening   5
through word-of-mouth—from another person who had heard about it.

JOBS OFFERED

Jobs Domestic   8200

AUPAIR L/I 2 kids 8 & 9 House-keeping & driving. H-(818)555-1890;

Accounting Manager Mountain Plumbing Contractor looking for an Asst to Controller. Ideal Candidate will have 3- 5 Yrs. Const. Acctng/Job Costing Exp. Handling Revenues $5MM & greater. Proficiency in Windows based-computer enviroment w/Exp. in Excel/Word a must. Fax Resume to 714-555-5870 Attn: Oscar

ACTORS Comedians and great personalitites to teach fun traffic school 16-24hrs/wk. $12/hr. 800-555-6463

Administrative Assistant City office of nat'l org dedicated to helping low-income communities find creative solutions to problems of

CHEF, Sushi - Select, clean, carve, & prepare traditional Japanese sushi & sashimi incl. tuna, yellowtail, salmon, albacore, octopus, snapper, mackerel, eel, shimp, squid, scallops, sea urchin, smelt roe, lobster, rice, seaweed, & vegetables. Requires 2 yrs exp. in job offered. $4200/mo. 11a-2p & 5-10p Wed-Sun. Interview & job in Long Beach, CA. Send this ad and your resume/letter of qualifs to Job #MM057000, PO Box 1256, Sacramento, CA 95826-1256

AUTOMOBILES

Automobiles   9000

'06 M Roadster Z-3 $37,988 Silver cert. to 100K 15K Mi. (vinLC90000) Exp. 12/31 Bob's BMW (818)555-1352

'04 Camaro Z28 Convertible auto, 16K mi, like new. (562)555-1397

'03 Lumina V6, Auto. 58Kmi.

REAL ESTATE

HOMES FOR SALE   9001

Older home in town. Great location, schools, shops nearby. Motivated to sell. 3BR/2BA 1300sqft. $199k 910-555-7799

BAYS COVE Updated home in a great neighborhood. 3 bedrooms, 2 baths, den, fireplace with gas logs, beautiful large kitchen, over 2200 sqft, 2 car garage and large lot. Only $269,000. Call 245-555-1930 or page

OWNER FINANCING. . .2BR, 1.5 BA condo, eat-in kit., deck, 129,000.

716 DOVER...3BR, 2BA custom built , great rm w/stone F/P, FR, 2 car gar., wooded lot. $299,000.

B&S REALTY AND AUCTION 753-555-1967

▲ Classified Ads

Topic: _____

Main idea: _____

_____

B   These days, job hunting is more complicated. The first step is to determine
what kind of job you want (which sounds easier than it is) and make sure that
you have the right education for it. Rapid changes in technology and science
are creating many professions that never existed until recently. It is important   10
to learn about them because one might be the perfect profession for you. The
fastest-growing areas for new jobs are in computer technology and health
services. Jobs in these fields usually require specific skills, but you need to
find out exactly which skills and which degrees are necessary. For example, it
may be surprising to learn that in the sciences, an M.S. is more marketable   15
than a Ph.D.! In other words, there are more jobs available for people with a
Master of Science degree than for people with a doctorate. (However, people
who want to do research still need a Ph.D.)

Topic: _____

Main idea: _____

_____

C   How do people learn about "hot" new professions? How do they
discover their "dream job"? Many people these days go to a career   20
counselor. In some countries, job hopping has become so common that
career counseling is now "big business." People sometimes spend large
amounts of money for this advice. In Canada and the United States, high
school and college students often have access to free vocational counseling
services on campus. There is even a career organization, the Five O'Clock   25
Club, which helps members to set goals. Members focus on this question:
what sort of person do you want to be years from now? The members then
plan their careers around that goal. All career counselors—private or
public—agree on one basic point: it is important for people to find a career
that they love. Everyone should be able to think, "I'm having such a good   30
time. I can't believe they're paying me to do this."

Topic: _____

Main idea: _____

_____

D   After people have determined what their dream job is, they need to find it. The biggest change in job hunting these days is the use of the Internet. More and more employers are advertising job openings on their computer websites. More and more job hunters are applying for jobs online. There are also several thousand job boards, among them HotJobs.com, Jobsjobsjobs.com, and Monster.com. Some people think that online job hunting is only for people in technology fields, but this isn't true. Over 65 percent of online job seekers are from nontechnical fields. Even truck drivers now find jobs on the Internet!

Topic: _____

Main idea: _____

_____

E   So how does this work? A job seeker can reply to a "Help Wanted" notice on a company's website. This person can also post his or her résumé (page with information about education and work experience) on one—or many—of the online job boards. If a company is interested, the person still has to take the next step the old-fashioned way—actually go to the job interview and perhaps take a skills test. However, even this might soon change. In the near future, companies will be able to give the person a skills test and check his or her background (job history and education) online. But what about the interview? Companies will soon be able to interview the person by videolink, so people can interview for jobs in other cities—or even other countries—without leaving home. Clearly, job hunting is not what it used to be.

Topic: _____

Main idea: _____

_____

After You Read

3 **Checking Your Answers** After you write the topic and main idea of each paragraph, exchange your answers with another student. Do you agree about the topics? Do you agree about the main ideas? If you don't agree, give reasons for your answers. One of you might want to change an answer!

4 **Understanding Pronoun Reference** Look back at the reading selection "Looking for Work in the 21st Century" to find the meaning of the following pronouns. What does each pronoun refer to?

1. they (Paragraph A, line 2) _____

2. them (Paragraph B, line 11) _____

3. it (Paragraph D, line 32) _____

4. them (Paragraph D, line 36) _____

5. this (Paragraph E, line 45) _____

6. it (Paragraph E, line 50) _____

5 **Discussing the Reading** Talk about your answers to these questions.

1. Have you ever gone job hunting? If so, what steps did you take?

2. Do you already know what your "dream job" is? If so, what will you need to do to get it?

3. Do people in most countries usually go to career counselors? Are there vocational counseling services in high schools and colleges? Have you ever gone to a career counselor for advice?

4. Have you ever visited an online job board? If so, tell your group about it.

Cultural Note

Globalization
There are 190 countries in the world. Which five do you think are the most **globalized?** These are the five countries with the most cell phones, computers, political involvement, and free movement of international visitors. Each also has a vibrant economy. Write your guesses here and check your answers at the end of this chapter on page 91.

_____

Responding in Writing

6 **Summarizing** Choose one of the following topics from the reading in Part 1, pages 75–77, to summarize.

- advantages and disadvantages of less job security (Paragraph C)
- telecommuting (Paragraph E)
- workaholism (Paragraph F)

Because a summary is shorter than the original, try to write only three or four sentences. To write this summary, follow these steps:

- Make sure that you understand the paragraph well.
- Identify the topic, main idea, and important details.
- Choose two or three important details.
- Do not include less important details.

In order to summarize this in your own words, *don't look at the original paragraph as you write*. When you finish writing, compare your summary with those of other students who summarized the same paragraph. Did you include the same main idea? The same details?

7 **Writing Your Own Ideas** Choose one of the topics below to write a paragraph about. Write your own thoughts. Try to use vocabulary from this chapter.

- your opinion about workaholism
- your opinion about telecommuting
- your experience with job hunting
- your idea of a "dream job"
- your opinion of telecommuting

What is the main idea of your paragraph? _____

_____

Talk It Over

8 **Discussing Proverbs and Quotations** Below are proverbs and quotations about work. Read them and then in small groups, discuss your answers to the questions that follow.

> **Proverbs and Quotations**
>
> - "All work and no play makes Jack a dull boy." (proverb)
> - "Ninety percent of inspiration is perspiration." (proverb)
> - "Work expands to fill the time available." (C. Northcote Parkinson)
> - "Laziness travels so slowly that poverty soon overtakes him." (Benjamin Franklin)
> - "It is neither wealth nor splendor, but tranquility and occupation, which give happiness." (Thomas Jefferson)

Questions

1. What does each proverb (or quotation) mean? (You might need to use a dictionary for a few words.)
2. Do you agree with each one?
3. What are some proverbs about work in your language? Translate them into English and explain them.

Part 3 | Building Vocabulary and Study Skills

1 Focusing on Words from the Academic Word List Fill in the blanks with words from the Academic Word List in the box. When you finish, turn back to page 75, Paragraph B, and check your answers.

areas	economy	jobs	traditionally
benefits	enormous	labor	varies
computer	job	secure	
creating	job security	temporary	

The situation _____*varies*_____ from country to country, but in

1

today's _____, there is generally less job security worldwide.

2

Even in Japan, where people _____ had a very

3

_____ job for life, there is now no promise of a lifetime

4

_____ with the same company. One reason for the lack of

5

_____ is the worldwide decrease in manufacturing

6

_____. Another reason is employers' need to hold down

7

costs. This has resulted in two _____ changes for the

8

workforce. First, employers are _____ more and more

9

_____ jobs because they don't need to pay health

10

insurance or other _____ to employees in these positions,

11

as they would to people in permanent posts. Second, more and more

companies are outsourcing. In other words, they are closing offices and

factories and sending work to other _____ of the country

12

or to other countries where _____ is cheaper. This

13

happens with factory work and _____ programming.

14

Also, the call center industry is on the move—mostly to India.

UNDERSTANDING ADJECTIVE AND NOUN PHRASES

Some words often appear together in phrases. In some phrases, there is a hyphen (-). If you have a question about whether to use a hyphen, look up the word in a dictionary.

Example

Many people have to accept **part-time** jobs.

The last word of a phrase is usually a noun or an adjective. The first word may be a noun, an adjective, or an adverb.

Example

city life (noun + noun)
social sciences (adjective + noun)
especially interesting (adverb + adjective)

---

2 **Understanding Adjective and Noun Phrases** In each sentence below, add a word to complete the adjective or noun phrase. Choose from the following words:

career	dream	personnel	unemployment
city	job	self	
classified	mass	shopping	
computer	part	traffic	

1. He looked through the _____*classified*_____ ads and hoped to find his

   _____ job.

2. In that country, the _____ rate is very high, and many people

   have to accept _____-time jobs temporarily. This sometimes

   causes depression and loss of _____-confidence.

3. Some advantages of _____ life are the _____

   centers and _____-transit systems. A disadvantage, though, is

   the problem of _____ jams.

4. Because she likes technology, her _____ counselor told her

   about the many possible jobs in _____ science.

5. When I began _____ hunting last year, I put in my application

   at the _____ office of many companies.

3 Creating Adjective and Noun Phrases Match a word on the left with a word on the right to create a new phrase.

1. old- ____d____

2. dream _____

3. cell _____

4. technology _____

5. job _____

6. career _____

7. employment _____

8. self- _____

a. job

b. opening

c. agency

d. fashioned

e. field

f. confidence

g. counseling

h. phone

UNDERSTANDING COMPOUND WORDS

Some words belong together in "compounds" (long words that consist of smaller words).

> **Example**
> I talked to a **salesclerk** at the **supermarket**.

4 Understanding Compound Words Read the compound words in Column A below. Draw a line between the two words of each compound word. Then match the compound words with the definitions in Column B. The first one is done as an example.

Column A

1. ____h____ over/seas

2. _____ drawback

3. _____ overcrowding

4. _____ gridlock

5. _____ worldwide

6. _____ overwork

7. _____ workforce

8. _____ upgrade

9. _____ online

10. _____ background

Column B

a. terrible traffic jam

b. too much work

c. people who are working

d. using the Internet

e. disadvantage

f. improve

g. one's experience and education

h. in another country across an ocean

i. everywhere in the world

j. too many people in one place

5 Creating Compound Words and Phrases How many compound words or phrases can you make from the words below? Work as fast as you can for five minutes and write the words on the lines. The group with the most *correct* words or phrases is the winner.

high	work	network
lab	exam	security
office	public	market
college	interview	department
self	tuition	confidence
science	school	job
Web	service	computer
life	city	planning

city life _____ _____ _____

_____ _____ _____

_____ _____ _____

_____ _____ _____

_____ _____ _____

_____ _____ _____

 6 Searching the Internet Look at some online job boards. Find one that looks interesting. How can that website help you with work-related questions? What can you do on that site? Tell the class about the site and list at least five helpful things people can do on that site.

Website: _____

Useful job-related information:

1. _____

2. _____

3. _____

4. _____

5. _____

FASTER READING SPEED—LEFT-TO-RIGHT EYE MOVEMENT

Slow readers look at the same words several times. Their eyes move back and forth over each sentence. Fast readers usually move their eyes from left to right one time for each line. They don't look back very often. A fast left-to-right eye movement increases reading speed. If you can read quickly, you may feel less nervous during tests.

There are exercises to help you improve reading speed. You will practice one below. This exercise is timed. It shows an underlined word on the left of each line. You will be asked to read across each line and underline the words in that line that are the same as the underlined word on the left.

Example

globe	globalize	globalization	globe	glide	global
workforce	work	workforce	workplace	workforce	worked
stress	stress	stressful	address	stressed	stress

1 Practice Your teacher will tell you when to begin each section. Quickly underline each word that is the same as the underlined word. At the end of each section, write down your time.

Section 1

banking	banks	banking	bank	banking	banking
challenge	challenges	challenging	challenge	challenge	challenged
savings	savings	save	savings	saving	saver
benefit	benefits	beneficial	benefited	benefit	benefit
employer	employ	employment	employee	employer	employed

Time:_____

Section 2

experience	experience	experienced	expertise	experience	expert
opening	opening	opening	opened	open	opened
excellent	excel	excelled	excellent	excellent	excellent
identity	indent	identity	identify	identity	indent
account	account	accounting	account	accounts	account

Time:_____

Section 3

part-time	part-time	partly	party	part-time
position	possible	position	positive	position
public	public	publicity	public	publicize
appointment	appoint	appointed	appoints	appointment
personnel	person	personal	personnel	personable

Time:_____

Section 4

salary	salary	celery	salaries	salaried	sales
apply	applied	apply	apply	apply	application
pleasure	pleasure	pleasant	pleasurable	pleased	pleasant
skills	skilled	skill	skills	skills	skillful
ability	ability	able	capable	ability	capability

Time: _____

Self-Assessment Log

Read the lists below. Check (✔) the strategies and vocabulary that you learned in this chapter. Look through the chapter or ask your instructor about the strategies and words that you do not understand.

Reading and Vocabulary-Building Strategies

❑ Getting meaning from context
❑ Previewing a reading
❑ Finding the main idea
❑ Finding important details
❑ Recognizing cause and effect
❑ Using the prefix *over-*
❑ Skimming for main ideas
❑ Understanding pronoun reference
❑ Understanding adjective and noun phrases
❑ Understanding compound words

Target Vocabulary

Nouns

❑ background
❑ career counselors
❑ cell phones
❑ classified ads
❑ drawback
❑ dream job
❑ employment agency
❑ globalization*
❑ job hopping
❑ job hunting
❑ job opening
❑ job security
❑ livelihood
❑ manufacturing jobs
❑ old-fashioned

❑ outsourcing
❑ personnel office
❑ posts
❑ self-confidence
❑ technology* field
❑ telecommuting
❑ ulcers
❑ workaholism
❑ workforce

Verbs

❑ distract
❑ keep up with
❑ overwork
❑ upgrade
❑ varies (vary)*

Adjectives

❑ flexible*
❑ leisure
❑ online
❑ passionate
❑ rigid*
❑ secure*
❑ temporary*
❑ worldwide

---

* These words are from the Academic Word List. For more information on this list, see www.vuw.ac.nz/lals/research/awl.

Answer to the Culture Note question on page 84:

#5: the Netherlands; #4: the United States; #3: Switzerland; #2: Ireland; #1: Singapore

5

Lifestyles Around the World

In This Chapter

Are you influenced by fashion? The first reading explores how trends and fads in many areas, including music, clothes, sports, and exercise, affect our lives. What fads are popular today? You will read about that in Part 2 and will have a chance to express your opinion about some popular trends. Then in Part 3, you will learn strategies to help you use a dictionary and improve your vocabulary by analyzing suffixes and prefixes. Last, the Focus on Testing section looks at test questions about vocabulary.

“ Great things are not accomplished by those who yield to trends and fads and popular opinion. **”**

—Jack Kerouac
American writer (1922–1969)

Connecting to the Topic

1 What do you see in the photo?

2 Where do you think this photo was taken? In what year?

3 How is this photo similar to or different from what you might see where you live?

Trendspotting

Before You Read

1   **Previewing the Topic**   Look at the photos and discuss the questions.

1. Describe each photo? What are the people wearing? What are they doing?

2. About when (what general time period) was each photo taken?

3. How are these scenes similar to (or different from) scenes in a country that you know well?

▲ Photo A

▲ Photo B

▲ Photo C

2 Previewing Vocabulary Read the words and phrases below. Listen to the pronunciation of each word. Put a check mark (✓) next to the words you know. For the words that you don't know, *don't* use a dictionary. Try to understand them from the reading. You'll work with some of these words in exercises in this chapter.

Nouns
- ❑ competitive edge
- ❑ essence
- ❑ fad
- ❑ influence
- ❑ lifestyle
- ❑ profit
- ❑ trend

- ❑ trendspotting

Verbs
- ❑ distinguish
- ❑ enroll
- ❑ influence
- ❑ invested
- ❑ spot

Adjectives
- ❑ gourmet
- ❑ slang

Adverbs
- ❑ enthusiastically
- ❑ suddenly

3 Previewing the Reading Look over the reading on pages 95–98. Discuss these questions with a partner.

1. What is the topic of the whole reading? (Look at the title of the reading.)
2. What are the seven subtopics? (Look at the heading of each paragraph.)
3. What do the pictures in the article lead you to expect?

Read

4 Reading an Article As you read the following selection, think about the answer to this question: *What are fads and trends, and why are they important?* Read the selection. Do not use a dictionary. Then do the exercises that follow the reading.

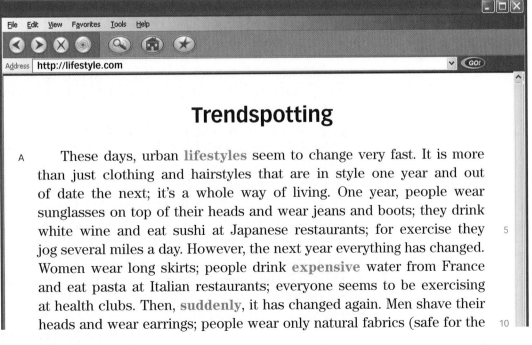

File Edit View Favorites Tools Help

Address http://lifestyle.com

Trendspotting

A   These days, urban **lifestyles** seem to change very fast. It is more than just clothing and hairstyles that are in style one year and out of date the next; it's a whole way of living. One year, people wear sunglasses on top of their heads and wear jeans and boots; they drink white wine and eat sushi at Japanese restaurants; for exercise they 5 jog several miles a day. However, the next year everything has changed. Women wear long skirts; people drink **expensive** water from France and eat pasta at Italian restaurants; everyone seems to be exercising at health clubs. Then, **suddenly**, it has changed again. Men shave their heads and wear earrings; people wear only natural fabrics (safe for the 10

▲ Are skateboard parks popular in your city?

environment); they drink **gourmet** coffee and eat Thai food; for both leisure and exercise, adults may go bicycling; and some younger people may go skateboarding.

Fads

B   Almost nothing in modern life escapes the **influence** of fashion: food, sports, music, exercise, books, slang words, movies, furniture, places to visit, even *names* go in and out of fashion. For a while, it seemed that all new parents in the U.S. were naming their babies Heather, Dawn, Mike, or Adam. These names were "in." Then, suddenly, these same names were "out," and Madison, Amber, and Jason were "in." It's almost impossible to write about specific **fads** because these interests that people **enthusiastically** follow can change very quickly.

The Essence of a Fad

C   This is the **essence**, the central quality, of a fad: it doesn't last long. Some fads disappear before we have even heard of them. How many people remember Green Peace swimsuits? (They changed color to indicate polluted water.) And then there was "Beethoven Bread." Popular in Japan in 1994, it was expensive—$20 for one loaf. It was made while classical music played in the kitchen. The woman who created this bread emphasized that "bread doesn't like rock music." In 2005, a company introduced a new toothbrush, "Tooth Tunes," which brought music "from the teeth to the ears." These fads quickly disappeared.

The Reason for Fads

D   What causes such fads to come and go? And why do so many people follow them? Although clothing designers and manufacturers influence fads in fashion because they want to make a **profit**, this desire for money doesn't explain fads in other areas, such as language. For example, why have English-speaking teenagers in the past 25 years used—at different times—the **slang** words groovy, boss, awesome, rad, or tubular instead of simply saying "wonderful"? According to Jack Santino, an expert in popular culture, people who follow fads are not irrational; they simply want to be part of something new and creative, and they feel good when they are part of an "in group." Santino believes that fads are common in any country that has a strong consumer economy. However, because of TV, movies, and the Internet, fads are now common worldwide and spread very fast. Increasingly, they seem to begin in Asia, especially in Hong Kong, Japan, and Korea.

Fads and Trends

E   Santino points out that it's sometimes difficult to see the difference between a fad and a **trend**. A fad, he says, lasts a very short time and

▲ Japanese anime: a fad or a trend?

is not very important. A trend lasts much longer. A recent trend is the interest in good health, but many fads come from this trend: aerobic exercise, kickboxing, organic vegetables, or special diets like carbohydrate-counting. A trend in the 1980s was the use of personal computers; certain computer games were fads. However, these days we can't really continue to call computers a "trend" because now they have become an essential part of everyday life.

Trendspotting

F   **Trendspotting** is the ability to identify a trend at an early stage—an extremely important skill in the business world. The first company that can correctly identify a new trend (and do something with it) has a **competitive edge**—an advantage—over other companies. The person who founded the Starbucks chain of coffeehouses was able to **spot** a trend—interest in quality and variety in coffee. Today, people buy Starbucks products in shopping centers, airports, and supermarkets

▲ Hybrid cars (gas/electric): a fad or a trend?

everywhere. But when a development in popular culture is new, it's difficult to **distinguish** between a fad and a trend. Trendspotters need to ask themselves: will this become an important global trend, or is it just a passing fad? "Hello Kitty" began as a fad but became a trend. People who **invested** their funds in Green Peace swimsuits, however, probably regret their decision. Clearly, they mistook a fad for a trend.

Popular Culture and the University

G   Possibly because of the importance of trendspotting in business, more and more universities are offering classes in popular culture. Some even offer a *major* in popular culture. Parents of students at New York University have sometimes been surprised to find their children taking such classes as "Inside the Mouse" (about the influence of Disney), "Golden Arches East" (about McDonald's in Asia), or "Hope in a Jar" (about the cosmetics industry). At Bowling Green State University, in Ohio, there has been a course on *Pokemon*, found in Japanese culture. At 95 other schools, students might **enroll** in "The History of Rock 'n' Roll," "Addiction in Literature," and "Smoking and Advertising." Many people don't take such classes seriously. However, companies are seeking out graduates of Bowling Green, which actually offers a master's degree in popular culture. These graduates find jobs in advertising, television, 100 publishing, and manufacturing. With an understanding of popular culture, these graduates are becoming the new trendspotters. The question now becomes this: Are courses in popular culture just a fad or a real trend?

After You Read

5 **Finding the Main Idea** Read the sentences below and select the main idea of the article, "Trendspotting." Remember, the topic is trendsetting, and the main idea is what the author wants to say about trendsetting.

(A) Fads in fashion are common because clothing manufacturers make more money if styles change every year.

(B) Trends, which are basically long-lasting fads, are important for both social and business reasons.

(C) Fads usually last a very short time, but they can be a lot of fun.

(D) People follow many different kinds of fads because they like to be part of something new and creative.

(E) The ability to distinguish between fads and trends is increasingly important in the business world.

6 **Identifying the Main Idea in Paragraphs** Go back to the passage. Underline one or two sentences in each paragraph that contain the main idea of that paragraph. When you finish, compare the sentences that you marked with those of other students. Did you choose the same sentences? Explain why you chose the sentences that you did.

 7 **Checking Your Understanding** Turn back to Activity 4 on page 95 and answer the question. Discuss your answer with a partner.

8 **Getting Meaning from Context: Vocabulary Check** Skim the reading passage to find the meaning of each of these words. On each line, write a definition or synonym—either one from the reading passage or in your own words. Do this exercise without a dictionary.

1. lifestyle: _____*a way of living, including fashion, food and exercise*_____

2. fads: _____

3. essence: _____

4. profit: _____

5. slang: _____

6. trend: _____

7. trendspotting: _____

8. competitive edge: _____

9. distinguish: _____

10. enroll: _____

9 **Finding Details** Go back to Paragraphs D and E in the reading passage to find examples of fads that come from the trends below. Write the fads in the boxes.

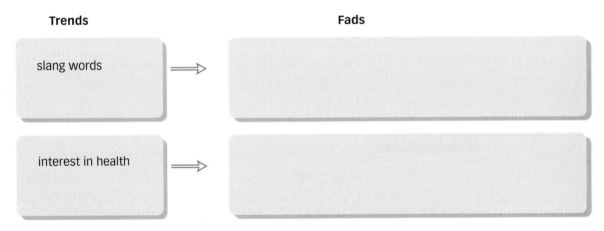

Trends

slang words

interest in health

Fads

10 **Discussing the Reading** What are some fads these days? Are these fads part of any longer-lasting trends? To help you answer these questions, fill in the chart on page 100. Then compare your charts in small groups and discuss your answers.

Current Fads

Clothing	Hairstyles	Food	Music	Activities

Part 2   Reading Skills and Strategies

Fads and Trends in the 21st Century

Before You Read

 1 Thinking Ahead Discuss your answers to these questions.

1. What are some fashions or forms of body decoration that are popular with teenagers these days?

2. What fashions do teenagers and their parents disagree about?

3. What sports are especially popular these days?

Strategy

Marking Text When You Read

Students—especially college students—often need to read so much material that they don't have time to reread it before an important exam. For this reason, it's necessary to learn how to mark a book. If you mark your reading material wisely, you can go back later and look over your markings to study for a test without reading the whole passage again. Try to use different colors for different purposes:

- one color for the topic
- a different color for the main idea(s)
- another color for important details or examples

You can also underline or circle important new vocabulary and phrases. You might add notes or question marks in the margin.

It's important to note that there is no one right way of marking a book. You need to find a style that is comfortable to you. However, if you mark too much, it's as bad as not marking anything. Marking too much may get confusing.

2 **Reading: Marking Text when You Read** Read the paragraphs below. As you read, mark the topic, main idea, and important details of each paragraph. Do not use a dictionary. When you finish, write the topic and the main idea of each paragraph. (The first paragraph is marked for you, as an example.)

Fads and Trends in the 21st Century

A The 19th-century American philosopher Henry David Thoreau was famous for saying, "Simplify, simplify." Unfortunately, the trend these days seems to be "complicate, complicate" instead. Many people are working longer hours, spending more money, and getting in more debt than ever before. They are also relaxing less and spending less time with family and friends. However, there is also a countertrend—a trend toward voluntary simplicity. People in the voluntary simplicity movement take various steps to make their lives both simpler and more enjoyable. Some people work fewer hours each week. Some move close to their workplace to avoid a long daily commute; they walk or ride a bike, instead. Some plant a vegetable garden; this gives them fresh air, exercise, and time with their families—not to mention organic produce. But all people in the voluntary simplicity movement try to cut back—to buy less; they cut up their credit cards and stop buying unnecessary items. In short, the priority for people in the voluntary movement is to follow Thoreau's suggestion: simplify.

Topic: _____ *voluntary simplicity* _____

Main idea: _____ *People in the voluntary simplicity movement take various steps to make their lives both simpler and more enjoyable.* _____

▲ *Mehndi*, a temporary decoration

B A popular fad for many teenagers is tattooing. Parents are usually horrified by these permanent designs on their children's skin, but the young people see them as a fashion statement. In the new millennium, some parents are greatly relieved when their teenage children turn to a new fad, a temporary form of decorating the hands, feet, neck, or legs—*mehndi*, a method of painting beautiful designs that last only about three weeks. This "new" fad is actually very old; for hundreds of years in India, a woman's friends have painted her to celebrate her wedding day. Another fad from India, however, causes parents more worry—*bidis*. Children and young teens are attracted to these thin cigarettes in candy flavors such as orange, chocolate, mango, and raspberry. The problem? *Bidis* contain more nicotine than regular cigarettes. Unfortunately, many children think these are "cool"—fashionable. So until a new fad comes along, "Indian chic is hot," as one radio commentator observed. 30

Topic: _____

Main idea: _____

_____

C   Another ancient art, aromatherapy, is also popular today. Of course, 35 people have always used perfume to make them more attractive to other people. And we all have experience with the power of smell in a different way—memory. When we smell something for the first time in many years, a sudden rush of memories comes to us. We remember where we were and how we felt all those years ago when we first smelled it. In aromatherapy, 40 floral scents and the smell of such things as lemon, pine, and mint are used to make people feel better in a variety of ways. Some scents make people more relaxed. Other scents make them more alert, more awake. As you might imagine, the market reflects interest in this trend. Businesspeople are happy to make scents available to their customers, for a price. 45

Topic: _____

Main idea: _____

_____

▲ Mountain bikes can go almost anywhere.

D   Another fad from the 1990s—dangerous sports—seems to be turning into a trend in the new millennium. People have begun to make traditional sports such as skiing and bicycling more challenging and dangerous. Instead of skiing, 50 there is now snowboarding, which is basically skateboarding on snow. Instead of using a regular bicycle, some people use a mountain bike, which can go almost anywhere. Some thrill seekers, people who want more and more excitement and 55 danger, have created new "extreme sports." One of these, sky-surfing, combines sky-diving (jumping out of an airplane with a parachute) with surfing.

In another, waterfall-running, a person rides a kayak off a high waterfall. The thrill seekers who are addicted to such sports don't seem to feel fear. They say they need to "focus 100 percent" in order to survive their experience. But they also say they feel "100 percent alive" only in those few moments of falling through air or water. But the question remains: Will this trend disappear, change into a different trend, or become part of the culture?

60

65

▲ Sky-surfing: a combination of sky-diving and surfing

Topic: _____

Main idea: _____

_____

After You Read

3 Checking Your Answers After you write the topic and main idea of each paragraph, compare your answers with another student's. Are your answers the same? Are your answers the same but perhaps in different words? Do you agree about the main ideas? If you don't agree, give reasons for your answers. Remember, you can change an answer if you wish!

Strategy

Studying for Exams: Organizing Information

After you have read and marked or highlighted material in a textbook, you usually need to study this material for an exam. You can absorb and remember more if you do something *active* with the material that you have marked. Here's what you can do:

- Open your book to the material that you have marked.

- Have a notebook next to your book.

- In the notebook, create a graphic organizer (see pages 10, 30, 33, 55, 79, 99, 104, and 178 for examples of graphic organizers) and write the information you highlighted in it.

- Study your graphic organizer. If you have chosen well the information to include, you won't need to read the material again.

4 **Studying for Exams: Organizing Information** Fill in this chart with the information that you marked in Paragraphs B, C, and D. You can copy directly from the text or put it in your own words—or both. Paragraph A is done as an example.

	Topic	Main Idea	Important Details
A	voluntary simplicity	People in this movement are trying to make their lives simpler.	■ work less ■ move close to work ■ walk or use a bike ■ plant a veg. garden ■ buy less ■ stop buying stuff they don't need
B			
C			
D			

5 **Discussing the Reading** Talk about your answers to these questions.

1. In a country you know well, is there a countertrend toward simplicity? If so, explain. What can people do to simplify their lives?

2. What "extreme sports" are popular these days? Have you tried any of these? Do you know anyone who has tried one? If so, tell your group about this sport. Why is it so thrilling—so exciting?

3. Are there any scents that cause you to experience a "sudden rush of memories"? Describe them.

Responding in Writing

6 **Summarizing** Read these two summaries of Paragraph A on page 101. Both are fine, but they are different. Compare them to the original paragraph. Write the points that are similar and the points that are different about the two paragraphs.

Summary 1
In a countertrend to the complexity of modern life, people in the voluntary simplicity movement take different steps to simplify their lives. Some may work fewer hours weekly; some walk or ride a bike to work. Others plant their own vegetable gardens. But all attempt to cut back—to buy less.

Summary 2
Voluntary simplicity is a countertrend to the complexity of modern life. The priority for people in this movement is to follow Thoreau's famous suggestion: "Simplify, simplify." These people focus on working less and spending less.

Similarities: _____

_____

Differences: _____

_____

7 **Writing Your Own Summary** Choose one of the following paragraphs to summarize. Remember that a summary is shorter than the original text.

- Paragraph E from Part 1, page 97
- Paragraph F from Part 1, page 97
- Paragraph B from Part 2, pages 101–102
- Paragraph C from Part 2, page 102

In order to summarize this in your own words, *don't look at the original paragraph as you write*. When you finish writing, compare your summary with those of other students who summarized the same paragraph. Note the similarities and differences.

8 **Responding in Writing** Choose one of the topics below to write a paragraph about. Write your own thoughts. Try to use vocabulary from this chapter.

- a crazy fad
- your opinion about the quotation at the beginning of the chapter, page 92
- your opinion about any fad or trend in Part 1 or 2
- your predictions about a future trend

What is the main idea of your paragraph? _____

_____

Cultural Note

Reality TV Worldwide

Reality TV, which began as a fad, has clearly become a trend, and it has swept the world. There are now dozens of reality TV programs. Some of the more popular shows in the United States are *Survivor, The Amazing Race, Extreme Makeover, Nanny 911, The Apprentice,* and *Extreme Makeover—Home Edition*. Here are some reality programs from other countries:

China:

- *Quest USA, Da Tiao Zhan*, was a 2004 show in which four bilingual teams (Mandarin Chinese and English) of three people each spent a week traveling in the United States and looking for various things. One group was from mainland China, one from Hong Kong, one from Taiwan, and one from the United States. In this competition, the team with the best "team spirit" won.

The Middle East

- *Arabic Big Brother* was similar to Big Brother programs in many countries (such as Mexico, France, Russia, Spain, and Australia, to name only a few). Twelve people from around the Arab world lived in a house in Bahrain. However, unlike the program in other countries, the house had separate sleeping rooms for men and women, a separate women's bathroom, and a prayer room.

Japan

- In what might be "extreme reality TV," a Japanese comedian named **Nasubi** spent eighteen months alone in a bare apartment with no furniture and no clothes. The only thing in the apartment was a large pile of postcards. To get out of the apartment (and to feed and clothe himself), he had to raise one million yen by sending in the postcards to enter contests and apply for free offers. By the end of the program, he had won such things as rice, steaks, and two vacuum cleaners . . . but no clothes.

Talk It Over

9 **Reality TV: What Do You Think?** You've just read some examples of reality TV programs in various countries. In small groups, discuss these questions.

1. Have you seen any reality TV programs? If so, which ones? What happens on each one?

2. Which reality shows are especially popular in your country?

3. What is your opinion of these types of shows?

4. Why do you think there are so many reality shows? Why are they so popular?

5. Are there specific groups of people who watch them and others who don't?

1 **Focusing on Words from the Academic Word List** Fill in the blanks with words from the Academic Word List in the box. When you finish, turn back to page 96, Paragraph D, and check your answers.

areas	culture	economy	irrational
creative	designers	expert	so

The Reason for Fads

What causes such fads to come and go? And why do _____ many people follow them? Although clothing
1

_____ and manufacturers influence fads in fashion
2

because they want to make a profit, this desire for money doesn't explain

fads in other _____, such as language. For example, why
3

have English-speaking teenagers in the past twenty-five years used—at

different times—the slang words groovy, boss, awesome, rad, or tubular

instead of simply saying "wonderful"? According to Jack Santino, an

_____ in popular _____, people who
4   5

follow fads are not _____; they simply want to be part of
6

something new and _____, and they feel good when they
7

are part of an "in group." Santino believes that fads are common in any

country that has a strong consumer _____. However,
8

because of TV, movies, and the Internet, fads are now common worldwide

and spread very fast. Increasingly, they seem to begin in Asia, especially in

Hong Kong, Japan, and Korea.

ANALYZING SUFFIXES

As you learned in Chapter 3, suffixes such as *-er, -sion, -ment* and *-ive*, often indicate the part of speech of a word (see the list on page 64). Here are some more suffixes, listed by the parts of speech that they usually indicate.

Nouns	Verbs	Adjective	Adverb
-ess	*-ate*	*-less*	*-ly*
-ship	*-ize*		
-ism	*-en*		

2 **Analyzing Suffixes** The words below include suffixes from this chapter and Chapter 3. Write the part of speech for each word: *n.* for nouns, *v.* for verbs, *adj.* for adjectives, and *adv.* for adverbs. In some cases, two answers are correct.

1. _n._ friendship

2. ____ suddenly

3. ____ actress

4. ____ specialize

5. ____ patriotism

6. ____ soften

7. ____ simplicity

8. ____ hopeless

9. ____ enthusiastically

10. ____ expensive

11. ____ participate

12. ____ individualism

13. ____ summarize

14. ____ worthless

15. ____ worsen

16. ____ frequently

17. ____ workaholism

18. ____ indicate

19. ____ organization

20. ____ pleasure

21. ____ hostess

22. ____ experience

23. ____ relationship

24. ____ flexible

ANALYZING PREFIXES

The prefix (beginning) of a word sometimes gives a clue to its meaning. Some prefixes create a word with an opposite meaning.

Example

We've **dis**covered many **un**usual hotels in our travels.

(*Discover* means to "uncover" information—i.e., to find out something that we didn't know before. *Unusual* means "not usual"—i.e., out of the ordinary.)

The following prefixes can have the meaning "no" or "not."

un-	(unpopular = not popular)
in-	(inconvenient = not convenient)
im-	(improbable = not probable)
ir-	(irresponsible = not responsible)
dis-	(disrespect = no respect)

3 **Analyzing Prefixes** Use one of the preceding prefixes to change each word into its opposite as in the example. Use your dictionary, if necessary. (The prefixes *in-* and *im-* have another meaning; they can both mean "in" or "into.")

1. _un_ pleasant

2. _____ patient

3. _____ expensive

4. _____ characteristic

5. _____ avoidable

6. _____ rational

7. _____ safe

8. _____ frequent

9. _____ desirable

10. _____ advantage

11. _____ possible

12. _____ interesting

MORE PREFIXES

Here are some other prefixes and their usual meanings:

con-/com-	= with, together	*pre-*	= first, before
counter-	= opposite	*re-*	= again, back
ex-/e-	= out of, from	*sur-*	= over, above
inter-	= between, among	*trans-*	= across
mis-	= wrong		

4 **Matching Words** The definitions on the right are based on the meanings of prefixes. Match them with the words on the left by writing the letters on the lines as in the example.

1. _g_ reflect

2. _____ survive

3. _____ transit

4. _____ international

5. _____ invest

6. _____ experience

7. _____ replace

8. _____ prevent

9. _____ combination

10. _____ counterclockwise

a. among other countries

b. get knowledge from life (not books)

c. moving people or things across places

d. stop something before it happens

e. put back, provide something again

f. in the opposite direction to the hands of a clock

g. throw back; give back an image of

h. joining together of people or things

i. continue to live or exist

J. put money into a business in the hopes of making a profit

5 **Understanding Dictionary Entries: Single Meanings** Some words have only one meaning. You can find the meaning in a dictionary entry, which sometimes includes an example. Read these two dictionary entries and answer the questions about them.

> **en·roll**, enrol /ɪnˈroʊl/ v. [I,T] to officially join a school, university, etc., or to arrange for someone else to do this.: *the students* **enrolled in** *honors classes* | *Nathan* **enrolled at** *City College.*

> **fad** /fæd/ n. [C] something that is very popular for a short period of time: *the newest fitness fad*

1. What part of speech is *enroll?* _____

2. What is the dictionary definition of the word? _____

_____

3. What word is related to it? _____

4. What part of speech is *fad?* _____

5. What is the dictionary definition of the word? _____

_____

6 **Understanding Dictionary Entries: Multiple Meanings** Most words, however, have more than one meaning. Often the same word can be more than one part of speech, and each part of speech can have different meanings.

Example

The word *style* is most commonly a noun. In the first dictionary entry to the right, it has four meanings. *Style* can also be a verb.

> **style**[1] /staɪl/ n. **1** [C,U] a way of doing, making, painting, etc. something that is typical of a particular period of time, place, or group of people: *He's trying to copy Van Gogh's* **style of** *painting.* | *architecture in the Gothic style* **2** [C] the particular way that someone behaves, works, or deals with other people: *Carolyn has an informal* **style of** *teaching.* | *Yelling at her students is* **not** *her* **style** (=is not the way she usually behaves). | *I don't like loud parties – a quiet night at home is* **more** *my* **style** (=I prefer quiet nights at home). **3** [C,U] a particular design or fashion for something such as clothes, hair, furniture, etc.: *They have over two hundred* **styles of** *wallpaper to choose from.* | *Long hair is* **in style/out of style** (=fashionable or not fashionable). **4** [U] the particular way you do things that makes people admire you: *You may not like him, but you have to admit that he* **has style.** | *an actor* **with style**
> **style**[2] v. [T] to cut someone's hair in a particular way

Refer to the previous dictionary entries to answer these questions.

1. What part of speech is the word *style* when it means "fashion, especially in clothes"? _____ Give an example of this use of the word in a phrase. _____

2. Write the part of speech of the word *style* in each of these sentences.

   a. When they travel, they go in style. _____

   b. The couple preferred a modern style of life. _____

   c. She usually styled her own hair. _____

3. Write the dictionary definition of the word *style* in each of these sentences.

   a. When they travel, they go in style.

   _____

   b. The couple preferred a modern style of life.

   _____

   c. She usually styled her own hair.

   _____

   d. In my travels, I saw many styles of furniture, clothing, and so on.

   _____

7 **Dictionary Practice** Read the following dictionary entries, paying close attention to the parts of speech, the different meanings, and the examples for each meaning. Then write the part of speech and the meaning of the underlined word in each sentence.

1. She wore a plain blue sweater for the interview.

   _____

   _____

   _____

2. The midwestern United States contains thousands of farms, set among countless acres of plains.

   _____

   _____

   _____

plain[1] /pleɪn/ *adj.* **1** very clear, and easy to understand or recognize: *It's quite **plain that** you don't agree.* | *Why don't you tell me **in plain English*** (=without using technical or difficult words)? **2** without anything added or without decoration [= **simple**]: *plain yogurt* | *a plain blue suit* | *a sheet of **plain paper*** (=paper with no lines on it) **3** showing clearly and honestly what you think about something: *Albright was known for her plain speaking.* **4** a woman or girl who is plain is unattractive – used in order to avoid saying this directly

plain[2] *n.* [C] **also plains** a large area of flat land: *a grassy plain* | *countless miles of plains*

3. It's important to get enough sleep so that you can be <u>alert</u> for the exam tomorrow.

_____

4. She <u>alerted</u> us about the new computer virus.

_____

5. They painted the wooden <u>posts</u> red and the rest of the fence white.

_____

6. They <u>posted</u> the job opening on the Internet.

_____

a·lert¹ /eˈlət/ _adj._ **1** always watching and ready to notice anything strange, unusual, dangerous, etc.: _Cyclists must always be **alert to** the dangers on a busy road._ **2** able to think quickly and clearly: _I didn't feel alert enough to do any more work._
alert² _v._ [T] to warn someone of a problem or of possible danger: _As soon as we suspected it was a bomb, we alerted the police._
alert³ _n._ [C] **1 be on the alert** to be ready to notice and deal with a problem: _Police are **on the alert for** trouble._ **2** a warning to be ready for possible danger: _a flood alert_

post¹ /poʊst/ _n._ [C] **1** a strong upright piece of wood, metal, etc. that is set into the ground, especially to support something: _a fence post_ | _the goal posts_ **2** _formal_ an important job, especially in the government or military: _She decided to leave her post at the Justice Department._ **3** the place where a soldier, guard, etc. is expected to be in order to do his or her job: _The guards cannot **leave** their **posts**._ **4** a military BASE
post² _v._ [T] **1 a)** to put a public notice about something on a wall or BULLETIN BOARD: _They've posted warning signs on the gate._ **b)** to put a message or computer document on the Internet so that other people can see it: _FBI agents have posted a message on the Internet describing the suspect._ **2** if someone who works for the government or military is posted somewhere, he or she is sent to work there, usually for several years: _His regiment have been **posted to** Germany._ **3** if a company posts its profits, sales, losses, etc., it records the money gained or lost in its accounts: _In the final quarter, the company posted $12.4 million in earnings._

8 **Searching the Internet**

Search the Internet for a website on reality TV shows. Type in a key term like "reality TV" or "reality TV (plus country)" in a search engine. Find reality shows (in any country) that you have never heard of before. Choose one that seems interesting to you. Read about it and summarize what the reality show is about. Share what you learned with the class. How many students would like to see the show?

Name of the reality TV show: _____

Country: _____

Summary: _____

_____

_____

_____

_____

Number of students who would like to see the show: _____

VOCABULARY QUESTIONS

The TOEFL® Internet-Based Test (iBT) asks vocabulary questions only about items that appear in a reading. None of the vocabulary questions targets an item by itself, without any context.

Because context is so important, many questions ask about items that could have several meanings in other contexts. Your task is to look at four multiple-choice options and choose the one that best matches the vocabulary item in its context. Be careful. At least one of the incorrect choices will be a meaning that the target item could have in a different context.

1 **Practice** Look again at the reading "Trendspotting" on pages 95–98. Read it again if necessary. Then answer the vocabulary questions below. Try to answer all the questions in ten minutes.

1. Which of the following is closest in meaning to *wear,* as it is used in Paragraph A?

- (A) show signs of being used very roughly
- (B) use as a piece of clothing or jewelry
- (C) remain useful for a long time
- (D) display publicly

2. Which of the following is closest in meaning to *out,* as it is used in Paragraph B?

- (A) far away
- (B) extended
- (C) discovered
- (D) unpopular

3. Which of the following is closest in meaning to *and then,* as it is used in Paragraph C?

- (A) also
- (B) in the past
- (C) however
- (D) at that time

4. Which of the following is closest in meaning to *follow,* as it is used in Paragraph D?

- (A) walk behind
- (B) come next
- (C) participate in
- (D) talk about

5. Which of the following is closest in meaning to *areas*, as it is used in Paragraph D?
  - Ⓐ parts of life
  - Ⓑ parts of the world
  - Ⓒ kinds of communication
  - Ⓓ kinds of business

6. Which of the following is closest in meaning to *lasts*, as it is used in Paragraph E?
  - Ⓐ comes to an end
  - Ⓑ continues to be present
  - Ⓒ influences society
  - Ⓓ remains good to eat

7. Which of the following is closest in meaning to *founded*, as it is used in Paragraph F?
  - Ⓐ bought
  - Ⓑ discovered
  - Ⓒ closed
  - Ⓓ started

8. Which of the following is closest in meaning to *taking*, as it is used in Paragraph G?
  - Ⓐ delivering
  - Ⓑ stealing
  - Ⓒ showing interest in
  - Ⓓ studying in

Self-Assessment Log

Read the lists below. Check (✔) the strategies and vocabulary that you learned in this chapter. Look through the chapter or ask your instructor about the strategies and words that you do not understand.

Reading and Vocabulary-Building Strategies

❑ Previewing the reading
❑ Finding the main idea
❑ Expressing an opinion
❑ Getting meaning from context: vocabulary check
❑ Finding details
❑ Marking text when you read
❑ Studying for exams
❑ Analyzing suffixes
❑ Analyzing prefixes
❑ Understanding dictionary entries

Target Vocabulary

Nouns

❑ areas*
❑ competitive edge
❑ culture*
❑ designers*
❑ economy*
❑ essence
❑ expert*
❑ fads
❑ lifestyles
❑ profit
❑ trend*
❑ trendspotting

Verbs

❑ distinguish
❑ enroll
❑ experience
❑ invested*
❑ spot
❑ survive*

Adjectives

❑ creative*
❑ irrational*
❑ slang

Adverbs

❑ enthusiastically
❑ so*
❑ suddenly

* These words are from the Academic Word List. For more information on this list, see www.vuw.ac.nz/lals/research/awl.

Global Connections

In This Chapter

The first reading selection discusses the advantages and disadvantages of global trade, including the gap between the rich and the poor. You will have a chance to learn about and discuss these issues. The second reading looks at some recent and exciting changes in global travel, highlighting a variety of ways that people travel and vacation, including working and studying abroad. In this chapter, you can discuss trips you have taken in the past and trips that you would like to take. Part 3 includes activities to help you develop your vocabulary. Last, the Focus on Testing section looks at inferencing, an important critical thinking skill.

> **❝** It has been said that arguing against globalization is like arguing against the laws of gravity. **❞**
>
> —Kofi Annan
> Ghanaian diplomat; seventh Secretary
> General of the United Nations (1938–)

Connecting to the Topic

1 Where do you think the people in the photo are from? Why are they together here?

2 What do you think they are talking about?

3 What might be some of the challenges a diverse group has? What might be some of the pleasant surprises?

Global Trade

Before You Read

1 **Previewing the Topic** In small groups, discuss these questions.

1. Look at all of the things around the room. What countries are the products from? (Include the clothing that you're wearing.)

2. What might be some reasons for the economic success of some cities (such as Dubai) and countries (such as Singapore)?

3. What might be some reasons for economic failure in other countries?

4. How can geography help or hurt a country's economy?

2 **Previewing Vocabulary** Read the words and phrases below. Listen to the pronunciation of each word. Put a check mark (✓) next to the words you know. For the words that you don't know, *don't* use a dictionary.

Nouns

- ❑ benefits
- ❑ consumers
- ❑ fuel
- ❑ gap
- ❑ goods
- ❑ harbor
- ❑ infotech (information technology)
- ❑ infrastructure
- ❑ nutrients

- ❑ obstacle
- ❑ priority
- ❑ protectionist policies (policy)
- ❑ soil
- ❑ standards
- ❑ subsidy
- ❑ tide

Verbs

- ❑ contribute
- ❑ created
- ❑ reduce

Adjectives

- ❑ economic
- ❑ global
- ❑ landlocked
- ❑ startling
- ❑ tropical

Idioms and Expressions

- ❑ goes without saying
- ❑ in turn

3 **Previewing** Look over the reading on pages 119–121. Discuss these questions.

1. What is the topic of the whole reading? (Look at the title of the reading.)

2. What are the five subtopics? (Look at the headings of each paragraph.)

3. Which workers in the photos probably have the highest yearly income?

Read

4 **Reading the Article** As you read the following selection, think about the answer to this question: *What seems to be the key to a country's economic success?*

Read the selection. Do not use a dictionary. Then do the exercises that follow the reading.

Global Trade

A   For the first time in history, almost the entire world is now sharing the same economic system. Communism began to fall in the late 1980s, and since then, capitalism has spread to most corners of the world. The basis of a "pure" capitalist economy is free trade, also called "open trade." There are **benefits** of open trade for both rich and poor countries. For developed   5
countries such as Japan and England, free trade brings with it more competition, which **in turn** brings advantages such as lower prices and more choices of products for **consumers**. For developing countries, open trade means that people have access to essential **goods** such as food, clothing, and **fuel** (for transportation and heat). An open economic system   10
can be a key to improving the lives of people in both poor and rich countries because it can **reduce** poverty and improve living conditions.

▲ Boats and ships in Hong Kong harbor

▲ Factory workers in India

"Leaking Boats"

B   This is apparently very good news. Optimists often say that "the rising **tide** lifts all boats." What do they mean by this? Imagine a **harbor** filled with boats—some small ones, some medium-sized, and some huge ships.   15
As the ocean tide comes in every twelve hours, the water rises and literally lifts all boats—both large and small. In economics, this expression means that in good economic times, poor countries benefit as much as rich countries do. However, pessimists point out that many of the "small boats" seem to be "leaking"—have holes in them—and so are going down instead of up.   20
In other words, the **gap** between rich and poor—the economic difference between them—is wider than it was in the past. The contrast can be **startling**. A former U.S. president, Jimmy Carter, once put it this way: "Globalization, as defined by rich people, . . . is a very nice thing. . . . You are

talking about cell phones, you are talking about computers." However, he 25
went on to point out that this "nice thing . . . doesn't affect two-thirds of the
people of the world." In fact, according to the World Bank, more than
1.1 billion people live on less than a dollar a day.

The Influence of Geography

C   Why is this happening? What causes this **gap** between rich and poor?
Many of the poorest countries are at a disadvantage because of geography, 30
which is the root of several problems. First, a country that is **landlocked**,
with no access to an ocean, has a disadvantage because it cannot easily
transport its products to other parts of the world. Second, many—but not
all—countries in **tropical** regions (near the equator) have the disadvantage
of heavy, heavy rains that often wash **nutrients** from the land. Without 35
these nutrients in the **soil**, agricultural development is more difficult.
Another **obstacle** for many countries is the problem of infectious diseases
such as malaria, schistosomiasis, and dengue fever, which are found only in
tropical climates. It **goes without saying** that people weak with disease
cannot **contribute** to the economy of the country. 40

Protectionist Policies

D   Another cause of the growing gap between rich and poor countries
is **protectionist policies**. In other words, many rich countries have
governmental plans that give special help to their own people, so trade isn't
actually completely "open." One example of a protectionist policy is an
agricultural **subsidy**. This is money that a 45
government gives to farmers; unfortunately,
governments in poor countries can't pay these
subsidies to their farmers. Therefore, the
farmers in rich countries have a competitive
edge in the global market. Other protectionist 50
policies are "hidden." For example, Country
X (a rich nation) might say their trade is
open. However, it will not buy products from
Country Y (a poor nation). Why? It says that
Country Y does not have high enough health 55
or safety **standards**.

A Way Out

E   It may sound as if the situation is
hopeless for developing countries ever to
have a competitive edge in **global** trade—
but perhaps not. East Asia, for example, has 60
found far more **economic** success than
Africa has. The key to success seems to
lie in each government's economic policy.

▲ Agricultural workers in Korea

▲ Infotech workers in India

Malaysia and Thailand have the same tropical climate as many African countries, but their economies—unlike those of Africa—are growing fast. The reason? Their governments have **created** an economic climate in which people can move from agriculture to manufacturing. Geography is not the terrible obstacle to manufacturing that it is to farming. To help new entrepreneurs, these governments pay careful attention to areas such as **infrastructure** (harbors, railroads, and so on) and telecommunication. In other countries, such as India, information technology (**infotech**) is driving the economy in some cities. Computer technology doesn't depend on geography, but it does require educated workers. Therefore, education must be a **priority**. In addition, governments of developing countries must work with developed countries and persuade them to drop protectionist policies. Clearly, it is possible for government policy to prepare a path out of poverty in even poor countries.

After You Read

5 **Finding the Main Ideas** Write *T* on the lines before the statements that are true, according to the reading. Write *F* on the lines before the statements that are false.

1. _____ Open trade has advantages for both developed and developing countries.

2. _____ The economic difference between rich and poor is narrower than it was in the past.

3. _____ Tropical countries without access to the ocean are usually at a disadvantage in the global economy.

4. _____ Protectionist policies help to keep global trade open.

5. _____ Some countries have more economic success than others because of their governments' policies.

Strategy

Understanding the Literal and Figurative Meanings of Words
Many words with one basic *literal* meaning have other *figurative* meanings.

Example
The woman with the sad **face** is worried about how to **face** the future. (The first usage of the noun *face* is used literally and means "the front part of the head." However, the second usage of the verb *face* is used figuratively and means "to meet a difficult situation.")

6 Understanding the Literal and Figurative Meanings of Words The underlined words in the sentences below are used figuratively. For each sentence, choose the appropriate meaning of the word in that context.

1. Information technology is <u>driving</u> the economy in some cities.
   - (A) guiding and controlling a car, bus, or truck
   - (B) taking someone in a car, bus, or truck
   - (C) forcing (someone) to leave
   - (D) providing the power for
   - (E) good

2. Communism began to <u>fall</u> in the late 1980s.
   - (A) lose power
   - (B) come down from a standing position
   - (C) become lower in level
   - (D) be killed in a battle
   - (E) become lower in quantity

3. Capitalism has spread to most <u>corners</u> of the world.
   - (A) points where two walls meet
   - (B) points where two roads meet
   - (C) distant places
   - (D) difficult positions from which there is no escape
   - (E) edges

4. Geography is the <u>root</u> of several farming problems.
   - (A) feeling of belonging to one place
   - (B) part of a plant that grows in the soil
   - (C) part of a tooth or hair that holds it to the rest of the body
   - (D) cause
   - (E) solution

5. An open economic system can be a <u>key</u> to improving the lives of people in developing countries.
   - (A) a metal instrument to unlock a door
   - (B) something that helps to find an answer
   - (C) important
   - (D) part of a piano, typewriter, or computer
   - (E) a list of answers to exercises in a textbook

6. Heavy rains <u>wash</u> nutrients from the land.
   - (A) clean with water
   - (B) water
   - (C) rain on
   - (D) cause to be carried off by water
   - (E) clean oneself in a bathtub

7. Their governments have created an economic <u>climate</u> in which people can move from agriculture to manufacturing.

- (A) weather
- (B) average weather condition in an area over a long time
- (C) urban area
- (D) condition, situation
- (E) temperature

8. It's possible for government policy to prepare a <u>path</u> out of poverty.

- (A) road for walkers
- (B) open space for people to move through
- (C) way
- (D) line that something (e.g., an arrow) moves along
- (E) road for runners

7 **Checking Vocabulary** Find the words and expressions in the reading selection "Global Trade" that have the following meanings and write the words on the lines.

1. advantages = _____ *benefits* _____

2. as a result = _____

3. things that people buy = _____

4. something that produces heat or power = _____

5. make less = _____

6. movement of the ocean toward the beach and away from the beach = _____

7. area of water where ships and boats are safe = _____

8. difference = _____

9. area with no access to an ocean = _____

10. natural chemicals that help plants grow = _____

11. something that prevents success = _____

12. obviously (idiom) = _____

13. governmental plans that give special help to a country's own people = _____

_____

14. money that the government gives people so that they can sell their products at a low cost = _____

15. system of roads, trains, harbors, and so on = _____

8 **Checking Your Understanding** Turn back to the beginning of Activity 4 on page 118 and answer the question that you were asked to think about.

Understanding Outlines

Many reading selections follow an outline. The outline is the plan, or the organization, of the material. It shows the relationship of the topics, main ideas, supporting details, and examples. Outlining reading material after you read can help you see clearly the relationships between and among ideas. You can also write an outline to organize your ideas when you are preparing to write a composition.

In an outline, the general ideas are labeled with Roman numerals such as I, II, III. The more specific ideas are labeled with capital letters (A, B, C) and are written below the general ideas. If there are more details or examples, label them with numbers (1, 2, 3) and write them below the specific idea. More specific ideas are indented to the right.

Example

The outline below is of the reading on pages 119–121.

Global Trade

I. Introduction: Benefits of Open Trade
  A. For developed countries
    1. More competition
    2. Lower prices
    3. More consumer choice
  B. For developing countries—access to essential goods
  C. For both
    1. Reduce poverty
    2. Improve living conditions

II. Disadvantages for Poor Countries
  A. *Apparent* advantage: "Rising tide lifts all boats"
  B. Problems with this idea
    1. "Leaking boats"
    2. Wide gap between rich and poor

III. The Disadvantage of Geography
  A. Landlocked countries
  B. Problems of tropical countries
    1. Rain washes nutrients from agricultural soil
    2. Diseases weaken workers

IV. Protectionist Policies
  A. Definition
  B. Examples
    1. Agricultural subsidies
    2. "Hidden" protectionist policies

V. Government Policies—Key to Economic Success
   A. East Asia (contrasted with Africa)
   B. Create a good economic climate in which people move from agriculture to
      1. Manufacturing
      2. Information technology
   C. Pay attention to
      1. Infrastructure
      2. Education
      3. Persuading developed countries to drop protectionism
   D. Conclusion: Path out of poverty

9 **Understanding Outlines** Answer these questions about the outline on this and the previous page.

1. What is the topic of the whole outline?

_____

2. What are three benefits of open trade for developed countries?

_____

3. What are two problems with the idea that "the rising tide lifts all boats"?

_____

4. What are two examples of protectionist policies?

_____

5. What two government policies can help developing countries to have a competitive edge?

_____

10 **Finding the Main Idea** What is the one main idea of the reading selection "Global Trade"?

(A) Almost the entire world now shares the same economic system—capitalism—which is based on the idea of open trade.

(B) Good economic times benefit poor countries, as well as rich ones, because "the rising tide lifts all boats."

(C) Geography is a serious disadvantage for many landlocked, tropical countries.

(D) The result of protectionist policies of rich countries is that "open" trade isn't actually open, and poor countries are at a disadvantage.

(E) Many developing countries are at a disadvantage in global trade, but they can find success with good government policies.

11 Discussing the Reading Talk about your answers to these questions.

1. Think of a country that you know well. Is geography in that country an obstacle to economic success? If so, is government policy moving the economy toward manufacturing or infotech?

2. Is the economy in that country better or worse than it was five or ten years ago? Why?

3. In your opinion, does the writer of "Global Trade" have more sympathy (agreement and understanding) for developed or developing countries? Why do you think this?

Part 2 | Reading Skills and Strategies

Global Travel . . . and Beyond

Before You Read

1 Thinking Ahead Discuss your answers to these questions.

1. What are some different types of travel? List as many as you can.

2. Do you like to travel? Where in the world would you like to go?

3. What are some obstacles to traveling?

Read

2 Identifying the Main Ideas Read the following paragraphs, without using a dictionary. After each paragraph, choose the sentence that best expresses the main idea.

Global Travel . . . and Beyond

A   When some people think of global travel, they think of expensive cruise ships and hotels or sightseeing tours to famous places. However, global travel has changed a lot in recent years. Now, not all travel is expensive, so lack of money doesn't have to hold people back. And these days there is an enormous variety of possibilities for people of all   5

▲ Have you ever been on a cruise?

interests. Are you looking for adventure? Education? Fun? Do you like to travel with a group? Do you prefer to travel on your own? Would you like to get "inside" another culture and understand the people better? Would you prefer to volunteer to help others? Are you in the market for something strange and different? There is something for almost everybody.

What is the main idea of Paragraph A?

- (A) Global travel doesn't have to be expensive.
- (B) Global travel offers more variety now than it did in past years.
- (C) Global travel includes cruise ships, hotels, and sightseeing.
- (D) There are now group tours for people with a variety of interests.
- (E) Global travel can now be strange and different.

B   Train travel used to be simply a means of getting from one place to another. Now, for people with money, it can also offer education or adventure. The Trans-Siberian Special, for example, is a tour that runs from Mongolia to Moscow. The train stops in big cities and small villages so that passengers can go sightseeing, and there is a daily lecture on board the train, in which everyone learns about history and culture. For people who are looking for fun and adventure, there are the Murder Mystery Trains of Western Australia. These trips interest people who love Sherlock Holmes, Hercule Poirot, and Miss Marple. They are for people who have always secretly dreamed of being a private eye and solving mysteries. The passengers on board have the opportunity to solve a murder mystery right there on the train. During the train ride, for instance, there might be a gunshot; soon everyone learns that there has been a "murder," and they spend the rest of the trip playing detective. They track down clues, exchange this information and their opinions, and solve the whodunit by the time the train has pulled into the station. Of course, no real crime takes place. The "murderer" and several passengers are actually actors. The trip is a very creative game.

What is the main idea of Paragraph B?

- (A) The Murder Mystery Trains allow passengers to solve a murder on the train.
- (B) The Trans-Siberian Special is a tour that offers sightseeing and lectures.
- (C) The Trans-Siberian Special and Murder Mystery Trains are expensive.
- (D) Train travel can offer education and adventure, in addition to transportation.
- (E) Train travel is one way to get from one place to another.

C   Many people don't realize that the world's largest industry is tourism. 35
Clearly, tourists have a big impact on the environment. Perhaps, then, it's

fortunate that there is interest in ecotourism; approximately 20 percent of all international travel is now nature travel. Serious ecotourists are interested in preserving the environment 40 and learning about wildlife. Most also want to experience a new culture. Although it's possible to be very comfortable on an ecotour, many travelers choose to rough it; they don't expect hot showers, clean sheets, gourmet food, or 45 air-conditioned tour buses. They live as villagers do. They get around on bicycles, on foot (by hiking or trekking), or on the water (on a sailboat or river raft).

▲ Ecotourists care about the environment.

What is the main idea of Paragraph C?

- (A) A popular form of travel, called ecotourism, is for people who are interested in nature.
- (B) Ecotours are not usually comfortable.
- (C) Ecotourists live as villagers do and do not travel by train, bus, or car.
- (D) The world's largest industry, tourism, is changing.
- (E) Most ecotourists want to experience another culture.

D   For people who want a valuable experience abroad, there are exciting 50
opportunities to study and volunteer—at the same time. Are you interested in
the arts or in learning about another culture? At the Vijnana Kala Vedi Cultural
Center in India, you can study two subjects from a list of possibilities
including Indian music, dance, theater, cooking, or yoga. The tuition for these
classes and room and board is very low because you volunteer one hour each 55
day to teach English to children in the village. Are you interested in science?
Through an organization called Earthwatch, you study a specific science in a
hands-on experience as you volunteer on a research project. The projects

change from year to year, but among typical possibilities are digging up dinosaur bones in Montana, U.S.A., building solar ovens in Indonesia, or studying medicinal plants in Kenya, bees in Brazil, or the ecology of Lake Baikal, Siberia. It may surprise some people that so many are willing to pay over $1,000 *and* agree to work hard, usually for two weeks. The Earthwatch director of Public Affairs says that there are two main reasons: "One—it's a really exciting vacation. And two—they can try out a potential career."

▲ Women dancing in India

What is the main idea of Paragraph D?

- (A) There are exciting opportunities for people who want to study and volunteer abroad.
- (B) Scientists in several fields need volunteers to help them.
- (C) It's possible to learn about Indian culture while volunteering in a village school.
- (D) Volunteering can offer a rich learning experience for people who can't afford tuition for classes.
- (E) Earthwatch volunteers have to pay for the opportunity to volunteer.

E   Volunteering is a good way to experience another country without paying for expensive hotels or tuition. But how can a person get to another country cheaply? One possibility is courier travel. For a low fee ($35–$50), a person can join an association that sends information about monthly courier opportunities. The passenger agrees to become a courier (i.e., carry materials for a business in his or her luggage) and can then receive huge discounts on airfare—for example, $250 from Los Angeles to Hong Kong round trip or $400 from London to Tokyo round trip. People who enjoy ocean travel but don't have money for a cruise ship might try a freighter. Although freighters carry cargo from country to country, most also carry eight to twelve passengers. For people who want to take their time, it's a relaxing way to travel and is less expensive than taking a crowded cruise ship.

What is the main idea of Paragraph E?

- (A) Volunteering is a good way to experience another country.
- (B) Courier flights and freighters are two ways to get to another country cheaply.
- (C) On a courier flight, a passenger carries something in exchange for cheap airfare.
- (D) A trip on a freighter is both cheap and relaxing.
- (E) It's possible to travel cheaply.

F   Travelers who return from a vacation often answer the question "How was your trip?" by saying, "Oh, it was out of this world!" By this idiom, they mean, of course, that their trip was amazing or wonderful. However, people will soon be able to use this expression literally, but it will be expensive. 85 Already, it's possible to go through the same training that astronauts go through. Just go to Star City, Russia. In addition to astronaut training, it's possible to experience one of their "Space Adventures." On one of these, for 90 example, you can enter a special plane that gives you the feeling of weightlessness that astronauts experience—several minutes of zero-gravity. (Gravity is the force that keeps us on the Earth.) Two private individuals have already spent a 95 week at the International Space Station, at a price of $20,000,000 each. A number of companies are now planning projects to commercialize space in various ways. A California company, Scaled Composites, and a British company, Virgin 100 Galactica, are working on the creation of reusable vehicles that could carry passengers in the near future. Even the Hilton Hotel chain is considering building a space hotel. The main attractions will be the view (of Earth), the feeling of weightlessness, and the chance to take a hike . . . on the Moon. It goes without saying that the price will also be "out of this world." 105

▲ Would you like to travel into space?

What is the main idea of Paragraph F?

- (A) People who want to go through astronaut training need to go to Russia.
- (B) People pay a lot of money to experience weightlessness, or zero-gravity.
- (C) Soon, it will be possible to take a flight to a space hotel.
- (D) There are three main attractions, not available on Earth, which people can experience at a space hotel.
- (E) Trips into space will soon be possible—but expensive.

UNDERSTANDING IDIOMS

An idiom is a phrase that means something different from the individual words in it. Idioms are most common in informal English but are found everywhere. The reading selections in this chapter contain several. Some phrases have both a literal meaning and an idiomatic meaning.

Example

Our trip was **out of this world**. We spent a fabulous week on the island of Bali.

In this case, *out of this world* is an idiom that means "wonderful." The context usually helps you figure out if the expression has a literal meaning or is an idiom, and you can often guess the meaning of an idiom from the context. Sometimes, as in the preceding example, it helps to visualize ("see" in your mind) the literal meaning of the expression.

3 **Understanding Idioms** For each of the following items, find an idiom in the reading selection "Global Travel . . . and Beyond" that has a similar meaning and write it on the line. The letters in parentheses indicate the paragraphs where the idioms appear.

1. stop the progress or movement of (A) = _hold (someone) back_

2. alone; not with a group (A) = _____

3. looking for; hoping to find (A) = _____

4. travels; goes (B) = _____

5. on a train (B) = _____

6. detective (B) = _____

7. look for and find (B) = _____

8. mystery (B) = _____

9. arrived in (B) = _____

10. travel in a simple and not comfortable way (C) = _____

11. go from place to place (C) = _____

12. with direct and active participation (D) = _____

13. travel slowly (E) = _____

Responding in Writing

4 **Summarizing** Choose one of the following paragraphs to summarize. Remember that a summary is shorter than the original.

- Any one of the paragraphs from Part 1, pages 119–121
- Any one of the paragraphs from Part 2, pages 126–130

In order to summarize this in your own words, make sure that you read and understand the paragraph. Then write the summary, but *don't look at the original paragraph as you write*. When you finish writing, compare your summary with those of other students who summarized the same paragraph.

5 **Writing Your Own Ideas** Choose one of the topics below to write about. Write a two-paragraph letter to a friend. In the first paragraph, explain one of the topics below. Tell your friend that you want to try this type of travel. In the second paragraph, try to persuade your friend to join you on the trip.

- a trip on a Murder Mystery Train
- an ecotour to _____ (Choose a country.)
- 2 weeks at the Vijnana Kala Vedi Cultural Center
- 2 weeks on an Earthwatch project (Choose one.)
- courier travel
- a trip on a freighter
- going to Star City, Russia, to experience zero-gravity

What is the main idea of each paragraph? _____

_____

6 **Discussing the Reading** Talk about your answers to these questions.

1. What kinds of travel are most interesting to you? Why?

2. Think of a country that you know well. Is tourism important there? If so, what kind of tourism? If not, why not?

3. Think of one trip that you've taken. (It could have been fun, exciting, boring, terrible, etc.) Tell your group about it.

7 **Searching the Internet** Search the Internet for the most interesting or unusual experience for international study, travel, or volunteering. (You can find the website for some opportunities that you read about on pages 126–130, if you want, or search for others.) Imagine that "money is no object." In other words, pretend that you don't need to worry about how much money you'll spend. Learn about this experience and tell a small group about it. Each group then chooses one experience to tell the whole class about.

Part 3 Building Vocabulary and Study Skills

1 **Focusing on Words from the Academic Word List** Fill in the blanks with words from the Academic Word List in the box. When you finish, turn back to pages 120–121, Paragraph E, and check your answers.

areas	global	policy	technology
created	infrastructure	priority	
economic	policies	require	

It may sound as if the situation is hopeless for developing countries ever to have a competitive edge in _____ trade—but perhaps not. East Asia, for example, has found far more _____ success than Africa has. The key to success seems to lie in each government's economic _____. Malaysia and Thailand have the same tropical climate as many African countries, but their economies—unlike those of Africa—are growing fast. The reason? Their governments have _____ an economic climate in which people can move from agriculture to manufacturing. Geography is not the terrible obstacle to manufacturing that it is to farming. To help new entrepreneurs, these governments pay careful attention to _____ such as _____ (harbors, railroads, and so on) and telecommunication. In other countries, such as India, information technology (infotech) is driving the economy in some cities. Computer _____ doesn't depend on geography, but it does _____ educated workers. Therefore, education must be a _____. In addition, governments of developing countries must work with developed countries and persuade them to drop protectionist _____. Clearly, it is possible for government policy to prepare a path out of poverty in even poor countries.

2 **Expressions and Idioms** Complete each sentence with the missing words. Choose from the expressions and idioms in the box. You will use only eight of them.

out of this world	whodunit	get around
goes without saying	hold back	on your own
on board	private eye	pull into
track down	in the market for	rough it

1. A fear of flying will _____ many people from traveling into space. Lack of money will cause many more to stay on Earth.

2. We're going to fly to Europe. Then, while we're there, we'll

   _____ by train.

3. I love to read mystery novels. Someday maybe I'll become a

   _____ and solve crimes myself.

4. She spent hours in the library, but she wasn't able to

   _____ the information that she needed.

5. His old car breaks down all the time, so he's _____ a new car.

6. I don't enjoy camping trips. I've never liked to _____.

7. It _____ that people who travel into space will need to enjoy the feeling of weightlessness.

8. Let's go to that new Thai restaurant next Saturday. The food is absolutely

   _____.

USING PARTICIPLES AS ADJECTIVES

Some adjectives come from verbs: *interest* → *interesting / interested; bore* → *boring/ bored; tire* → *tiring/ tired*. Present participles (*-ing*) are used for the cause of an emotion. (The book is *interesting*.) Past participles (*-ed*) are used for the result or effect. (I'm *interested* in that book.)

Examples

The contrast between rich and poor is **astonishing**.
You might be **astonished** to learn that "the wealth of the world's 200 richest people is greater than the combined incomes of the poorest 41 percent of humanity." (These participles come from the verb *astonish*.)

3 Using Participles as Adjectives Read the verbs in the box and the sentences below it. Fill in the blanks with the present or past participles of the verbs in the box. (Use a dictionary if necessary.) You will have opinions on which words to choose, but let the context guide your choice. You will use some words more than one time.

addict	excite	horrify	relax	thrill
challenge	frighten	interest	terrify	tire

1. Ecotourism is a type of travel for people who are ——————— in preserving the environment. They enjoy a ——————— hike through a tropical rainforest and don't mind roughing it.

2. My job has been very stressful and ——————— this year. I've been working too hard and not sleeping enough. I'm so ———————! I need a ——————— vacation someplace restful, where I can just lie on a beach and do absolutely nothing. After two weeks, when I come back to work, I want to be completely ——————— and free of stress.

3. I guess most people think that a trip into space would be ———————. They would sign up for such a trip right now, if they could afford it. But I couldn't get ——————— about a trip like this. I don't even like to fly on a regular airplane. I'm ——————— of planes, so I'm pretty sure that space travel would be ——————— to me.

4. Dangerous sports are ——————— to some people, who love excitement and are ——————— to danger. They are ——————— to be able to jump out of a plane or off a waterfall. Other people are just the opposite. They're ——————— at the thought of doing anything so dangerous.

Part 4 Focus on Testing

UNDERSTANDING INFERENCES

In previous chapters you learned about and practiced making inferences. This skill is important to help you understand the meanings of reading passages. It is also important for test taking because questions about implied meaning are common on tests. In this section there are two exercises, one from each reading in this chapter, that will help you practice your inferencing skills.

1 **Practice** Complete each sentence by choosing the answers that the reading selection "Global Trade" on pages 119–121 either states or implies.
Note: Each item has more than one answer.

1. Landlocked countries are at a disadvantage because _____.
   - (A) they have no access to the ocean
   - (B) they are in tropical countries
   - (C) it is difficult for them to transport their products to other countries
   - (D) many products must be transported by ship
   - (E) their agricultural land is of poor quality

2. Protectionist policies _____.
   - (A) are a cause of the gap between rich and poor countries
   - (B) include agricultural subsidies
   - (C) are most common in poor countries
   - (D) help everyone
   - (E) are sometimes hidden

3. Malaysia and Thailand _____.
   - (A) are now developed countries
   - (B) have a tropical climate
   - (C) have fast-growing economies
   - (D) are moving from farming to manufacturing
   - (E) have protectionist policies

4. Information technology _____.
   - (A) is important to the economies of some cities in developing countries
   - (B) does not depend on government policies
   - (C) does not depend on geography
   - (D) is difficult to have in landlocked countries
   - (E) depends on educated workers

2 **Critical Thinking: Identifying Inferences** Read the statements below about the article "Global Travel . . . and Beyond" on pages 126–130. Put a check mark (✓) by the statements that you can infer from the reading selection. Do not check the other statements, even if you think they are true. Then, on the line after each inference, write the phrases from which you inferred the information. Leave the other statements blank.

Paragraph A

1. _✓_ You don't have to be rich in order to travel.

   not all travel is expensive, so lack of money doesn't have to hold
   people back

2. _____ It costs a lot of money to take a cruise.

   _____

   _____

3. _____ There is greater variety today in types of travel than there used to be.

_____

_____

4. _____ It's better to travel on your own than in a group.

_____

_____

Paragraph B

1. _____ Today, train travel is more than just a way to get from place to place.

_____

_____

2. _____ The Trans-Siberian Special is a lot of fun.

_____

_____

3. _____ The Murder Mystery Trains are expensive.

_____

_____

4. _____ The Murder Mystery Trains are fun.

_____

_____

Paragraph C

1. _____ Ecotourism is popular with some people.

_____

_____

2. _____ Ecotours are often not very comfortable.

_____

_____

3. _____ Serious ecotourists care about animals.

_____

_____

4. _____ Ecotourists don't enjoy comfortable hotels.

_____

_____

Paragraph D

1. _____ Earthwatch doesn't have any projects in the arts.

_____

_____

2. _____ There are a variety of subjects that people can study in different countries.

_____

_____

3. _____ Rich people prefer to take courses, and people without money prefer to volunteer.

_____

_____

4. _____ An Earthwatch project is an experience for a person who is trying to decide what subject to major in in college.

_____

_____

Paragraph E

1. _____ Cruise ships are expensive.

_____

_____

2. _____ A freighter is a kind of ship.

_____

_____

3. _____ Freighters are as exciting as cruise ships.

_____

_____

4. _____ Travel by freighter is probably not good for people who are in a hurry.

_____

_____

Paragraph F

1. _____ The expression _out of this world_ has both a literal and a figurative meaning.

_____

_____

2. _____ The feeling of weightlessness is always enjoyable for all people.

_____

_____

3. _____ Most people probably cannot afford a week on the International Space Station.

_____

_____

4. _____ Space hotels will be comfortable.

_____

_____

Language and Communication

In This Chapter

How do animals communicate? In Part 1 of this chapter, you will read about recent research in animal communication—how different animals communicate and how some of these communication patterns are similar to those of humans. The second reading selection discusses how humans communicate. For example, do you think women or men talk more? Read and discuss this and other interesting findings from research in Part 2. After working on vocabulary development in Part 3, the final part includes a reading about how the English language is changing as it spreads around the world.

❝ Language shapes the way we think and determines what we can think about. **❞**

—Benjamin Lee Whorf
American linguist (1897–1941)

Connecting to the Topic

1. What two species do you see in the photo?
2. How does each species communicate?
3. What do you think they are "saying" to each other?

If We Could Talk with Animals . . .

Before You Read

1 **Previewing the Topic** Look at the photos and discuss the questions.

1. What might be some ways in which these animals communicate?

2. In your opinion, what is the difference between communication and language?

3. Do you think animals can learn language? Can they learn grammar?

▲ How do ants communicate?

▲ A whale in the ocean

▲ Primatologist Jane Goodall with chimps in the wild

▲ Working with dolphins

2 Previewing Vocabulary Read the words and phrases below. Listen to the pronunciation of each word. Put a check mark (✓) next to the words you know. For the words that you don't know, *don't* use a dictionary. Try to understand them from the reading.

Nouns
- ❏ brain
- ❏ chatter
- ❏ creatures
- ❏ degree
- ❏ echo
- ❏ gender
- ❏ gestures
- ❏ grin
- ❏ lexigrams

- ❏ mammals
- ❏ organs
- ❏ pod
- ❏ prey
- ❏ primates
- ❏ species
- ❏ subjects
- ❏ swagger

Verbs
- ❏ acquire
- ❏ claims
- ❏ coin
- ❏ echoes
- ❏ feeds
- ❏ reassure
- ❏ vocalize
- ❏ wagging

Adverb
- ❏ upright

Idioms and Expressions
- ❏ head (of something)
- ❏ head back
- ❏ picked up
- ❏ shedding light on

3 Previewing the Reading Look over the reading on pages 143–147. Answer these questions with a partner.

1. What is the topic of the reading? (Look at the title.)
2. What are the seven subtopics? (Look at the headings of each paragraph.)
3. What do the pictures in the article lead you to expect?
4. What are at least three questions you have about the reading after previewing it?

Read

4 Reading the Article As you read the following selection, think about the answer to these questions: *How do animals communicate? Do animals have the capacity to learn language?* Read the selection. Do not use a dictionary. Then do the exercises that follow the reading.

If We Could Talk with Animals . . .

A   In a famous children's story, Dr. Doolittle is able to talk to—and understand—animals. This has long been a dream of many people—to be able to communicate with animals and know what they're thinking. For almost as long, scientists have wondered if animals actually have language. It seems clear to anyone who has a dog or cat or who closely observes animals that there is certainly communication going on. But how do animals communicate? What do they "say"? And is it truly language?

5

Recent research into everything from ants to chimpanzees is **shedding light on** animal communication.

The "Language" of Smell

B   Many animals produce chemicals called pheromones, which send "smell-messages" to other animals of the same species. These odors have different meanings. One odor attracts a mate. Another sends a warning. Another marks a territory. A honeybee, for example, makes over thirty-six different pheromones to communicate such information as where to find good flowers. An ant that has found food will take a bit of it and then **head back** "home" to the anthill. As it carries the food, it wipes its stomach on the ground. This leaves a chemical trail or path so that other ants will know where to go for more food.

Body Language

C   Just as humans do, animals communicate with body language and sometimes **gestures**. In addition to using odors, for example, a honeybee uses its entire body in a complex "dance" to give other bees exact directions to flowers. A dog expresses happiness by **wagging** his tail, as most people know. But what is the dog in the photo "saying"? His stomach is on the ground; his rear end is up in the air, and his tail is **wagging**. This means "I want to play." Chimpanzees in the wild communicate a wide variety of gestures and facial expressions, as we learn from the research of primatologist Jane Goodall. To express anger, for example, a chimp stands **upright** on two legs, moves with a **swagger** —a proud walk, swinging from side to side—and waves her arms or throws branches. A nervous chimp who is afraid of a more powerful chimp will lower himself to the ground. Then he either holds out his hand or shows his rear end to the other chimp. Interestingly, when a chimp "smiles," it is not a smile of happiness. Instead, it is an expression similar to the nervous, fearful **grin** that a human makes in a tense or stressful situation. A powerful chimp will **reassure** a nervous, fearful chimp by touching, hugging, or kissing him.

▲ What is this dog "saying"?

Vocalizations

D   Like humans, many animals **vocalize**, but we are only beginning to understand the meaning of these sounds. As they move through the ocean, some whales make use of echolocation—first they make clicking noises that travel through the water as sound waves. When these sound waves

▲ Is this chimp nervous, angry, or happy?

encounter an object such as a boat or **prey** such as fish, they rebound or **echo**. The whales use these **echoes** to locate and identify the objects the echoes are bouncing from, even in cloudy water, where it's difficult to see. Some whales also produce mysterious "songs." These are probably calls to communicate with other members of their **pod**, or group, and to know where each member is. So far, we don't know much more than that. Research into whale communication is especially difficult because different populations of whales have different songs—even if those whales are of the same **species**. 50 55

E We have a better understanding of the **chatter** of prairie dogs. A professor at Northern Arizona University, Con Slobodchikoff, has spent over ten years studying one colony of prairie dogs in the wild. He records their sounds. He also carefully observes their actions and all events that happen at the same time as the sounds. He then **feeds** the data into a computer. The computer puts together the chatter—the "talking"—and the actions. By utilizing the computer in this way, Slobodchikoff **claims** that he has identified about 50 words. So what are these prairie dogs talking about? They often alert each other when they spot danger from such **creatures** as a human, dog, or coyote. Surprisingly, in their chatter, they can apparently distinguish shapes, colors, and sizes. They might "say," for example, "There's a tall blue human coming from the north" about a person wearing blue clothes. Slobodchikoff believes that they can distinguish **gender** (a man from a woman) and a dog from a coyote. Their chatter also varies according to the **degree** of danger: Is this creature very dangerous or just something to be careful about? 60 65 70 75 80

▲ Can prairie dogs really communicate?

The Use of Symbols by Dolphins

F Many scientists wonder about animals' capacity to understand a system of symbols, such as language. At the University of Hawaii, studies with dolphins have been going on since 1979. Researchers are teaching these ocean **mammals** a language of hand signals that includes nouns (*ball, basket, pipe*), adjectives (*big, small, red*), directions (*left, right*), verbs (*go, take*), 85 and prepositions (*in*, *under*). The dolphins prove that they understand by following commands such as "Go to the ball on your right and take it to the basket." There is even clear evidence that dolphins understand the grammatical difference between subjects and objects. The **head** of the research program, Dr. Louis Herman, says that with a vocabulary of about 50 words, the dolphins demonstrate their intelligence by following new commands that they have never before experienced or practiced.

The Use of Symbols by Primates

G   Since the 1970s, other researchers have been studying the capacity for language among **primates**—especially among chimpanzees. Because chimps don't have vocal **organs** that allow them to form spoken words, researchers decided to teach them other types of language. One of the earliest **subjects**, a chimp named Washoe, began to learn ASL (American Sign Language, the hand signals of deaf Americans) when she was less than a year old. By age four, she understood and used 132 ASL signs.

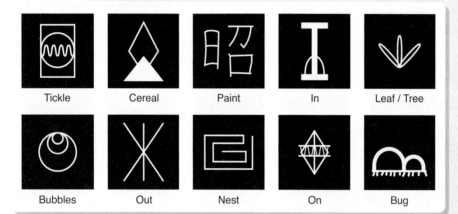

| Tickle | Cereal | Paint | In | Leaf / Tree |
| Bubbles | Out | Nest | On | Bug |

▲ Lexigrams

In other studies, researchers have been communicating with chimps by using a keyboard with special symbols called **lexigrams**. One chimp named Kanzi **picked up** this language naturally; in other words, he watched as people tried (unsuccessfully) to teach this language to his mother.

H   How much can chimps understand? And what can they do with these words? They understand the difference between "take the potato outdoors" and "go outdoors and get the potato." They understand adjectives such as *good*, *funny*, *hungry*, and *stupid*. They can combine words into short sentences: "You me out"; or "Me banana you banana me you give." Perhaps most interestingly, they can **coin** new words or phrases when they don't know a word—for example, "water bird" for a swan and "green banana" for a cucumber. And they can express emotion: "Me sad."

▲ What kind of birds are these?

Language?

But is this language? What distinguishes communication from true language? Do chimps actually have the capacity for language? There is much disagreement about this. Some people argue that chimps can acquire only the vocabulary of a 2 1/2-year-old human. They also point out that a sentence such as "Lana tomorrow scare snake river monster" is not exactly Shakespearean English. It goes without saying that there is a gap between the language ability of chimps and humans. But clearly, this gap is not as wide as we used to think it was. Recent research is now focusing on the structures and activity of the brain. Biologists have looked at one small area of the brain, the *planum temporale*, which humans use to understand and produce language. In chimps, this is larger on the left side of the brain than on the right. In the journal *Science*, researchers tell us that this is "essentially identical" to the *planum temporale* in humans. This is not surprising to people who believe that chimps do have the capacity for language. After all, they say, 99 percent of the genetic material in chimps and humans is identical, making chimps our closest relative.

Conclusions

It is clear, then, that animals certainly communicate in various ways. However, the question "Is it language?" is still open. The famous linguist Noam Chomsky believed that what distinguishes communication from true language is *syntax*—that is, the use of grammar and word order, so he believed that only humans can have language. However, now we know that some animals (dolphins, chimps) have at least simple syntax. Louis Herman suggests, "Some people think of language like pregnancy—you either have it or you don't." But he and other researchers prefer to see language as "a continuum of skills." In other words, some animals simply have more than others.

After You Read

5 **Getting the Main Ideas** Write *T* on the lines before the statements that are true, according to the reading. Write *F* on the lines before the statements that are false. Write *I* before the statements that are impossible to know from the reading.

1. _____ Some animals communicate by producing odors for other animals to smell.

2. _____ Chimpanzees, like humans, smile when they are happy.

3. _____ We know a lot about the communication of whales.

4. _____ With their vocalizations, prairie dogs can warn each other of specific dangers.

5. _____ Dolphins can understand only sentences that they have memorized.

6. _____ Chimps can understand much more vocabulary and grammar than researchers previously thought they could.

7. _____ Researchers agree that all animals communicate but that only humans have a capacity for language.

6 **Checking Your Understanding** What did you learn from the reading? Answer these questions with a group.

1. What are ways in which animals communicate in the wild (that is, in their natural environment)? List them.

2. What are ways in which dolphins and chimps have been taught by humans to communicate? List them.

3. What are examples of the body language of dogs and chimps, and what do these specific movements mean?

4. What is evidence that indicates the similarity of chimpanzees to humans?

Language Tip

The **context** of a reading can give clues to the meaning of vocabulary items. Use information between commas, dashes, or parentheses or after connecting expressions such as **in other words,** or **that is (i.e.).** Also, use information in another sentence or sentence part and your own logic.

7 **Getting Meaning from Context** Read the definitions below and write the correct words and expressions from the reading "If We Could Talk with Animals . . ." that fit these definitions.

1. making (something) clear = _shedding light on_ _____

2. return (verb) = _____

3. movements that communicate meaning = _____

4. moving a tail = _____

5. straight up; standing on two feet = _____

6. a proud walk, from side to side = _____

7. a smile = _____

8. make someone feel better = _____

9. make sounds = _____

10. an animal that another animal hunts = _____

11. group of whales = _____

12. animals of the same type = _____

13. rapid "talk" (noun) = _____

14. says; expresses an opinion = _____

15. male or female = _____

16. animals with warm blood = _____

17. get; obtain; learn = _____

18. the part of the body with which we think = _____

8 Categorizing On each line, write the category that the items are examples of.

1. humans, dogs, coyotes (E) = _____

2. chimpanzees (G) = _____

UNDERSTANDING HOMOPHONES

Some words are pronounced the same, but have different meanings. These types of words are called **homophones**. These words are also sometimes spelled the same.

Examples
I **read** a great book last week. / We painted the door **red**.
She bought a new *blue* car. / The wind *blew* so hard that the newspaper flew out of my hands!

9 Understanding Homophones Write a word from the reading that fits both definitions.

1. gives food to; puts (information) into (E) = *feeds* _____

2. amount; title that a university gives students who have completed their

studies (E) = _____

3. part of the body; director or leader (F) = _____

4. musical instruments in churches; parts of the body (G) = _____

5. topic; person or animal in an experiment (G) = _____

6. lifted from a lower place; learned (G) = _____

7. piece of metal money; create (a word or term) (H) = _____

UNDERSTANDING ITALICS AND QUOTATION MARKS

Writers use *italics* (slanted letters) in English for several reasons:
- for emphasis—to stress an important word
- to mean *the word* _____, or *the term* _____ (Example: *Red* sounds the same as the past tense verb *read*.)
- for the title of a magazine, newspaper, or book
- for words in foreign languages

Writers use quotation marks for two main reasons:
- to quote direct speech—someone's exact words
- to show that the word in quotation marks really means something different from its literal meaning

Examples
There is certainly communication going on. But *how* do animals communicate? What do they "say"?
(The word *how* is in italics for emphasis. The word *say* is in quotation marks because the writer believes that animals don't really say anything.)

10 Understanding Italics and Quotations Look through the reading on pages 144–147 beginning with Paragraph B. Highlight every example of italics and quotation marks. In each case, decide why the writer used them. Then compare your answers with those of other students.

11 Finding Details Read the types of communication in the chart below. Go back to the selection and find examples of each type. Fill in this information to complete the chart.

Types of Communication	Examples
smell	*Smells have different meanings: to attract a mate, send a warning, mark a territory, or communicate where to find food.*
body language	
vocalizations	
chatter (by prairie dogs)	
symbols (used by dolphins)	
symbols (used by primates)	

12 Checking Your Vocabulary Turn back to the Vocabulary Preview on page 143. How many words do you know now? Work with a small group. Go through the list and briefly explain each word in one of these possible ways:
- Give a synonym or definition.
- Use gestures or body language.
- Give an example.
- Point to a picture in this chapter.

13 Discussing the Reading Discuss your answers to the question in the last paragraph of the reading: *Is it language?* Specifically, discuss the following: *What is the difference between communication and language?*

1. Brainstorm possible kinds of communication. Then brainstorm the characteristics of language. List them in the T-chart on the next page.

Communication	Language

2. Now discuss three species. Complete the chart below.

Species	Do they have capacity for language? (*yes/no/not sure*)	Evidence
prairie dogs		
dolphins		
chimps		

Culture Note		

Animal Sounds

In every language, we imagine that animals make certain sounds. We create words for these sounds. These are words that you often see in children's books. Below are some in English.

Animal	What This Animal "Says" in English	What This Animal "Says" in Another Language
cat	meow	
dog	bow-wow (or woof-woof)	
pig	oink	
small bird	cheep! cheep! (or tweet! tweet!)	
duck	quack	
owl	whoo (or hoot)	
rooster	cock-a-doodle-doo	

It's sometimes fun to compare these in different languages. What do animals "say" in another language you know? Write these sounds in the chart.

"Parentese"

1 ■ **Previewing the Topic** Discuss your answers to these questions.

1. In your opinion, who talks more—men or women?

2. In school, who is better at language skills—boys or girls?

3. Do parents talk differently with their sons than they do with their daughters? Do mothers talk differently to their children than fathers do? If so, how?

4. What kinds of toys do parents usually give to their sons? What kinds of toys do parents usually give to their daughters?

5. In your opinion, what is more important in determining what we are—genetics (biology) or our education and environment?

2 ■ **Identifying the Main Ideas** The following paragraphs are about the language that parents use with their young children—what some people are calling "parentese." Read these paragraphs, without using a dictionary. After each paragraph, choose the sentence that best expresses the main idea.

"Parentese"

A   Who talks more—men or women? Most people believe that women talk more. However, linguist Deborah Tannen, who has studied the communication style of men and women, says that this is a stereotype. According to Tannen, women *are* more verbal, or talk more, in private situations, where they use conversation as the "glue" to hold relationships 5 together. But, she says, *men* talk more in public situations, where they use conversation to exchange information and gain status. Tannen points out that we can see these differences even in children. Little girls often play with one "best friend"; their play includes a lot of conversation. Little boys often play games in groups; their play usually involves more *doing* than 10 talking. In school, girls are often better at verbal skills; boys are often better at mathematics.

What is the main idea of Paragraph A?

    (A) Women talk more than men.

    (B) Women talk more in private, and men talk more in public.

    (C) Little girls and little boys have different ways of playing.

    (D) Men and women have different styles of talking, which may begin in childhood.

B   A recent study at Emory University helps to shed light on the roots of this difference. Researchers studied conversation between children age 3–6 and their parents. They found evidence that parents talk very differently to [15] their sons than they do to their daughters. The startling conclusion was that parents use far more language with their girls. Specifically, when parents talk with their daughters, they use more descriptive language and more details. There is also far more talk about emotions, especially sadness, with daughters than with sons. [20]

What is the main idea of Paragraph B?

    (A) Researchers have studied the conversations of children and their parents.

    (B) A research study found that parents talk differently to their sons and daughters.

    (C) An Emory University study found that parents talk more with their daughters than with their sons.

    (D) Parents don't talk about emotions with their sons.

C   Most parents would be surprised to learn this. They certainly don't *plan* to talk more with one child than with another. They don't even realize that this is happening. So why do they do it? Interestingly, it begins when the children are newborn babies. It is a known fact that at birth, males are a little less developed than females are. They don't vocalize, or make noises, [25] as much as girls do, and they don't have as much eye contact. Female babies vocalize, look at their parents, and remain alert longer. The result? Parents respond by talking more to the baby girls, who seem to be paying attention and "talking" back to them. Apparently, then, biology determines the amount of language that parents use. [30]

What is the main idea of Paragraph C?

    (A) Parents who talk more to their baby girls are responding to the fact that girls are a little more developed at birth than boys are.

    (B) Most parents don't know that they talk more with their girls and would be surprised to learn this.

    (C) Baby girls make noises and have eye contact a little more than baby boys do.

    (D) Baby boys don't remain alert as long as baby girls do.

D   There is always this question: what determines our character, personality, and behavior—nature (biology) or nurture (environment and education)? The research with babies seems to suggest that *nature* causes the amount and quality of language use. However, a study from the University of California at Santa Cruz provides evidence that the *situation* [35] or *context* also influences the conversation. For example, parents usually give gender-stereotyped toys to their children. A boy gets a car that he can take apart and put back together, for instance. A girl gets a toy grocery store. The type of talk depends on the toy the child is playing with. A toy grocery store naturally involves more conversation. If we consider this, we [40] might decide that *nurture* determines language ability because we *choose* which toys to give our children.

What is the main idea of Paragraph D?

- (A) The toys that parents give their son or daughter may influence the child's language ability.
- (B) From research with babies, we know that biology determines language use.
- (C) Parents usually give gender-stereotyped toys to their children.
- (D) Education determines language ability.

E   Campbell Leaper, a researcher at the University of California, believes that the choice of toys is important. Both boys and girls, he says, need "task-oriented" toys such as take-apart cars. With these toys, they practice [45] the language that they will need, as adults, in work situations. Both boys and girls also need "social, interactive" toys such as a grocery store. With these toys, they practice the kind of conversation that is necessary in relationships with friends and family. The data suggest that biology does not have to be a self-fulfilling prophecy. Leaper concludes that verbal [50] ability is the result of both nature and nurture. Parents might naturally respond to their baby's biology, but they can choose a variety of toys and can choose how to talk with this child.

What is the main idea of Paragraph E?

- (A) Boys usually receive toys with which they practice language that they will use in work situations.
- (B) Girls usually receive toys with which they practice language that is necessary in relationships.
- (C) Biology is not a self-fulfilling prophecy.
- (D) Biology influences language ability, but environment also does, so parents need to give both their boys and girls a variety of types of toys.

3 **Getting Meaning from Context** For each definition, find a word in the reading selection that has a similar meaning and write it on the line.

Paragraph A

1. connected with the use of spoken language = _____

2. sticky liquid that joins things together = _____

Paragraph B

3. feelings = _____

Paragraph C

4. understand and believe = _____

5. to act in return or in answer = _____

6. it seems that = _____

Paragraph D

7. biology = _____

8. environment and education = _____

9. proof; support for a belief = _____

4 **Critical Thinking: Identifying Inferences** Read the statements below about the article "Parentese" on pages 152–154. Put a check mark (✓) by the statements that you can infer from the reading selection. Do not check the other statements, even if you think they are true. Then, on the line after each inference, write the phrases from which you inferred the information. Leave the other statements blank.

Paragraph A

1. _✓_ According to Deborah Tannen, the belief that women talk more is partly right but mostly wrong and oversimplified. _Most people believe that women talk more . . . but this is a stereotype._

2. _____ Women talk more in some situations; men talk more in others.
_____

Paragraph B

3. _____ Parents enjoy talking more with their daughters than with their sons.
_____
_____

4. _____ Girls have more practice discussing sadness than boys do.
_____
_____

Paragraph C

5. _____ Vocalization and eye contact are evidence of development in babies.

_____

_____

6. _____ Little girls, like baby girls, are more alert than little boys are.

_____

_____

Paragraph D

7. _____ People naturally talk more in some situations than in others.

_____

_____

8. _____ A toy car probably doesn't involve boys in much conversation.

_____

_____

Paragraph E

9. _____ According to Campbell Leaper, we should prepare both boys and girls for the adult world of work and relationships.

_____

_____

10. _____ If parents choose their child's toys carefully, biology won't influence the child's verbal ability.

_____

_____

Strategy

Distinguishing Facts from Assumptions

In reading textbooks, students need to be able to determine the difference between a fact (information that has been proven to be accurate) and an assumption (an idea that might or might not be true but has not been proven). One way to do this is to be aware of certain "signal words."

Some words and expressions that indicate a fact are these:

    found proof   a known fact   evidence

Some words that indicate an assumption are these:

    believe   suggest

    apparently   may/might

    seem

5 **Distinguishing Facts from Assumptions** For each statement below, write *fact* or *assumption*, according to the presentation of information in the reading selection "Parentese." (Look back at the selection for words that indicate fact or assumption.)

1. _____ Women talk more than men.

2. _____ Parents talk very differently to their sons and daughters.

3. _____ At birth, males are a little less developed than females are.

4. _____ The situation in which conversation takes place—in addition to a child's gender—influences the amount of talk.

5. _____ The choice of toys that parents give their children is important.

6. _____ Biology does not have to be a self-fulfilling prophecy.

6 **Discussing the Reading** Talk about your answers to these questions.

1. According to the reading, what might cause some schoolchildren to be better at language skills than other children?

2. Did anything in the reading surprise you? If so, what?

3. Complete this diagram with information from both the reading and your own experience. What makes us the people we are? In other words, which of our characteristics come from nature? Which come from nurture? Which come from both?

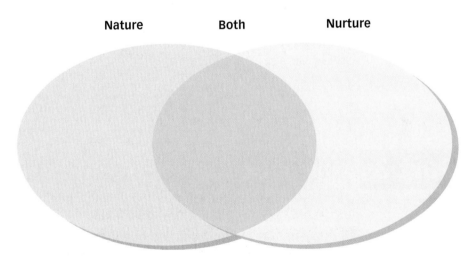

Nature   **Both**   **Nurture**

Responding in Writing

7 **Summarizing** Choose one paragraph from "Parentese" on pages 152–154. Write a short summary of it (two or three sentences). Follow these steps:

- Make sure that you understand the paragraph well.
- Identify the topic, main idea, and supporting details.
- Find the most important details.

In order to summarize this in your own words, *don't look at the original paragraph as you write*. When you finish writing, compare your summary with those of other students who summarized the same paragraph.

8 **Writing Your Own Ideas** Choose one of these topics to write about.

- animal communication
- "parentese"
- the influence of toys on children

What did you learn about this topic from Part 1 or 2? Write two paragraphs. In the first, tell what you learned about your topic. In the second paragraph, write about one of the following:

- something that especially interested you or surprised you about this topic (and why)
- an experience in your own life that is related to your topic.

What is the main idea of each paragraph? _____

_____

_____

Talk It Over

9 **Toys** Make a list of the toys that you played with most often as a child. What were they? What kind of conversation did they involve you in? (Task-oriented? Social and interactive?) Do you think these toys influenced your language ability? Discuss your answers with a small group.

Part 3 Building Vocabulary and Study Skills

1 **Focusing on Words from the Academic Word List** Fill in the blanks with words from the Academic Word List in the box. When you finish, turn back to page 147, Paragraph I, and check your answers. You will use one word twice.

acquire	focusing	research
capacity	identical	structures
communication	journal	percent

But is this language? What distinguishes _____ from 1 true language? Do chimps actually have the _____ for 2 language? There is much disagreement about this. Some people argue that chimps can _____ only the vocabulary of a 2 1/2-year-old 3 human. They also point out that a sentence such as "Lana tomorrow scare snake river monster" is not exactly Shakespearean English. It goes without saying that there is a gap between the language ability of chimps and humans. But clearly, this gap is not as wide as we used to think it was. Recent _____ is now _____ on the 4 5 _____ and activity of the brain. Biologists have looked at 6 one small area of the brain, the *planum temporale*, which humans use to understand and produce language. In chimps, this is larger on the left side of the brain than on the right. In the _____ *Science*, 7 researchers tell us that this is "essentially _____" to the 8 *planum temporale* in humans. This is not surprising to people who believe that chimps do have the _____ for language. After all, 9 they say, 99 _____ of the genetic material in chimps and 10 humans is identical, making chimps our closest relative.

PREFIXES AND SUFFIXES

Below is a partial list of word **prefixes** and their approximate meanings. On the next page are **suffixes**. These were all introduced in previous chapters.

Prefix	Meaning
com-/con-	together; with
im-/in-/un-/dis-	not
inter-	between; among
mis-	wrong
pre-	before; first
re-	again; back

Suffix	Part of Speech	Meaning
-al	adjective	having the quality of
-ar	adjective	of or relating to; resembling
-i(an)	noun	belonging to; characteristic of
-ed	adjective	passive participle
-en	verb	to make; to become
-ence/-ance	noun	state; quality
-ent/-ant	adjective	having the quality of
-er	adjective	comparative form
-er/-or/-ist	noun	a person who
-ess	noun	a person (female)
-est	adjective	superlative form
-ful	adjective	full of
-ible/-able	adjective	having the quality of; able to be
-ic	adjective	having the quality of; affected by
-ing	noun, adjective	active participle; gerund
-ion	noun	state; condition
-ive	adjective	having the quality of; relating to
-less	adjective	without
-ly	adverb	manner (how)
-ment/-ness/-ship	noun	state; condition; quality
-(i)ous	adjective	full of
-ure	noun	state; result
-y	adjective	having the quality of; full of

2 **Working with Prefixes and Suffixes** In the parentheses after each word in the following list, write its part of speech (n. = noun; v. = verb; adj. = adjective; adv. = adverb). Then complete the sentences that follow with the appropriate words.

1. converse (*v.*), conversation (*n.*), conversational (*adj.*)

   Recent studies show that there is more _____*conversation*_____ between parents and their daughters than with their sons. This begins at birth, when parents _____*converse*_____ more with baby girls, who tend to have more eye contact and make more noises than baby boys do. It continues in childhood, when girls' play is more _____ than boys' is.

2. linguist (   ), linguistic (   ), linguistics (   )

   The field of _____ has several branches. In one of these, _____s study how children acquire language. In another branch, they work to discover if some animals have _____ ability.

3. reassurance (   ), reassure (   ), reassuringly (   )

   The mother chimp hugged her frightened baby to _____ him. Then she kissed him to give him further _____. These actions are similar to those of a human, who, in addition, speaks _____ to a fearful child.

4. able (   ), ability (   ), ably (   )

   Many people wonder if animals have the _____ to learn language. Studies with dolphins and chimps indicate that they are _____ to learn a certain amount of vocabulary. They also _____ follow a number of directions.

5. appear (   ), apparent (   ), apparently (   )

   _____, both nature and nurture decide a child's linguistic ability. It is _____ that boys and girls vocalize to a different degree from birth. However, it also _____s that parents can influence the amount and type of conversation that their children have.

6. simple (   ), simplify (   ), simplified (   )

When humans _____ their language, chimps are able to understand a certain amount. The chimps can also use _____ grammar to put together _____ sentences.

7. vocal (   ), vocalize (   ), vocalization (   )

Members of a pod of whales frequently _____ with each other. We believe they are _____ in this way to make sure where each member is, but we really don't know much, yet, about their _____s.

3 **Understanding Words in Phrases** As you read, it's important to notice words that often go together. Go back to the reading on pages 152–154. Find words to complete the following phrases.

Paragraph A

1. hold relationships _____

2. _____ status

3. points _____ that

4. are often better _____ (mathematics)

Paragraph B

5. shed _____ _____

Paragraph C

6. a _____ fact

7. _____ contact

8. _____ attention

Paragraph D

9. _____ evidence

10. take _____ and put _____ _____

11. depends _____

Paragraph E

12. a _____-_____ prophecy

Learning New Vocabulary: Making a Vocabulary Log

While you are reading, you need to understand vocabulary, but you do not need to learn it actively. Sometimes, however, you may want to remember new vocabulary for use in conversation and writing. A vocabulary log may prove useful. Follow these steps to create one:

1. Divide a sheet of paper into three columns. (This will become your Vocabulary Log.) Write these headings at the top of the three columns: Word, Definition, Example. Write the new word or expression and its pronunciation in the first column. In the middle column, write the definition and the part of speech. In the third column, write a sentence that illustrates the meaning of the item. (You can find these sample sentences in the readings in this book.)

2. Look up the words in a dictionary and write related words on the same piece of paper.

3. Pronounce the words to yourself. Try to "see" their spelling in your mind as you learn them. Repeat examples to yourself and make up other examples.

4. Cover the words and examples and try to remember them when you read the definitions.

5. Review your list regularly.

Pay special attention to *how* the word is used. For example, if the word is a verb, is it transitive? (Does it need an object?) Is a preposition used after the word? If this is a noun, is it a count noun (like *teacher*) or a noncount noun (like *water*)?

Example

Word	Definition	Example
respond (rĭ-spŏnd′)	(v.) answer	Parents **respond** to their baby's vocalizations.
response (rĭ-spŏns′)	(n.) answer	Her **response** was immediate.
responsive (rĭ-spŏn′sĭv)	(adj.) answering willingly with words or actions	They were **responsive** to their child's needs.

4 **Making a Vocabulary Log** Choose a few words from Chapters 1–7 in this book. Follow the directions in the box above to make your own Vocabulary Log. Focus on the words that you had a hard time learning or are having a hard time remembering. Each day, as part of your homework, spend a few minutes adding new words to your Vocabulary Log.

5 Searching the Internet Search the Internet for information about one of the topics below. Share this with a small group.

- Communication among animals and people
  How do they communicate? What words do they know?
  (Tip: You can look for Jane Goodall, chimps in the wild; Con Slobodchikoff, prairie dog communication; Louis Herman, dolphin communication; or Deborah Tannen, human male-female communication.)
- Popular toys
  Find out what the five most popular toys are these days. Which of these toys are task-oriented? Which are social or interactive?

Part 4 | Focus on Testing

COMPREHENSION QUESTIONS ABOUT DETAILS

Standardized tests often give a reading passage followed by questions about it. Many of these questions are about details. You'll be able to answer some from memory, after one quick reading. You'll need to look back and scan for the answers to others.

Hints

- You can usually find the items in the same order in which they appear in the selection, so look for the answer to number 1 near the beginning.
- It usually helps to quickly look over the questions before reading, if possible.

1 Practice First, read the questions that follow the article (page 166). Then read the article. Try to keep some of the questions in mind as you read and mark the answers with a felt-tip pen. Don't worry if you don't understand every word. When you finish reading, answer the questions. Work as quickly as possible, as you would on a test. Your teacher may give you a time limit.

As English Spreads, Speakers Morph It into World Tongue

"English is probably changing faster than any other language," says Alan Firth, a linguist at the University of Aalborg in Denmark, "because so many people are using it."

More than 1 billion people are believed to speak some form of English. For every native speaker, there are three nonnative speakers. Three-quarters of the world's mail is in English and four-fifths of electronic information is stored in English.

5

As more nonnative speakers converse with each other, hundreds of . . . varieties of English are taking on lives of their own around the world.

But the uncontrolled, global germination of so many "Englishes" has 10 some worried. English purists, led by Britain's Prince Charles, bemoan the degradation of the language as they see it.

Multiculturalists, meanwhile, say the . . . spread of English effectively commits "linguistic genocide" by killing off dozens of other languages.

These differing views lead to the question: Is the world taking English 15 by storm or is English taking the world by storm?

Tom McArthur, editor of the *Oxford Companion to the English Language*, says that in 20 to 30 countries around the world, English is merging with native languages to create hybrid Englishes.

"The tensions between standard English and hybrid Englishes are going 20 to become very, very great," says Mr. McArthur, who calls the process neither good nor bad. "We are going to have to keep on our toes. Some standard form of English [should be maintained] . . . as a tool of communication."

Prince Charles recently warned of a creeping degradation of the English language, lashing out at Americans for cheapening it with bad grammar. 25

"People tend to invent all sorts of nouns and verbs and make words that shouldn't be," said Prince Charles at the March launching of a five-year British effort to preserve "English English."

"I think we have to be a bit careful, otherwise the whole thing can get rather a mess," he added. 30

Danish Professor Firth, who studies conversations between nonnative speakers when they conduct business, says businessmen tend to . . . use simplified grammar and develop and use their own English terms to cut a deal.

"People develop their own ways of doing business with each other, of talking and even writing . . . that native speakers might not understand," 35 Firth says. "And native speakers join in and start to speak that way also."

But those who seek to preserve native cultures warn that in many parts of the world, English is taking more than it is giving. Some linguists attending the 1995 global Cultural Diversity Conference held in Sydney last month warned of accelerating global "linguicide." 40

Schools in former European colonies still use English or French to assimilate ethnic populations, eradicating dozens of native languages, they warn. . . .

Oxford Companion editor McArthur says the spread of English can't be halted. The globalization of the world, mostly driven by economics, is 45 inevitable.

"It's the [world's] need for a unified language of trade, politics, and culture," he says. "We're going to lose a lot of languages around the world, but if it's not English, it would be something else."

Source: Adapted from "As English Spreads, Speakers Morph It into World Tongue" from David Rohde, *The Christian Science Monitor*.

1. According to the article, how many people probably speak English?
   - (A) three-fourths of the world
   - (B) four-fifths of the world
   - (C) more than 1 billion people
   - (D) one in three people

2. Two groups of people with differing views are _____.
   - (A) purists and multiculturalists
   - (B) native speakers and nonnative speakers
   - (C) businessmen and linguists
   - (D) linguists and multiculturalists

3. People who believe that the spread of English is harming (hurting) English are _____.
   - (A) linguists
   - (B) multiculturalists
   - (C) purists
   - (D) editors

4. The article indicates that Prince Charles _____.
   - (A) leads the English purists
   - (B) does not like the changes in the English language
   - (C) does not appear to like American English
   - (D) all of the above

5. *Linguicide* (line 40) probably means _____.
   - (A) the teaching of languages
   - (B) the preservation of languages
   - (C) the killing of languages
   - (D) the teaching of linguistics

6. Tom McArthur, editor of the *Oxford Companion to the English Language*, believes that _____.
   - (A) English is joining with other languages to create something new
   - (B) it's not necessary to have a standard form of English
   - (C) the spread of English is unavoidable
   - (D) a and b

Beyond the Reading

2 Interviewing Choose one of these projects. When you finish, report your findings to the class.

- Interview ten people who are not native speakers of English. Ask them if the spread of English is having any effect on their culture or language, and if so, *what* effect?
- Interview ten native speakers of English. Ask them if they notice any recent changes in the English language (vocabulary, grammar, etc.) due to the influence of other languages, and if so, *what changes?*

Self-Assessment Log

Read the lists below. Check (✓) the strategies and vocabulary that you learned in this chapter. Look through the chapter or ask your instructor about the strategies and words that you do not understand.

Reading and Vocabulary-Building Strategies

- ❏ Getting the main ideas
- ❏ Getting meaning from context
- ❏ Understanding homophones
- ❏ Understanding italics and quotation marks
- ❏ Finding details
- ❏ Identifying the main ideas
- ❏ Identifying inferences
- ❏ Distinguishing fact from assumption
- ❏ Working with prefixes and suffixes
- ❏ Understanding words in phrases
- ❏ Making a vocabulary log

Target Vocabulary

Nouns

- ❏ brain
- ❏ capacity*
- ❏ chatter
- ❏ communication*
- ❏ context*
- ❏ creatures
- ❏ degree
- ❏ emotions
- ❏ evidence*
- ❏ gender*
- ❏ gestures
- ❏ glue
- ❏ grin
- ❏ journal*
- ❏ mammals
- ❏ nature
- ❏ nurture
- ❏ organs
- ❏ pod
- ❏ prey
- ❏ primates
- ❏ research*
- ❏ situation
- ❏ species
- ❏ structures*
- ❏ subjects
- ❏ swagger

Verbs

- ❏ acquire*
- ❏ claims
- ❏ coin
- ❏ feeds
- ❏ focusing*
- ❏ realize
- ❏ reassure
- ❏ respond*
- ❏ vocalize
- ❏ wagging

Adjectives

- ❏ identical*
- ❏ verbal

Adverbs

- ❏ apparently*
- ❏ percent*
- ❏ upright

Idioms and Expressions

- ❏ head (of something)
- ❏ head back
- ❏ picked up
- ❏ shedding light on

* These words are from the Academic Word List. For more information on this list, see www.vuw.ac.nz/lals/research/awl.

8

Tastes and Preferences

In This Chapter

Goods and products have moved around the globe for centuries. Along with this exchange of products comes an exchange of culture. The Silk Road was a huge area, or route, where such exchanges took place. The first reading selection explores the history and significance of the Silk Road. Part 2 includes a reading selection that describes things that people do in different societies to make themselves more attractive, in both modern and ancient times. The final two parts will help you develop vocabulary and test-taking strategies.

❝ Science and art belong to the whole world, and before them vanish the barriers of nationality. ❞

—Johann Wolfgang von Goethe
German philosopher and poet (1749–1832)

Connecting to the Topic

1. What do you see in the photo?

2. What is the mood of the woman? What do you think she is feeling? What is she thinking?

3. What types of art do you like to look at? To buy?

The Silk Road: Art and Archaeology

Before You Read

1 Previewing the Topic Look at the photos and discuss the questions.

1. Compare the map of the ancient Silk Road to the modern map of the same area. What countries exist in this region today?

2. What was the purpose of caravans? Do people still have caravans today? Why or why not?

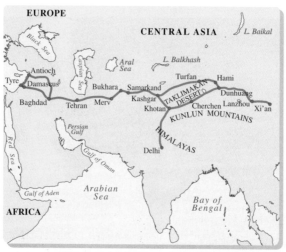

▲ A map of the Silk Road, from about 2000 years ago to about the 16th century

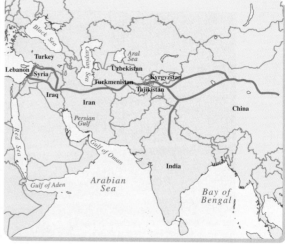

▲ A map of the Silk Road countries today

▲ A **caravan** of camels, from the 19th century

2 **Previewing Vocabulary** Read the words and phrases below. Listen to the pronunciation of each word. Put a check mark (✓) next to the words you know. For the words that you don't know, *don't* use a dictionary. Try to understand them from the reading.

Nouns

- ❑ arabesques
- ❑ archaeologists
- ❑ architecture
- ❑ armor
- ❑ calligraphy
- ❑ caravans
- ❑ caves
- ❑ cowry shells
- ❑ destination
- ❑ documents

- ❑ fabric
- ❑ frescoes
- ❑ mausoleums
- ❑ merchants
- ❑ mosques
- ❑ mummy
- ❑ network
- ❑ oasis
- ❑ pitcher

- ❑ silk
- ❑ spices
- ❑ statues

Verbs

- ❑ decorated
- ❑ depict
- ❑ flowered
- ❑ spread

Adjectives

- ❑ exquisite
- ❑ fertility
- ❑ holy
- ❑ significant
- ❑ vast

Expression

- ❑ to this end

3 **Previewing the Reading** Look over the reading on pages 171–175.

1. What is the topic of the reading? (Look at the title.)

2. What are the five subtopics? (Look at the headings of each section.)

3. What do the photos in the article lead you to expect?

Read

4 **Reading the Article** As you read the following selection, think about the answer to these questions: *What was the Silk Road? What can we learn about ancient life in this region from a study of the art and archaeology?* Read the selection. Do not use a dictionary. Then do the exercises that follow the reading.

The Silk Road: Art and Archaeology

Cross-Cultural Evidence

A   In the ruins of the ancient Roman city of Pompeii, which was destroyed by a volcano in the year 79 C.E.,* a mirror was found. It had an ivory handle in the shape of a female **fertility** goddess. The mirror was from India. In the tomb of Li Xian, a Chinese military official who died in 569 C.E.,

---

* C.E. = *Common Era;* 79 C.E. = 79 A.D.

archaeologists found a water pitcher in the shape of a vase. The pitcher had a combination of different styles: the shape was from Persia (today's Iran), many details were from Central Asia, and the figures on the side were Greek stories from the Trojan War. In the Japanese city of Nara, the 8th century Shosoin Treasure House holds thousands of exquisite objects of great beauty—furniture, musical instruments, weapons, fabric, and military armor. These objects come from what is today Vietnam, western China, Iraq, the Roman Empire, and Egypt. Clearly, long before the globalization of our modern world, trade was going on between very distant lands, and the objects tell a story about a place and time.

What Was the Silk Road?

B   Along the famous Silk Road, cultures have influenced each other from ancient times, although it was not truly one continuous road. Instead, it was a 5,000-mile series or network of trails that connected East Asia to the Mediterranean. In ancient times, it was never called the "Silk Road." The term *Silk Road* was coined in the 19th century by a German explorer. He was thinking of one of the goods that people in the West found especially desirable—silk fabric from China. For centuries, the Chinese kept as a secret the way in which silk is produced. They exchanged this fabric for Mediterranean glass, whose production was also kept secret by the Romans. However, merchants also moved many other goods along these trade routes: spices (such as cinnamon), musical instruments, tea, valuable stones, wool, linen, and other fabrics. Ideas and knowledge also moved along the Silk Road. Travelers to foreign regions took with them ideas about art, architecture, styles of living, and religion.

C   In a sense, there were *two* Silk Roads—the literal, historical one and the figurative one. The historical network of trails was used from approximately 100 B.C.E.* until the 16th century C.E. Almost nobody actually made a complete trip from one end to the other. Instead, merchants used to carry goods along one section of the road and sell them to other merchants at an oasis in the desert or a town in the mountains. These merchants, in turn, took the goods to the next stop, and so on. The figurative Silk Road is a symbol of the cross-cultural exchange of knowledge. This continues

▲ A desert oasis

* B.C.E. = *Before the Common Era;* 100 B.C.E. = 100 B.C.

even today. In short, the Silk Road was the way that goods and ideas moved across a **vast** area of Asia and southeastern Europe.

Art, Religion, and the Silk Road

D   Art and architecture reflect the movement of religion from region to region. At various times, Buddhism, Zoroastrianism, Judaism, Christianity, and Islam, among other religions, **spread** along the Silk Road. 50 Buddhism and Islam were an especially **significant** influence. Buddhism moved north and east from India beginning in the 4th century C.E. When Buddhism entered China, the Buddhist love of painting and **statues** moved with it. However, there was at least one change in style: the bare chest of the figure of the Buddha in India was not considered proper by the 55 Chinese, who created figures of the Buddha wearing a robe.

E   As in many religions worldwide, **caves** deep inside mountains seem to have been important **holy** places for 60 Buddhists. For example, in Dunhuang, China, a desert oasis far from towns or cities, Buddhists dug a series of caves and **decorated** them 65 with exquisite **frescoes**— wall paintings—and statues. In these caves, called *Mogaoku* in Chinese, the frescoes are not all religious. 70

▲ The Mogaoku, "Peerless Caves," in Dunhuang, China

Many **depict** scenes of daily life. Also, evidence of some of the many Silk Road cultures was discovered. In one cave, **documents** were found that were written in five languages: Chinese, Uigur, Sogdian, Tibetan, and Sanskrit.

F   The spread of Islam toward the east, in the 7th 75 century C.E., contributed to the disappearance of some art but the creation of other art. Islam played a role in the destruction of many Buddhist 80 statues because the Koran (the book of Islam) taught that images of humans were unholy. However, during this period, Islamic art and 85 architecture **flowered** in

▲ Gur-i Amir Mausoleum in Samarkand, Uzbekistan

many areas along the Silk Road. For example, in Samarkand—in what is Uzbekistan today—the military leader Timur built **mosques** (for Islamic religious worship), **mausoleums** (in which to bury the dead), and palaces. The creators of such buildings followed Islamic law by decorating them with **arabesques**—exquisite designs of great beauty with images of flowers, geometric forms (such as circles, squares, and triangles), and Arabic **calligraphy**, or writing. In brief, it is possible to follow the rise and fall of religions by studying the art and architecture along the Silk Road.

A Question of Time: Two Views

G   Most historians have dated the Silk Road from about 100 B.C.E., when the Chinese emperor Wu Di first sent a representative, General Zhang Qian, with a **caravan** of 100 men on a long, dangerous trip. His **destination** was the Western Territories. Zhang returned 13 years later, with only one of his men but with much information. Recent discoveries, however, shed light on a period long *before* this. These discoveries suggest that people were on the move

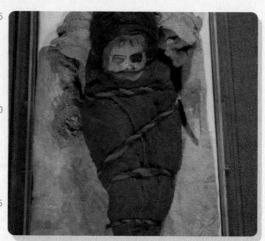

▲ **Mummy** of a baby from 1000 B.C.E.; the bright colors of the clothing are due to the preserving powers of the very dry, salty land. Blue stones were placed on the eyes.

and trading goods as early as 1000 B.C.E. Archaeologists have found tombs of people in the Takla Makan Desert, in Central Asia, in what is today the northwestern region of China. The dry, salty earth preserved the people's bodies and the goods that were buried with them in these tombs. We have learned that these people had horses and sheep. They ate bread, although wheat did not grow in this area. They had **cowry shells** from the ocean, although the region is landlocked. They wore brightly colored clothing. They wore leather boots and wool pants. Some were tall: a woman was 6 feet tall (1.83 meters), and a man 6 feet 6 inches (1.98 meters). Perhaps most astonishing, they had long noses and reddish hair, and the men wore beards. Thus, archaeologists are beginning to ask, Were people moving along the Silk Road long before we thought they were?

The Silk Road Today

H   Today, there is new interest in the history and culture of the Silk Road, which the famous Chinese-American musician Yo-Yo Ma has called "the Internet of antiquity." New technology is helping us to learn more about this ancient "Internet." Special radar on the space shuttle allows archaeologists to "see" objects and ruined cities 1–2 meters under the dry desert sand, for example. Tourists now come from all over the world to ¹³⁰ follow the old trade routes. And experts want to make sure that the customs in the vast region do not die out as the world modernizes. **To this end**, Yo-Yo Ma has founded the Silk Road Project, which encourages the living arts of these traditional lands. The result is that the people along the ancient Silk Road continue to learn from each other.

After You Read

5 Checking Your Understanding What did you learn from the reading? Answer these questions.

1. What are three pieces of evidence that indicate trade between distant lands was occurring before the 9th century?

2. What were the two opposite ends of the Silk Road?

3. What were two goods whose method of production was kept a secret?

4. What was moved along the Silk Road?

5. How did merchants move goods along the Silk Road?

6. What is evidence of the movement of Buddhism to China?

7. What is evidence of the spread of Islam to the east?

8. What was found in tombs of people in the Takla Makan Desert, in Central Asia?

9. What is Yo-Yo Ma's Silk Road Project encouraging?

6 Getting Meaning from Context Read the sentences below. Answer the questions and write a definition for each underlined vocabulary word. When you finish, check your definitions in a dictionary.

1. Many of the wall paintings <u>depict</u> scenes of everyday life.

   What part of speech is *depict* (noun, verb, adjective)? _____

   In this example, what *depicts* something? _____

   What does *depict* mean? _____

2. Timur built <u>mosques</u> for Islamic religious worship.

   What part of speech is *mosques*? _____

   What did Timur do? _____

   What happens in *mosques?* _____

   What does *mosques* mean? _____

7 **Getting Meaning from Context** Read the sentences below. Highlight the words that give clues to the meanings of the underlined words. Then write a definition of the underlined word. When you finish, check your definitions in a dictionary.

1. As in many religions worldwide, caves deep inside mountains seem to have been important holy places for Buddhists.

   People dug a series of caves and decorated them with exquisite wall paintings.

   What are *caves*? _____

2. They were important holy places for Buddhists.

   The Koran (the book of Islam) taught that images of humans were unholy, so many statues were destroyed.

   What does *holy* mean? _____

3. In the Japanese city of Nara, the 8th century Shosoin Treasure House holds thousands of exquisite objects of great beauty.

   The creators of such buildings followed Islamic law by decorating them with arabesques—exquisite designs of astonishing beauty with images of flowers and geometric forms.

   What does *exquisite* mean? _____

8 **Checking Your Vocabulary** Read the definitions below and write the correct words and expressions from the reading.

1. people who study ancient cultures = _____*archaeologists*_____

2. something that a soldier wears to protect the body in a battle = _____

3. material for clothing = _____

4. people who sell things = _____

5. a place with water and trees in the desert = _____

6. important = _____

7. official papers with written information = _____

8. grew and spread = _____

9. buildings where dead people are buried = _____

10. beautiful decoration with images of flowers and geometric forms = _____

11. writing as an art form = _____

12. a place that someone is trying to reach = _____

13. in order to do this = _____

9 **Recognizing Summaries** Copy or paraphrase the sentences from the reading selection that begin with the connecting words below. Then circle the number of the sentence below that best expresses the main idea of the entire reading.

1. Clearly, _____

_____

2. In short, _____

_____

3. In brief, _____

_____

4. Thus, _____

_____

5. The result is _____

_____

10 **Understanding Outlines** Complete the outline below of the reading selection "The Silk Road: Art and Archaeology." The general topics are filled in, but the reading also contains many subtopics that serve as supporting material. Write these specific topics in the correct places. Some are done for you. Use the list of subtopics on page 179. You will need to look back at the reading to see where they belong.

The Silk Road: Art and Archaeology

I. Introduction: Cross-Cultural Evidence

   A. _____

   B. _____

   C. _____

   D. _____ trade between distant lands long before today's globalization

II. What Was the Silk Road?

   A. _____

      1. _____

      2. _____ exchange of ideas and knowledge

   B. _____

      1. _____

      2. _____ figurative

III. Art, Religion, and the Silk Road

   A. _____

   B. _____ the spread of Islam toward the east

IV. A Question of Time: Two Views

   A. _____

      1. _____ 100 B.C.E.

      2. _____

   B. _____ archaeological view

      1. _____

      2. _____

V. The Silk Road Today

   A. _____

   B. _____

   C. _____

1. the spread of Buddhism north and east from India

2. two Silk Roads

3. new technology

4. example: Indian mirror in Roman Pompeii

5. historical view

6. series or network of trails that connect East Asia to the Mediterranean

7. example: pitcher with styles from three cultures in a Chinese tomb

8. exchange of goods (silk, glass, spices, etc.)

9. 1000 B.C.E

10. tourism

11. example: the Shosoin Treasure House in Japan

12. literal

13. General Zhang Qian, sent by emperor

14. encouragement of living arts

15. tombs in the Takla Makan Desert

11 Checking Your Understanding Turn back to the beginning of Activity 4 on page 171 and answer the two questions.

12 Making Inferences Look at Paragraph G on page 174 to answer these questions.

1. What were the physical characteristics of the people buried in the Takla Makan Desert?

2. What inference can you make about this? In other words, what does the reading not say directly but instead *imply?*

 13 Discussing the Reading Talk about your answers to these questions.

1. Have you been to any places along the Silk Road? If so, tell you group about them.

2. Do you know of any other long road that connected distant places in ancient times? If so, tell your group about it.

3. What is one type of art from ancient times in your country? Tell your group about it.

4. What kinds of art do you like? Why?

Fashion: The Art of the Body

Strategy

Identifying Main Ideas by Analyzing Details
The main idea is not always clearly expressed in a paragraph. Instead, the details may *imply* the main idea, which sums up all the information in the paragraph.

Example

For various reasons, clothing of some type has been worn by human beings since the beginning of time. The Inuit (Eskimos) wear animal fur to protect them against the cold winter weather. Nomadic desert people wear long, loose clothing for protection against the sun and wind of the Sahara. But is clothing really essential for protection? Perhaps not. Scientists point out the absence of clothing among certain Indians of southern Chile, where the temperature is usually 43°F (7°C) and often colder. Similarly, the tribal people of Australia, where the weather is like that of the Sahara Desert, wear almost no clothing.

(The topic of the paragraph is clothing. The important details are that some groups wear clothing for protection against the weather, while others do not. Thus, the main idea of the paragraph is that protection is one function of clothing, but not an essential one.)

 1 Identifying Main Ideas by Analyzing Details Read each paragraph. Then to help you figure out the main idea, answer the three questions that follow each paragraph.

Fashion: The Art of the Body

A   The enormous and fascinating variety of clothing may express a person's status or social position. Several hundred years ago in Europe, Japan, and China, there were many highly detailed sumptuary laws—that is, strict regulations concerning how each social class could dress. In

Europe, for example, only royal families could wear fur, purple silk, or gold cloth. In Japan, a farmer could breed silkworms, but he couldn't wear silk. In many societies, a lack of clothing indicated an absence of status. In ancient Egypt, for instance, children—who had no social status—wore no clothes until they were about twelve. These days, in most societies (especially in the West), rank or status is exhibited through

▲ A street in Paris

regulation of dress only in the military, where the appearance or absence of certain metal buttons or stars signifies the dividing line between ranks. With the exception of the military, the divisions between different classes of society are becoming less clear. The clientele of a Paris café, for example, might include both working-class people and members of the highest society, but how can one tell the difference when everyone is wearing denim jeans?

1. What is the topic of Paragraph A?
   - (A) the military
   - (B) sumptuary laws
   - (C) uniforms
   - (D) status

2. What details about the topic does the paragraph provide? (Choose more than one answer.)
   - (A) Strict laws in some countries used to regulate what people of each social class could wear.
   - (B) Rich people wear more beautiful clothing than poor people do.
   - (C) In many societies, the absence of clothing indicated an absence of status.
   - (D) Today, the divisions between social classes are becoming less clear from the clothing that people wear.

3. What do the answers to numbers 1 and 2 have in common? That is, what is the main idea of Paragraph A?
   - (A) Today, the differences between various social classes can be seen only in military uniforms.
   - (B) Laws used to regulate how people could dress.
   - (C) Clothing (or its absence) has usually indicated status or rank, but this is less true in today's world.
   - (D) Clothing has been worn for different reasons since the beginning of history.

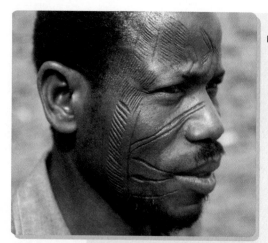

▲ Scarification

▲ Modern tattooing

B   Three common types of body decoration are *mehndi*, tattooing, and scarification. *Mehndi* is the art of applying dye (usually dark orange or dark brown) to the skin of women in India, Islamic cultures, and Africa. The dye comes from the henna plant and is applied in a beautiful design that varies from culture to culture—fine, thin lines in India and large flower patterns in the Arab world, for example. (See page 101 for a photo of a *mehndi* design.) A tattoo is also a design or mark made with a kind of dye (usually dark blue); however, unlike henna, it is put into a *cut* in the skin. In scarification—found mainly in Africa—dirt or ashes are put into the cuts instead of dye; the result is a design that is unique to the person's tribe. Three lines on each side of a man's face identify him as a member of the Yoruba tribe of Nigeria, for example. A complex geometric design on a woman's back identifies her as Nuba (from Sudan) and also makes her more beautiful in the eyes of her people. In the 1990s, tattooing became popular among youth in urban Western societies. Unlike people in tribal cultures, these young people had no tradition of tattooing, except among sailors and criminals. To these young people, the tattoos were beautiful and were sometimes also a sign of rebellion against older, more conservative people in the culture. These days, tattooing has become common and is usually not symbolic of rebellion.

30
35
40
45
50
55

1. What is the topic of Paragraph B?

    (A) the Yoruba people

    (B) geometric designs

    (C) dirt and ashes

    (D) body decoration

2. What details about the topic does the paragraph provide? (Choose more than one answer.)

    (A) *Mehndi,* tattooing, and scarification are types of body decoration.

    (B) Tattoos and scarification indicate a person's tribe or social group, although youth in Western societies sometimes use tattoos as a form of rebellion.

    (C) Scarification is very painful and is symbolic of strength.

    (D) Designs on a person's face or body are considered beautiful.

3. Which idea below includes all the details that you chose in number 2? In other words, what is the main idea of the paragraph?

    (A) Everyone who wants to be beautiful should get a tattoo.

    (B) People decorate their bodies for the purposes of identification, beauty, and sometimes rebellion.

    (C) *Mehndi* and tattoos are designs made by putting dye on or in the skin.

    (D) Men more often decorate their faces; women often decorate their backs.

C   In some societies, women overeat to become plump because large women are considered beautiful, while skinny women are regarded as unattractive. A woman's plumpness is also an indication of her family's wealth. In other societies, by contrast, a fat person is considered unattractive, so men and women eat little and try to remain slim. In many 60 parts of the world, people lie in the sun for hours to darken their skin, while in other places light, soft skin is seen as attractive. People with gray hair often dye it black, whereas those with naturally dark hair often change its color to blond or green or purple.

1. What is the topic of Paragraph C?

    (A) hair

    (B) skin

    (C) body shape

    (D) body changes

2. What details about the topic does the paragraph provide? (Choose more than one answer.)

    (A) It is unhealthy to lose or gain too much weight.

    (B) Some societies consider large people attractive; others, slim ones.

    (C) Some people prefer dark hair or skin; others, light.

    (D) Most wealthy people try to stay thin.

3. What is the main idea of Paragraph C?

- (A) Individuals and groups of people have different ideas about physical attractiveness.
- (B) Lying in the sun darkens the skin.
- (C) In some societies, thinness is an indication that a family is poor.
- (D) Dark-skinned people usually have dark hair.

D   In the West, most people visit a dentist regularly for both hygiene and beauty. They use toothpaste and dental floss daily to keep their teeth clean. They have their teeth straightened, whitened, and crowned to make them more attractive to others in their culture. However, "attractive" has quite a different meaning in other cultures. In the past, in Japan, it was the custom for women to blacken, not whiten, the teeth. People in some areas of Africa and central Australia have the custom of filing the teeth to sharp points. And among the Makololo people of Malawi, the women wear a very large ring—a *pelele*—in their upper lip. As their chief once explained about peleles: "They are the only beautiful things women have. Men have beards. Women have none. What kind of person would she be without the pelele? She would not be a woman at all." While some people in modern urban societies think of tribal lip rings as unattractive and even "disgusting," other people—in Tokyo or New York or Rome—might choose to wear a small lip ring or to pierce their tongue and wear a ring through the hole.

1. What is the topic of Paragraph D?

- (A) dentistry
- (B) blackening or whitening the teeth
- (C) changes to the human mouth
- (D) peleles and beards

2. What details about the topic does the paragraph provide? (Choose more than one answer.)

- (A) White teeth are attractive to all cultures.
- (B) In the West, people visit dentists and have their teeth straightened, whitened, and crowned.
- (C) In some cultures, people blacken their teeth or file them to sharp points, and in other cultures young people wear lip rings or tongue rings.
- (D) Makololo women wear a large ring in their upper lip.

3. What is the main idea of Paragraph D?

- (A) People can easily change the color or shape of their teeth.
- (B) What is *attractive* has different interpretations.
- (C) The human mouth suffers change and abuse in many societies.
- (D) Some methods of changing the appearance of the mouth are dangerous, but others are safe.

▲ Papua New Guinean man wearing tribal face paint

▲ Woman wearing modern "face paint"

E Body paint or face paint is used mostly by *men* 80 in preliterate societies in order to attract good health or to ward off disease. Anthropologists explain that it is a form of magic protection against the dangers of the world outside the village, where men have to go for the hunt or for 85 war. When it is used as warpaint, it also serves to frighten the enemy, distinguish members of one's own group from the enemy, and give the men a sense of identity, of belonging to the group. *Women* in these societies have less need of body 90 or face paint because they usually stay in the safety of the village. Women in Victorian society in England and the United States were expected to wear little or no makeup. They were excluded from public life and therefore didn't need 95 protection from the outside world. In modern societies, however, cosmetics are used mostly by women, who often feel naked, unclothed, without makeup when out in public—like a tribal hunter without his warpaint. 100

1. What is the topic of Paragraph E?
- (A) body and face paint
- (B) men's warpaint
- (C) modern women's cosmetics
- (D) magic protection

2. What details about the topic does the Paragraph provide? (Choose more than one answer.)
- (A) Body or face paint is usually worn by men in tribal societies.
- (B) People wear body or face paint to make them more attractive.
- (C) Makeup ("face paint") is usually worn by women in modern societies.
- (D) When women are excluded from public life, they wear little or no makeup.

3. What is the main idea of Paragraph E?
- (A) Body paint gives men a sense of identity.
- (B) Women in modern times wear makeup to be more beautiful.
- (C) In the past, men wore face paint, but in modern times, women wear it.
- (D) Body or face paint may be worn as a sort of protection by people who leave the home or village.

2 **Critical Thinking: Identifying Inferences** Read the statements below about the article "Fashion: The Art of the Body." Put a check mark (✓) by the statements that you can infer from the reading selection. Put an X by the other statements, even if you think they are true. Then, on the line after each inference, write the phrases from which you inferred the information. Leave the other statements blank. The first two are done as examples.

1. __X__ All people wear clothing to keep warm.

_____

_____

2. __✓__ Fur provides warmth, while long, loose clothing is useful in hot weather.
The Inuit (Eskimos) wear animal fur to protect them against
the cold winter weather. Nomadic desert people wear long, loose
clothing for protection against the sun and wind of the Sahara.

3. _____ Rich people wear more clothing than poor people do.

_____

_____

4. _____ Social status might be less important now than it was in the past.

_____

_____

5. _____ Some methods of body beautification may be uncomfortable or painful.

_____

_____

6. _____ Body or face paint may make people feel protected.

_____

_____

7. _____ Women are more interested in looking good than men are.

_____

_____

8. _____ There are some similarities between tribal people and modern urban people in their views of body decoration.

_____

_____

3 Discussing the Reading Talk about your answers to these questions.

1. Why are people often unhappy with their bodies? What are their reasons for changing their appearance?

2. What do you think of the methods of body beautification that are described in the reading selection? Why?

3. What methods of "body art" are common in your culture? (makeup? tattoos? ear piercing? hair dyeing? etc.) What do you think of them?

Responding in Writing

4 Summarizing Choose one paragraph—B, F, or G—from pages 172–174. Write a short summary of it (two or three sentences). To write this summary, follow these steps:

- Make sure that you understand the paragraph well.
- Choose the main idea.
- Find the most important details.

In order to summarize this in your own words, *don't look at the original paragraph as you write*. When you finish writing, compare your summary with those of other students who summarized the same paragraph.

5 Writing Your Own Ideas Choose one of these topics to write about:

- clothing and status
- your society's views on weight
- tattooing
- *mehndi* designs
- body piercing

What is your opinion about the topic you chose? Write a one-paragraph letter to your teacher in which you explain your opinion.

What is the main idea of your paragraph? _____

_____

Cultural Note

Beauty and the Past

In ancient Egypt, both rich and poor people used many kinds of scented oils to protect their skin from the sun and wind and to keep it soft. These oils were a mixture of plants and the fat of crocodile, hippo, or cat. Many people shaved their heads and wore wigs. Other people dyed their hair black when it began to turn gray. Men, women, and children all wore kohl—black eye liner—both for beauty and to protect their eyes from disease. On special occasions, people wore exquisite jewelry, especially necklaces and earrings, and on top of their wigs wore a white cone made of sweetly scented ox fat. As the evening went on, the cone melted, and the fragrance dripped down over their wigs, faces, and clothes.

▲ Egyptians on a special occasion: notice the white cones on their heads.

Talk It Over

6 Art and Beauty Below are some quotations about art and beauty. Read them and discuss your answers to each of the questions that follow.

Quotations

- "Beauty is in the eye of the beholder." Margaret Hungerford
- "Alas, after a certain age, every man is responsible for his own face." Albert Camus
- "Remember that the most beautiful things in the world are the most useless: peacocks and lilies, for instance." John Ruskin
- "I'm tired of all this nonsense about beauty being only skin-deep. That's deep enough. What do you want, an adorable pancreas?" Jean Kerr
- "Form follows function." motto of the Bauhaus (a German school of design)
- "Great artists have no country." Alfred de Musset

Questions

1. What does the quotation mean? (You might need to use a dictionary.)

2. Do you agree with it?

3. What are some proverbs or quotations about art or beauty in your language? Translate them into English and explain them.

7 **Analyzing Advertisements** Bring to class advertisements about beauty treatments and methods (hairstyling salons, makeup, plastic surgery, etc.). Discuss new vocabulary. Tell the class about the most interesting ads and your opinions of them.

Part 3   Building Vocabulary and Study Skills

Strategy

Recognizing Words with Similar Meanings
Although words with similar meanings can often be substituted for one another, they may have somewhat different definitions.

Examples
I'm taking a geography **course**. The **class** meets twice a week and there is a different **lesson** at each meeting.

(*course* = series of lessons on a subject; *class* = a meeting of a course or the students who are taking a course; *lesson* = a separate piece of material on a subject or the amount of teaching at one time)

1 **Recognizing Words with Similar Meanings** The words in each of the following groups have similar meanings, but they are not exactly the same. Match the words with their definitions by writing the letters on the lines as in the examples. If necessary, check your answers in a dictionary.

1. ___*b*___ study   **a.** gain knowledge or skill in a subject

   _____ memorize   **b.** make an effort to learn

   _____ learn   **c.** to know something exactly from memory

2. _____ depict   **a.** show in the form of a picture

   _____ indicate   **b.** point out; make known

   _____ express   **c.** put (thoughts, etc.) into words

3. _____ target

_____ goal

_____ destination

a. objective; purpose

b. the place where someone is going

c. an object or mark someone tries to reach or hit

Strategy

Understanding General and Specific Words
The meaning of one word can _include_ the meanings of many others.

Example
Beautiful art can be found in different kinds of **structures**: churches, mosques, and palaces.

(Churches and mosques are religious buildings, and palaces are buildings for royalty. The word _structures_ can mean "buildings," so it includes the meanings of the three other words.)

2 **Understanding General and Specific Words** In each of the following items, circle the one word that includes the meanings of the others. The first one is done as an example.

1. (art)   statue   painting

2. script   calligraphy   writing

3. architecture   house   building

4. traveler   tourist   passenger

5. bus   subway   transportation

6. cosmetics   lipstick   dye

7. Christianity   religion   Islam

8. murder   crime   theft

Strategy

Understanding Connotations
Sometimes words with similar meanings have different connotations (implied meanings, "feelings"). Some of the meanings can be positive; some can be negative.

Examples
In some societies, women overeat to become **plump** because **large** women are considered beautiful. In other cultures, a **fat** person is considered unattractive.

(The words _plump_, _large_, and _fat_ all mean "over normal weight." However, to say someone is _fat_ is an insult, while _plump_ and _large_ are more polite ways of referring to the same characteristic.)

Some dictionaries provide information on usage of words in different situations and on connotations of words with similar meanings.

3 **Understanding Connotations** Read the dictionary entries below and complete the following exercises.

thin[1] /θɪn/ *adj.* comparative **thinner,** superlative **thinnest**
1 something that is thin is not very wide or thick
[≠ **thick**]: *a thin slice of cheese* | *The walls here are* **paper-thin** (=very thin). **2** having little fat on your body [≠ **fat**]: *He's tall, very thin, and has dark hair.*

THESAURUS
slim and **slender** – used about someone who is thin in an attractive way
skinny – used about someone who is very thin in a way that is not attractive
lean – used about someone who is thin in a healthy way: *He has a runner's physique: long legs and a lean body.*
underweight – used, especially by doctors, about someone who is too thin, in a way that is not healthy
emaciated – used about someone who is extremely thin and weak because of illness or not eating
→ FAT

3 if someone has thin hair, they do not have very much hair [≠ **thick**] **4** air that is thin is difficult to breathe because there is not much OXYGEN in it **5** a substance that is thin has a lot of water in it [≠ **thick**]: *thin broth* —**thinness** *n.* [U]

beau·ti·ful /ˈbyutəfəl/ *adj.* **1** extremely attractive to look at: *She was the most beautiful woman I've ever seen.* | *a beautiful baby* | *The views from the mountaintop were beautiful.*

THESAURUS
attractive, good-looking, pretty, handsome, gorgeous, stunning, nice-looking, cute
→see Thesaurus box at ATTRACTIVE

2 very good or giving you great pleasure: *beautiful music* | *The weather was beautiful.*

Write a plus sign (+) before the words with positive connotations and a negative sign (−) before the words with negative ones.

1. _____ slim   **3.** _____ skinny   **5.** _____ fat

2. _____ emaciated   **4.** _____ slender   **6.** _____ overweight

Next, circle the words that have a polite connotation.

1. underweight   **3.** plump   **5.** obese

2. emaciated   **4.** chubby   **6.** heavy

For each pair of words, circle the one with the stronger meaning. The first one is done as an example.

1. (beautiful)/pretty   **4.** ugly/plain

2. ugly/hideous   **5.** beautiful/good-looking

3. attractive/beautiful   **6.** unattractive/ugly

4 **Choosing the Appropriate Words** Choose all of the possible answers for each blank to complete each sentence.

1. He's a very _____ man.
  (A) pretty
  (B) handsome
  (C) attractive
  (D) ugly

2. What a _____ baby!
- (A) beautiful
- (B) handsome
- (C) pretty
- (D) good-looking

3. This is a very _____ garden.
- (A) good-looking
- (B) plain
- (C) pretty
- (D) attractive

5 **Writing Words with Similar Meanings** On a separate piece of paper, write words with meanings similar to the following words. Use your dictionary for help. Then write the lists of similar words on the board and discuss with your classmates differences in meanings, connotation, and usage.

1. woman	**3.** talk	**5.** old
2. thief	**4.** believe	**6.** small

6 **Recognizing Words in Phrases** As you read, it's important to notice words that often go together. Go back to the paragraphs on pages 171–175. Find words to complete the following phrases.

Paragraph A

_____ the shape _____ (a female fertility goddess)

Paragraph B

a network _____ (trails)

Paragraph C

was used _____ (approximately 100 B.C.E.)

_____ (the 16th century)

Paragraph D

_____ (region) _____ (region)

Paragraph E

a desert _____

Paragraph F

1. contributed _____ the disappearance of (some art)

2. _____ brief

Paragraph H

_____ _____ end

7 Focusing on Words from the Academic Word List Fill in the blanks with words from the Academic Word List in the box. When you finish, turn back to pages 174–175, Paragraph H, and check your answers.

called	founded	region	traditional
culture	over	routes	under
experts	project	technology	

Today, there is new interest in the history and _____culture_____ [1] of the Silk Road, which the famous Chinese-American musician Yo-Yo Ma has _____ [2] "the Internet of antiquity." New _____ [3] is helping us to learn more about this ancient "Internet." Special radar on the space shuttle allows archaeologists to "see" objects and ruined cities 1–2 meters _____ [4] the dry desert sand, for example. Tourists now come from all _____ [5] the world to follow the old trade _____ [6]. And _____ [7] want to make sure that the customs in the vast _____ [8] do not die out as the world modernizes. To this this end, Yo-Yo Ma has _____ [9] the Silk Road _____ [10], which encourages the living arts of these _____ [11] lands. The result is that the people along the ancient Silk Road continue to learn from each other.

8 **Searching the Internet** Search the Internet for one of the topics below. Explore one website and find something that interests you. Share this with a small group.

Choose from these topics:
- tours of the Silk Road
- the meaning of tattooing or scarification among tribal peoples
- *mehndi* designs in different cultures
- the latest fashions in "body art" these days

Part 4 Focus on Testing

QUESTIONS ABOUT BASIC COMPREHENSION

In the Focus on Testing section of Chapter 1, the three types of reading questions on the TOEFL ® Internet-Based Test (iBT) are listed. One type is the *basic comprehension question*, which focuses on the understanding of facts, what facts mean, and how language ties one fact to others. You must understand not only words and phrases but entire groups of sentences. You must also be able to find main ideas and recognize how they are supported in the reading.

Vocabulary questions make up 20 to 25 percent of all TOEFL® iBT reading questions. These are considered *basic comprehension questions.* To answer them, you have to understand the context, not just the words themselves.

1 **Practice** Read again the Focus on Testing reading selection in Chapter 7, "As English Spreads, Speakers Morph It into World Tongue," on pages 164–165. Answer the basic-comprehension questions below. You may refer to the reading as often as you want. Try to answer all five questions in five minutes or less.

1. Which pair names groups that, according to the article, both dislike the spread of "Englishes" around the world?
   - (A) purists and multiculturalists
   - (B) native speakers and nonnative speakers
   - (C) businesspersons and linguists
   - (D) linguists and multiculturalists

2. According to the article, which of the following statements would Tom McArthur, editor of the *Oxford Companion to the English Language,* agree with?
   - (A) People invent too many new words.
   - (B) Hybrid Englishes are not really English.
   - (C) The spread of English is unstoppable.
   - (D) The British should stop the degradation of English.

3. Professor Firth's comments indicate that people involved in international business often think which of the following?

- (A) Any communication strategy is good if it helps business get done.
- (B) Nonnative speakers of English invent terms so that native speakers won't understand them.
- (C) Nonnative speakers of English should let native speakers cut most deals.
- (D) English is changing too fast for businesses.

4. Which of the following is closest in meaning to *hybrid,* as it used in this reading?

- (A) foreign
- (B) mixed
- (C) incorrect
- (D) grammatical

5. Which of these other terms from the reading is closest in meaning to *linguistic genocide*?

- (A) creeping degradation
- (B) tension
- (C) linguicide
- (D) global germination

Self-Assessment Log

Read the lists below. Check (✓) the strategies and vocabulary that you learned in this chapter. Look through the chapter or ask your instructor about the strategies and words that you do not understand.

Reading and Vocabulary-Building Strategies

- ❏ Getting meaning from context
- ❏ Understanding outlines
- ❏ Recognizing summaries in a reading
- ❏ Identifying main ideas by analyzing details

- ❏ Critical thinking: identifying inferences
- ❏ Recognizing words with similar meanings
- ❏ Understanding general and specific words
- ❏ Understanding connotations

Target Vocabulary

Nouns

- ❏ arabesques
- ❏ archaeologists
- ❏ architecture
- ❏ armor
- ❏ calligraphy
- ❏ cosmetics
- ❏ culture*
- ❏ destination

- ❏ documents*
- ❏ experts*
- ❏ mausoleums
- ❏ merchants
- ❏ mosques
- ❏ oasis
- ❏ project*
- ❏ region*

- ❏ silk
- ❏ statues
- ❏ technology*

Verbs

- ❏ called*
- ❏ depict
- ❏ flowered
- ❏ founded*

Adjectives

- ❏ significant*
- ❏ traditional*

Prepositions

- ❏ over*
- ❏ under*

Expression

- ❏ to this end

* These words are from the Academic Word List. For more information on this list, see www.vuw.ac.nz/lals/research/awl.

New Frontiers

In This Chapter

What parts of the brain are active as you read these words and comprehend their meaning? In this chapter you will read about how the complex human brain works and what recent studies are finding. The second selection looks into what influences our personality—the age-old nature/nurture question. Is our personality developed from our environment (parents, family, society) or do our genes determine it? In Part 3, you will continue to practice valuable vocabulary and study skills. The chapter ends with a review of an important reading strategy—getting meaning from context.

> **❝** If the brain were so simple [that] we could understand it, we would be so simple [that] we couldn't. **❞**
>
> —Lyall Watson
> Africa-born biologist and writer (1939–)

1. What do you think the man in the photo is doing? Why is he doing it?

2. What problems do you think he might be trying to solve?

3. What kind of research do you think is important? Why?

The Human Brain—New Discoveries

Before You Read

1 **Getting Started** Look at the diagram and the photos. Discuss the questions.

1. Which areas of the brain might a person use to compose music? To throw a ball? To paint a picture?

2. If you feel cold and want to put on a sweater, which area of the brain is probably active?

3. Which person might be in better health—the man in photo A or one of the people in photo B? Why do you think so?

4. What do you think is typical or atypical about photos C and D?

5. It has been observed that little boys and little girls play, speak, and act differently from each other. What do you think causes these differences?

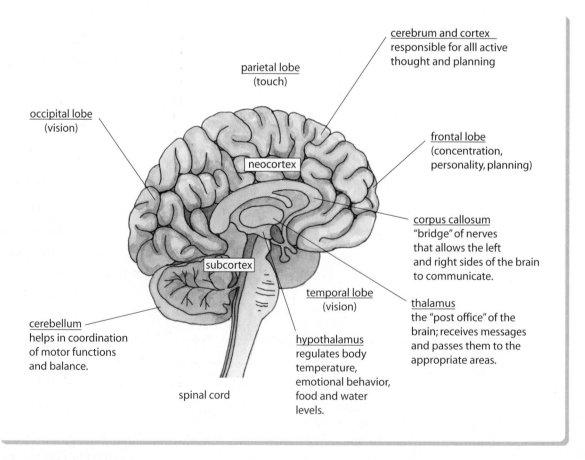

parietal lobe
(touch)

occipital lobe
(vision)

cerebrum and cortex
responsible for alll active
thought and planning

neocortex

frontal lobe
(concentration,
personality, planning)

corpus callosum
"bridge" of nerves
that allows the left
and right sides of the brain
to communicate.

subcortex

temporal lobe
(vision)

cerebellum
helps in coordination
of motor functions
and balance.

hypothalamus
regulates body
temperature,
emotional behavior,
food and water
levels.

thalamus
the "post office" of the
brain; receives messages
and passes them to the
appropriate areas.

spinal cord

Photo A

Photo B

Photo C

Photo D

2 **Previewing the Reading** Look over the reading on pages 200–203 and answer these questions with a partner.

1. What is the topic of the reading?

2. What are the eight subtopics?

3. List three things that you expect to learn from the reading.

_____

_____

_____

3 **Preparing to Read** Asking yourself questions before and during reading often helps you understand and remember the material. Look again at the illustration of the brain on page 198 and at the headings in the following reading. Then check (✓) the questions in the following list that you think the reading selection might answer.

1. _____ What is the function of different parts of the brain?

2. _____ How are human brains different from animal brains?

3. _____ Why do some people seem to be more creative than others?

4. _____ What is the difference between the left and right side of the brain?

5. _____ Are the happiest memories of most people's lives from their childhood?

6. _____ Is it possible to have a memory of something that never happened?

7. _____ How can we improve our memories?

8. _____ Are teenagers' brains different from adults' brains?

9. _____ How do men and women communicate with each other?

10. _____ What activities may make people less intelligent?

11. _____ What activity may make people more relaxed?

 4 **Previewing Vocabulary** Read the words and phrases below. Listen to the pronunciation. Put a check mark (✓) next to the words you know. For the words that you don't know, *don't* use a dictionary. Try to understand them from the reading.

Nouns

❑ blood vessels
❑ colleagues
❑ hemispheres
❑ insights
❑ intuition
❑ logic
❑ maturation

❑ maturity
❑ memory
❑ neuroscientists
❑ origin
❑ toxins
❑ wiring

Verb

❑ rotate

Adjectives

❑ cognitive
❑ exposed
❑ logical
❑ mature

❑ precise
❑ repressed

Expression

❑ going into training

Read

5 **Reading an Article** As you read the following selection, think about the answers to the questions that you checked in Activity 3. Read the selection. Do not use a dictionary. Then do the exercises that follow the reading.

The Human Brain—New Discoveries

A   Most of us learn basic facts about the human brain in our middle or high school biology classes. We study the subcortex, the "old brain," which is found in the brains of most animals and is responsible for basic functions such as breathing, eating, drinking, and sleeping. We learn about the neocortex, the "new brain," which is unique to humans and is where complex brain activity takes place. We find that the cerebrum, which is responsible for all active thought, is divided into two parts, or **hemispheres**. The left hemisphere, generally, manages the right side of the body; it is responsible for **logical** thinking. The right hemisphere manages the left side of the body; this hemisphere controls emotional, creative, and artistic functions. And we learn that the corpus callosum is the "bridge" that connects the two hemispheres. Memorizing the names for parts of the

5

10

brain might not seem thrilling to many students, but new discoveries in
brain function *are* exciting. Recent research is shedding light on creativity,
memory, **maturity**, gender, and the possibility of changing the brain.   15

Left Brain/Right Brain: Creativity

B   Psychologists agree that most of us have creative ability that is greater
than what we use in daily life. In other words, we can be more creative than
we realize! The problem is that we use mainly one hemisphere of our brain—
the left. From childhood, in school, we're taught reading, writing, and
mathematics; we are **exposed** to very little music or art. Therefore, many of   20
us might not "exercise" our right hemisphere much, except through dreams,
symbols, and those wonderful **insights** in which we suddenly find the answer
to a problem that has been bothering us—and do so without the need for
logic. Can we be taught to use our right hemisphere more? Many experts
believe so. Classes at some schools and books (such as *The Inner Game of*   25
Tennis and *Drawing on the Right Side of the Brain*) claim to help people to
"silence" the left hemisphere and give the right a chance to work.

Memory—True or False?

C   In the 1980s in the United States, there were many cases of adults who
suddenly remembered, with the help of a psychologist, things that had
happened to them in childhood. These memories had been **repressed**—   30
held back—for many years. Some of these newly discovered memories
have sent people to prison. As people remember crimes (such as murder or
rape) that they saw or experienced as children, the police have re-opened
and investigated old criminal cases. In fact, over 700 cases have been filed
that are based on these repressed memories.   35

D   However, studies in the 1990s suggested that many of these might
be *false* memories. At a 1994 conference at Harvard Medical School,
neuroscientists discussed how memory is believed to work. It is known
that small pieces of a memory (sound, sight, feeling, and so on) are kept in
different parts of the brain; the limbic system, in the middle of the brain, pulls   40
these pieces together into one complete memory. But it's certain that people
can "remember" things that have never happened. Even a small suggestion
can leave a piece of memory in the brain. Most frightening, according to Dr.
Michael Nash of the University of Tennessee, is that "there may be no
structural difference" in the brain between a false memory and a true one.   45

The Teen Brain

E   Parents of teenagers have always known that there is something, well,
different about the teen years. Some parents claim that their teenage children
belong to a different species. Until recently, neuroscience did not support this
belief. The traditional belief was that by the time a child was eight to twelve,
the brain was completely **mature**. However, very recent studies provide   50
evidence that the brain of a teenager differs from that of both children and

adults. According to Jay Giedd of the National Institute of Mental Health, "**Maturation** does not stop at age ten, but continues into the teen years" and beyond. In fact, Giedd and his **colleagues** found that the corpus callosum "continues growing into your 20s." Because, it is believed, the corpus callosum is involved in self-awareness and intelligence, the new studies imply that teens may not be as fully self-aware or as intelligent as they will be later. Other researchers, at McLean Hospital in Massachusetts, have found that teenagers are not as able (as adults are) to "read" emotions on people's faces.

Differences in Male and Female Brains

F   Watch a group of children as they play. You'll probably notice that the boys and girls play differently, speak differently, and are interested in different things. When they grow into men and women, the differences do not disappear. Many scientists are now studying the **origins** of these gender differences. Some are searching for an explanation in the human brain. Some of their findings are interesting. For example, they've found that more men than women are left-handed; this reflects the dominance of the brain's right hemisphere. By contrast, more women listen equally with both ears while men listen mainly with the right ear. Men are better at reading a map without having to **rotate** it. Women are better at reading the emotions of people in photographs.

G   One place to look for an explanation of gender differences is in the hypothalamus, just above the brain stem. This controls anger, thirst, hunger, and sexual desire. One recent study shows that there is a region in the hypothalamus that is larger in heterosexual men than it is in women and homosexual men. Another area of study is the corpus callosum, the thick group of nerves that allows the right and left hemispheres of the brain to communicate with each other. The corpus callosum is larger in women than in men. This might explain the mystery of "female **intuition**," which is supposed to give women greater ability to "read" and understand emotional clues.

A Change of Mind?

H   We all know the expression *to change your mind*. But is it possible *literally* to change your mind—or, to be more **precise**, to change your *brain*? Reports from 2005 say yes. First, the bad news, at least for smokers: a study from the University of Aberdeen and the University of Edinburgh, in Scotland, concludes that smoking makes people less intelligent. On **cognitive** tests (that is, tests that involve judgment), smokers did significantly worse than nonsmokers. The theory is that **toxins**—poisons—in the smoke enter the blood and damage **blood vessels** providing the brain with oxygen. And there is more bad news, for most of us: a study from the University of London says that "infomania"—the constant flood of information from cell phones, emails, and text messaging—can reduce intelligence by ten points on an IQ test.

However, there is also good news: meditation seems to change the "wiring" in the brain in several positive ways. In a study that compared the brains of eight lifelong Buddhist meditators who work with the Dalai Lama with the brains of beginning meditators, scientists discovered that there were significant differences. The expert meditators had higher levels of gamma brain waves, which improve memory, learning, and concentration. Meditation appears to do for the brain what physical training does for the body. The researcher Richard Davidson said, "The trained mind, or brain, is physically different from the untrained one." Perhaps we should consider "going into training."

▲ Does meditation change the brain?

After You Read

6 **Getting the Main Ideas** Read the statements below. Write *T* on the lines before the statements that are true, according to the reading. Write *F* on the lines before the statements that are false. Write *I* on the lines before the statements that are impossible to know from the reading.

1. _____ Different parts of the brain control different activities or parts of the body.

2. _____ Most people probably don't use all their creative ability.

3. _____ Newly discovered memories from childhood are false memories.

4. _____ The human brain is mature by the age of 12.

5. _____ There is no real difference between the brains of males and females.

6. _____ Certain activities might make us more or less intelligent.

7 **Vocabulary Check** Turn back to the vocabulary preview on page 200. Which words do you now know? Check them off (✓). With a partner, discuss what you think each word means. For words that you aren't sure of, look through the reading to find them in bold and try to guess the meaning.

Strategy

Distinguishing Facts from Assumptions

As you saw in Chapter 7, certain words or expressions in statements usually indicate the existence of facts—that is, information that has been proven accurate. Here are some more words that indicate facts:

certain	objective	scientific
clear	positive	show
know	prove	sure

Other words can indicate assumptions—that is, ideas that are believed by some people but have not been proven to be true. Here are some more words that indicate assumptions:

claim	imply	possibly	theorize
(dis)agree	likely	probably	think
doubt	possible	subjective	

8 **Distinguishing Facts from Assumptions** For each statement below, write *fact* or *assumption*, according to the presentation of information in the reading selection "The Human Brain—New Discoveries" on pages 200–203. (You'll need to look back at the selection for words that indicate fact or assumption.)

1. _____ Most of us have creative ability that is greater than what we use in daily life.

2. _____ Many of us don't "exercise" our right hemisphere much.

3. _____ We can be taught to use our right hemisphere more.

4. _____ Some books help people "silence" the left hemisphere and use the right hemisphere.

5. _____ Over 700 cases have been filed that are based on newly discovered memories.

6. _____ Many newly discovered memories are false.

7. _____ Small pieces of memory are kept in different parts of the brain.

8. _____ People "remember" things that have never happened.

9. _____ There is no structural difference between a false memory and a true one.

10. _____ The brain of a teenager differs from that of both children and adults.

11. _____ Teens are not as fully self-aware as adults are.

12. _____ There is a region in the hypothalamus that is larger in heterosexual men than in women and homosexual men.

13. _____ Women have a greater ability to understand emotional clues because they have a larger corpus callosum than men do.

14. _____ In smokers, toxins damage the blood vessels that take oxygen to the brain, so the brain doesn't get enough oxygen.

15. _____ Meditation changes the wiring in the brain.

9 **Checking Your Understanding** Turn back to Activity 3 on pages 199–200 and answer the questions that are answered in the reading selection.

10 **Critical Thinking: Application** If you want to improve your brain, what can you do? Turn back to the selection and find at least one way. In a small group, discuss what you can or will do to improve your brain.

Part 2 Reading Skills and Strategies

Personality: Nature or Nurture?

Before You Read

1 **Identifying the Main Idea by Analyzing Details** Read each paragraph and answer the questions that follow. Then combine the answers to express the main idea of each paragraph. Answers for Paragraph A are given as examples.

Personality:
Nature or Nurture?

A   The nature/nurture question is not a new one. Its roots go back at least several hundred years. In the 1600s, the British philosopher John Locke wrote that a newborn infant was a "blank slate" on which his or her education and experience would be "written." In other words, Locke believed that environment alone determined each person's identity. In the 5 1700s, the French philosopher Jean Jacques Rousseau claimed that "natural" characteristics were more important. Today, we realize that both play a role. The question now is, to what degree? To answer this question, researchers are studying identical twins, especially those who grew up in 10 different environments.

1. What is the main topic of Paragraph A?
   - (A) John Locke
   - (B) Jean Jacques Rousseau
   - (C) newborn infants
   - (D) the nature/nurture question
   - (E) identical twins

2. What details about the topic does the paragraph provide? (Choose more than one answer.)
   - (A) People have just recently begun to discuss the nature/nurture question.
   - (B) John Locke believed in "nurture."
   - (C) Jean Jacques Rousseau believed in "nature."
   - (D) Today, we know that both nature and nurture determine a person's identity.
   - (E) Researchers are studying identical twins to learn the degree to which nature and nurture determine personal characteristics.

3. The main idea of the paragraph is that _both nature and nurture play a role in determining a person's identity._

B   Jim Lewis and Jim Springer are identical twins who were separated five weeks after birth. They grew up in different families and didn't know about each other's existence. They were reunited at the age of 39. It is not surprising that they were physically alike—the same dark hair, the same height and weight. They both had high blood pressure and very bad headaches. But they also moved in the same way and made the same gestures. They both hated baseball. They both drank the same brand of beer, drove the same make of car, and spent their vacations on the same small beach in Florida. They had both married women named Linda, gotten divorced, and then married women named Betty. Studies of these and other separated twins indicate that genetics (biology) plays a significant role in determining personal characteristics and behavior.

▲ Pairs of identical twins

1. What is the main topic of Paragraph B?
- (A) a reunion
- (B) twins
- (C) similarities in twins who grew up in different environments
- (D) genetics
- (E) personal characteristics and behavior

2. What details about the topic does the paragraph provide? (Choose more than one answer.)
- (A) Jim Lewis and Jim Springer were identical twins who grew up together.
- (B) Jim Lewis and Jim Springer were identical twins who grew up separately.
- (C) They have similar physical characteristics, interests, and preferences for specific products.
- (D) They married the same woman.
- (E) Their example indicates the significance of genetics in determination of identity.

3. The main idea of the paragraph is that _____

_____

C   Various research centers are studying identical twins in order to discover the "heritability" of behavioral characteristics—that is, the degree   35 to which a trait is due to genes ("nature") instead of environment. They have reached some startling conclusions. One study found, for example, that optimism and pessimism are both very much influenced by genes, but only optimism is affected by environment, too. According to another study, genes influence our coffee consumption, but not consumption of tea.   40 Anxiety (nervousness and worry) seems to be 40 to 50 percent heritable. Another study tells us that happiness does not depend much on money or love or professional success; instead, it is 80 percent heritable! Among the traits that appear to be largely heritable are shyness, attraction to danger (thrill seeking), choice of career, and religious belief.   45

1. What is the main topic of Paragraph C?
- (A) research centers
- (B) optimism and pessimism
- (C) behavioral characteristics
- (D) happiness
- (E) heritability of behavioral characteristics

2. What details about the topic does the paragraph provide? (Choose more than one answer.)

- (A) Researchers want to understand "heritability."
- (B) Researchers are studying identical twins.
- (C) Most behavioral characteristics are the result of genes, not environment.
- (D) A person who has money, love, and success will probably be happy.
- (E) Examples of characteristics that are heritable to some degree are optimism, pessimism, happiness, thrill seeking, and choice of career.

3. The main idea of the paragraph is that _____

_____

D   It is not easy to discover the genes that influence personality. The acid that carries genetic information in every human cell, DNA, contains just four chemicals: adenine, cytosine, guanine, and thymine. But a single gene is "spelled out" by perhaps a million combinations. As the Human Genome Project (which provided a "map" of human genes) was nearing completion 50 in the spring of 2000, there were a number of newspaper headlines about specific discoveries: "Gene Linked to Anxiety," "Gay Gene!" and "Thrill Seeking Due to Genetics." The newspaper articles led people to believe that a single gene is responsible for a certain personality trait, in the same way a single gene can be responsible for a physical characteristic or disease. 55 However, one gene alone cannot cause people to become anxious or homosexual or thrill seeking. Instead, many genes work together, and they direct the combination of chemicals in the body. These chemicals, such as dopamine and serotonin (which affect a person's mood), have a significant influence on personality. 60

1. What is the main topic of Paragraph D?

- (A) the Human Genome Project
- (B) the effect of genes on personality
- (C) chemicals
- (D) DNA
- (E) thrill seeking

2. What details about the topic does the paragraph provide? (Choose more than one answer.)

- (A) It's difficult to find out which genes influence personality.
- (B) A single gene is responsible for each personality trait such as thrill seeking.
- (C) Many genes work together.
- (D) Genes direct the combination of chemicals in the body.
- (E) Chemicals have a significant influence on personality.

3. The main idea of the paragraph is that _____

_____

E   If, indeed, personality traits are, on average, about 50 percent heritable, then environment still plays an important role. Unlike other animals, human beings have choice. If our genes "program" us to be anxious, we can choose a low-stress lifestyle or choose to meditate or do relaxation exercises. But because of the powerful influence of genes, most psychologists believe that there is a limit to what we can choose to do. Thomas Bouchard, a psychologist and the director of one twin study, says that parents should not push children in directions that go against their nature. "The job of a parent," he says, "is to look for a kid's natural talents and then provide the best possible environment for them."

65

70

1. What is the main topic of Paragraph E?
   (A) the role of environment
   (B) personality traits
   (C) anxiety
   (D) psychologists
   (E) what parents should do

2. What details about the topic does the paragraph provide? (Choose more than one answer.)
   (A) Environment still plays an important role.
   (B) Human beings have choice.
   (C) Human beings can choose to do anything they want.
   (D) Psychologists say that parents should not push children against their nature.
   (E) Parents should provide their child with the best environment for the child's natural talents.

3. The main idea of the paragraph is that _____

_____

After You Read

2 **Critical Thinking: Making Inferences** Read the statements below about the article "Personality: Nature or Nurture." Put a check mark (✓) by the statements that you can infer from the reading selection. Put an X by the other statements, even if you think they are true. Then, on the line after each inference, write the phrases from which you inferred the information. Leave the other lines blank.

1. _____ The philosophical question of nature/nurture is an old one.

_____

_____

2. _____ The environments in which Jim Springer and Jim Lewis grew up had no effect on their behaviors or personalities.

_____

_____

3. _____ The goal of twin studies is to identify the amount of influence from genes and the amount from education and experiences that determine our identity.

_____

_____

4. _____ The possibility of being happy is mostly a result of our genes, not our situations in life.

_____

_____

5. _____ A single gene determines each personality characteristic.

_____

_____

6. _____ The genetic contribution to personality is complicated.

_____

_____

7. _____ Human beings are able to change their genetics.

_____

_____

3 **Discussing the Reading** Talk about your answers to these questions.

1. Do you know any identical twins? If so, how are they similar or different?

2. What characteristics are found in many of your family members or members of other families you know well? Think of characteristics such as the following:

- interests
- health
- optimism or pessimism
- anxiety
- happiness
- shyness
- thrill seeking
- choice of career
- religious belief

Responding in Writing

4 **Summarizing** Choose one paragraph from pages 200–203 or one from pages 205–209. Write a short summary of it (two or three sentences). To write this summary, follow these steps:

- Make sure that you understand the paragraph well.
- Choose the main idea.
- Find the most important details.

In order to summarize this in your own words, *don't look at the original paragraph as you write*. When you finish writing, compare your summary with those of other students who summarized the same paragraph.

5 **Writing Your Own Ideas** Choose one of these topics to write about:

- a memory you have that is different from a family member's memory of the same event
- what you can do to improve your brain
- how you and your brother or sister are similar (or different)
- how nature has influenced you and/or how your environment has influenced you

Write a one- to two-paragraph letter to one of your family members in which you explore your topic.

What is the main idea of your letter? _____

Talk It Over

6 **Genes for Crime?** It is highly possible that there is a genetic link or contribution to violence or criminality. In other words, our genes may contribute to the possibility that we will become a thief, murderer, or other type of criminal.

Psychologist David Lykken believes that people who want to become parents should be tested and given a license. If both the man and the woman have genes for violence or criminality, they should not be allowed to have a baby. He says that this will reduce crime in society. What do you think? Discuss this with a group.

Part 3 Building Vocabulary and Study Skills

1 **Understanding Words with Similar Meanings** The words in each of the following groups have similar meanings, but they are not exactly the same. Match the words with their definitions by writing the letters on the lines. If necessary, check your answers in a dictionary.

1. _____ brain

_____ mind

_____ memory

a. the faculty of thinking, reasoning, or feeling
b. the ability to remember
c. an organ of the body that controls thought and feeling

2. _____ identity

_____ personality

_____ behavior

a. the qualities of a person specific to him or her
b. the way a person is recognizable as a member of a particular group
c. the way that someone acts

3. ____ insight

    ____ knowledge

    ____ logic

a. thinking and reasoning with formal methods

b. understanding that comes from experience and learning

c. the power of using one's mind (especially the right brain) to understand something suddenly

4. ____ colleague

    ____ peer

    ____ co-worker

a. a person of equal status or age

b. a person who works in the same place as another

c. a person who works in the same profession as another

Strategy

Putting Words in Categories

It often helps to learn words in groups (words with the same stem, words with similar meanings, words with opposite meanings, etc.). One method of grouping words is to put them together in categories, such as people, animals, buildings, and so on. One kind of category is a "content area"—the subject with which all the words are associated.

Example

The following are words associated with the content area of science: *laboratory, neuroscientist, subjects, experiment*

2 **Putting Words in Categories** Cross out the word in each line that does not belong, as in the example. Write the category or content area of the words that belong together.

1. genes   ~~nurture~~   nature   biology

    genetics

2. infant   maturity   baby   newborn

3. doctor   neuroscientist   psychologist   musician

4. creativity   cerebrum   hypothalamus   corpus callosum

5. meditation   disease   insomnia   headache

6. height   eye color   weight   anxiety

7. reading   writing   dreams   mathematics

ANALYZING WORD ROOTS AND AFFIXES

It is often possible to guess the meanings of new words from affixes (prefixes and suffixes) and word roots (also called "stems.") There is a list of many affixes in Chapter 7 on pages 159–160. Below are some more affixes and word roots and their meanings.

Prefix	Meaning
a-, an-	no, without
ante-	before
micro-	small
poly-	many

Suffix	Meaning
-ism	belief in; act or practice
-ist	a person who believes in or performs a certain action

Word Root	Meaning
anthro, anthropo	man, human
ced	go, move
chrom	color
chron	time
graph	write, writing
hetero	different
homo	same
metr, meter	measure; an instrument for measuring
morph	form
phil	love
psych	mind
somn	sleep
sphere	round; ball-shaped
tele	far
theo, the	god

3 **Analyzing Word Roots and Affixes** Without using a dictionary, guess the meaning of each underlined word. Use the list of word roots and affixes. (Not all the underlined words are common.)

1. It is believed that an earthquake <u>anteceded</u> the fire.
   a. caused
   b. happened after
   c. happened before
   d. put out; worked against
   e. was caused by

2. There were some <u>amorphous</u> clouds in the sky.
   a. without form or shape
   b. thick and dark
   c. beautiful
   d. related to rain
   e. bright white

3. Many ancient peoples were <u>polytheists</u>.
   a. very well educated
   b. people with many culture centers
   c. people who studied many languages
   d. people who believed in many gods
   e. people who believed in having several wives

4. Movies often <u>anthropomorphize</u> creatures from other planets.
   a. study
   b. give human form or characteristics to
   c. present in a terrible way
   d. depict
   e. try to imagine

5. The actors wore <u>polychromatic</u> body paint.
   a. beautiful
   b. symbolic
   c. complex
   d. made of natural dyes
   e. of many colors

6. My teacher didn't appreciate my <u>heterography</u>.
   a. talking a lot in class
   b. different ideas in the speech that I gave in class
   c. logic
   d. spelling that was different from the rule
   e. answers on my geography examination

7. She sometimes has a problem with <u>somnambulism</u>.
   a. sleepwalking
   b. drinking
   c. lying
   d. breathing
   e. anxiety

8. He used a <u>telemeter</u>.
   a. instrument for seeing something very small
   b. instrument for finding directions
   c. instrument for measuring time
   d. instrument for measuring how far away an object is
   e. instrument for measuring a person's level of anxiety

4 Focusing on Words from the Academic Word List Fill in the blanks with words from the Academic Word List in the box. When you finish, turn back to pages 201–202, Paragraph E, and check your answers.

adults	intelligence	mental
colleagues	intelligent	researchers
evidence	involved	traditional
imply	maturation	
institute	mature	

A Parents of teenagers have always known that there is something, well, different about the teen years. Some parents claim that their teenage children belong to a different species. Until recently, neuroscience did not support this belief. The _____ belief was that by the
                  1
time a child was 8 to 12, the brain was completely _____.
                                2
However, very recent studies provide _____ that the
                    3
brain of a teenager differs from that of both children and adults. According to Jay Giedd of the National _____ of
                           4
_____ Health, "_____ does not stop
     5   6
at age 10, but continues into the teen years" and beyond. In fact, Giedd and his _____ found that the corpus callosum "continues
        7
growing into your 20s." Because, it is believed, the corpus callosum is _____ in self-awareness and _____,
     8   9
the new studies _____ that teens may not be as fully
          10
self-aware or as _____ as they will be later. Other
          11
_____, at McLean Hospital in Massachusetts, have found
   12
that teenagers are not as able (as _____ are) to "read"
                13
emotions on people's faces.

5 Searching the Internet Choose one of the questions below and search the Internet for the most recent information. Share this information (and any new vocabulary that you learn) with a group of students who chose different questions.

- What are techniques to improve your memory?
- What are ways to reduce stress?
- Are there differences between the brain of a musician and a nonmusician?
- What are other stories of twins who were separated at birth but reunited?
- When a man and woman are in love, do their brains "work" in different ways?

Part 4 | Focus on Testing

TOEFL® iBT

GETTING MEANING FROM CONTEXT

In the Focus on Testing section of Chapter 2, we saw some vocabulary questions like those on the TOEFL® Internet-Based Test (iBT). Those questions are all related to vocabulary that is defined or explained in a reading passage. Many of the TOEFL® iBT's vocabulary questions will be about words that are not defined or explained for you.

The TOEFL® Internet-Based Test, like many other tests, does not allow you to use a dictionary. If a term without an in-text definition or explanation comes up, you must use context to figure out its meaning. Often, you need more than the information in one sentence to discover this meaning. You may need several sentences or even paragraphs to figure it out.

1 Practice Look again at the reading, "The Human Brain—New Discoveries" on pages 200–203. Answer the following TOEFL® iBT-style questions without using a dictionary.

1. Which of the following is closest in meaning to *shedding light on*, as it is used in Paragraph A?
   - (A) learning about
   - (B) turning on a light
   - (C) making understandable
   - (D) experimenting

2. Which of the following is closest in meaning to the sentence in Paragraph B, *We are exposed to very little music or art*?
   - (A) We cannot hear or see truly important music or art.
   - (B) We are taught a little bit about music and art.
   - (C) Music and art are uncovered for everyone to observe.
   - (D) Music and art are not taught very much.

3. Which of the following is closest in meaning to *insights*, as it is used in Paragraph B?
   - (A) the dreams we have while sleeping
   - (B) moments when we suddenly understand something
   - (C) moments when we are very logical
   - (D) the abilities of the human eye

4. Which of the following pairs is closest in meaning to the two uses of *cases* (lines 28 and 34) in Paragraph C?

    Ⓐ examples and memories

    Ⓑ memories and crimes

    Ⓒ examples and events that need police attention

    Ⓓ crimes and people who belong in prison

5. Which of the following is closest in meaning to *rotate*, as it is used in Paragraph F?

    Ⓐ change jobs

    Ⓑ look at

    Ⓒ understand

    Ⓓ turn around

6. Which of the following is closest in meaning to *intuition*, as it is used in Paragraph G?

    Ⓐ mystery

    Ⓑ the ability to read quickly and accurately

    Ⓒ the ability to understand without using logic

    Ⓓ emotions

7. Which of the following is closest in meaning to *read*, as it is used in Paragraphs E, F, and G?

    Ⓐ understand the meaning of

    Ⓑ understand writings about

    Ⓒ show to someone

    Ⓓ make announcements about

Self-Assessment Log

Read the lists below. Check (✓) the strategies and vocabulary that you learned in this chapter. Look through the chapter or ask your instructor about the strategies and words that you do not understand.

Reading and Vocabulary-Building Strategies

❑ Previewing the reading

❑ Distinguishing facts from assumptions

❑ Skimming for main ideas

❑ Understanding words with similar meanings

❑ Putting words in categories

❑ Understanding word roots and affixes

Target Vocabulary

Nouns

			Adjectives
❑ adults*	❑ institute*	❑ neuroscientists	❑ involved*
❑ colleagues*	❑ intelligence*	❑ personality	❑ mature*
❑ evidence*	❑ logic*	❑ psychologist*	❑ mental*
❑ identity*	❑ maturation*	❑ researchers*	
❑ infant	❑ maturity*	**Verb**	
❑ insights*	❑ memory	❑ imply*	

* These words are from the Academic Word List. For more information on this list, see www.vuw.ac.nz/lals/research/awl.

Ceremonies

When did you last go to a wedding? What was it like? The first reading selection explores universal rituals called "rites of passage." Weddings are just one type of rite of passage. Funerals and graduations are other types. In Part 2, you will read about and discuss modern variations on traditional rituals. There are unique ways that cultures all around the world are celebrating and marking rites of passage. You will be able to discuss some of your favorite ceremonies. Part 3 includes activities to help you develop and build your vocabulary. The final part of this chapter focuses on comprehension of a reading selection that deals with a rite of passage that many teenagers anticipate—driving.

❝ When humans participate in ceremony, they enter a sacred space. Everything outside of that space shrivels in importance. Time takes on a different dimension. **❞**

—Sun Bear
Medicine Chief of the Bear Tribe Medicine Society (1929–1992)

Connecting to the Topic

1. What do you think these people are celebrating? Why?

2. Name ten adjectives to describe this photo.

3. What are some of your favorite ceremonies or celebrations? Describe one of them.

Rites of Passage

Before You Read

1 Getting Started Discuss these questions in small groups.

1. What are some ceremonies or rituals that you are familiar with?

2. What kinds of birthday celebrations have you been a part of? Do you know of any cultures that don't celebrate birthdays?

3. Is there any ceremony or ritual that people perform differently now from the way they performed it in the past? Explain.

2 Previewing the Reading Look over the reading and the photos on pages 221–224. Discuss the questions below with a partner.

1. What is the topic of the reading? What are the five subtopics?

2. Describe the photos. What is new or interesting to you in the photos?

3. Write six questions that you expect the reading to answer.

_____

_____

_____

_____

_____

_____

3 Previewing Vocabulary Read the words and phrases below. Listen to the pronunciation. Put a check mark (✓) next to the words you know. For the words that you don't know, *don't* use a dictionary. Try to understand them from the reading.

Nouns
- ❑ bride
- ❑ coffin
- ❑ coming-of-age
- ❑ rituals
- ❑ cremation
- ❑ deceased
- ❑ delivery
- ❑ funerals
- ❑ groom
- ❑ guidance
- ❑ incorporation
- ❑ monks
- ❑ negotiations
- ❑ pregnancy
- ❑ proposal
- ❑ pyre
- ❑ rite of passage
- ❑ scriptures
- ❑ taboos
- ❑ trousseau
- ❑ vision

Verbs
- ❑ chant
- ❑ regain
- ❑ vary
- ❑ wail

Adjectives
- ❑ indigenous
- ❑ nomadic
- ❑ previous

Expression
- ❑ ask for (a woman's) hand

4 **Reading an Article** As you read the following selection, think about the questions that you wrote in Activity 2. Can you find the answers in the reading? Read the selection. Do not use a dictionary. Then do the exercises that follow the reading.

Rites of Passage

A   **A**mong many **indigenous** peoples of North America, a 16-year-old boy leaves his family and experiences a ritual in which he spends four days and nights alone in a small cave dug into the side of a mountain. He experiences cold, hunger, thirst, fear, and sleeplessness. He has with him several objects of symbolic value. One of these is a pipe. The belief is that the   5 smoke from the pipe goes up to the spirit world and allows power to come down. His hope is to have a **vision** in which he receives insight and **guidance** for his way in life. At the beginning of the ritual, he is a boy, with a boy's name. At the end, when he comes out of the cave, he is a man, with an adult name, and he knows what his livelihood will be. This ritual, called a **vision quest**, is   10 an example of a rite of passage. Rites of passage are not found only in indigenous cultures. They are universal, found in all cultures, and include certain birthdays, **coming-of-age** rituals, weddings, and **funerals**.

What Are Rites of Passage?

B   Anthropologists use the term **rite of passage** for a ceremony or ritual of transition that marks a person's change from one status or social   15 position to another. Although such rites differ in details, they share certain characteristics. All rites of passage include three stages: separation, transition, and **incorporation** of the person back into the society. In the first stage, the person is separated from his or her **previous** status. Sometimes in this stage, as in a vision quest, the person is *literally* and   20 *physically* separated from the community. In the transition stage, the person is in between—not in either status. In the last stage, the person re-joins the society, now with the new status.

Birth Rituals in Korea

C   Many cultures have a rite of passage that marks the birth of a baby. In Korean tradition, the rituals begin during the woman's **pregnancy**. Some of   25 these rituals are still practiced today, but some are not. There are food taboos—certain foods that pregnant women are not supposed to eat. These include hot and spicy foods and broken crackers or cookies. In the past, close

▲ The first birthday celebration for this Korean baby

to the time of birth, there were various symbolic actions that signified an easy **delivery** of the baby. For example, family members left doors open, and did not repair rooms, doors, or fireplaces in the kitchen. Today, as in the past, there is special care to keep the mother and baby well after the birth. The mother traditionally eats seaweed soup, full of iron, to **regain** her strength. She is also not supposed to drink cold water for 21 days.

D   At the age of 100 days, there is a special ceremony. Family, friends, and neighbors gather to admire the baby, give thanks for the baby's health, and have a big meal. More important is the first birthday. At this time, the baby, dressed in a traditional outfit, is seated in front of a table with all kinds of objects on it. For example, they may include a bow and arrow (which represents the military), money (wealth) string (a long life), and a pencil and a book (knowledge). These days, people can add any object, such as a baseball, if they want their child to be a great baseball player. The parents encourage the baby to choose something. Everyone is very interested in which object the baby reaches for because the belief is that this object indicates something about the baby's future. Now the baby is truly a person, a member of the family and the community.

Islamic Weddings

E   A wedding in any culture is an important rite of passage. In Islam, the specific stages of a wedding ceremony may **vary** from country to country, but most share certain characteristics. Typical is the traditional wedding of the Bedouin—**nomadic** Arabs who move from place to place (although these days many are settling in urban areas). A Bedouin wedding can last up to a week and reflects the ancient Arab belief that marriage is not just a joining of two people; it is the joining of two families.

▲ A Bedouin bride with henna

F   The first step in a Bedouin wedding is the **proposal**, in which the father of the **groom** (the man) and their close relatives visit the home of the **bride** (the woman) to **ask for her hand** in marriage. The next step involves **negotiations** between the two families and a marriage contract—a formal, legal agreement. The third step is the henna party, for just the bride and her female friends and relatives. At this party, there is song and dance, and the bride's hands and feet are exquisitely decorated with henna, a dark brown paste. The henna is more than just skin paint. It is associated with health, beauty, and luck. After this, the groom's relatives arrive at the bride's house. Men perform a special dance with swords while women admire the bride's **trousseau**—the personal objects that she will bring to her marriage such as clothing, gifts from the groom's family, and jewelry. The jewelry is usually large, made of silver and expensive stones, and decorated with calligraphy. In the fifth step, the men and women sit separately, and guests bring gifts. In the last step, as the bride enters her new home, she and her new husband meet for the first time. They are officially married. Actually, there is perhaps one more step. One week after the wedding, the bride visits her parents and brings them gifts. This is a symbol of her comfort in her new home.

Funerals in Thailand

G   A person's final passage is death. Every culture has rituals in which the person and his or her family make this transition. In Thailand, a Buddhist country, people believe that after death, the person is born again, in another body. Everything the person did in life—both good and bad—determines whether the next life will be a good one or not. Of course, family members and friends want to achieve a good

▲ Buddhist monks chanting at a funeral pyre

rebirth for the **deceased**, and this is a major goal of a Thai funeral.

H   As a Thai person is dying, the family members encourage him or her to think about Buddhist **scriptures**—holy writing—or to repeat one of the names of the Buddha. Then, after the person dies, the family takes the deceased to the temple. They lay the body down, cover him or her, and place one hand outside of the blanket. The family and friends show respect by washing the hand of the deceased. Then they put the body in a **coffin**. People burn candles and sweet-smelling incense around the coffin, and Buddhist **monks** come to **chant**—recite prayers. In the next step, perhaps three days, one week, or 100 days later, friends, relatives, and monks take the coffin to the cemetery for the **cremation**, at which there is more chanting. The coffin is placed on a funeral **pyre**. At this point, people come up to it with white paper flowers, candles, and incense. One by one, they light the pyre, and the body is burned. It is believed that when the body still exists, the spirit can benefit from the chanting; however, when the body is cremated, the spirit is cut off from the world. After the cremation, people go home. The family usually takes some of the ashes home, but some families keep the ashes at the temple.

The Timelessness of Rites of Passage

The origin of such rites of passage is unclear. However, there is reason 115 to believe that such rites existed long before the beginning of history, before there was any system of writing to record the rituals. In caves and on rock walls all over the world, there are paintings from the Paleolithic Era (Old Stone Age)—exquisite art that may have been part of the people's rituals. In the graves of even these very ancient people, objects have been 120 carefully placed. Anthropologists believe that this may be evidence of early religion and of the human need to mark the transitions from one stage to another in their lives—a universal, timeless need.

After You Read

5 Getting the Main Ideas Fill in this chart with information from the reading about four rites of passage. The first one is done for you.

Rite of Passage	Previous Status	Transition	New Status
vision quest	a boy	4 days isolated in a cave, not a boy or a man	a man with an adult name

6 Checking Vocabulary Turn back to the vocabulary preview on page 220. Which words do you now know? Check them off (✓). With a partner, discuss what you think each word means. For words that you aren't sure of, look through the reading to find them in bold and try to guess the meaning.

7 Making Inferences Put a check mark next to each statement below that you can infer from the reading selection. Do not check the other statements, even if you think they are true. Then, after the checked statements, write the phrases from which you inferred the information.

1. _____ In a vision quest, a boy finds out about his future career from his vision.

_____

_____

2. _____ Korean parents might put a soccer ball in front of their one-year-old if they want him or her to be a great soccer player.

_____

_____

3. _____ The Bedouin marriage contract involves money.

_____

_____

4. _____ People who put objects in the graves of the dead may have religious beliefs.

_____

_____

UNDERSTANDING CHRONOLOGY

Time words show the relationship between events and their order in time. Here are just a few examples.

first	beginning	after that	after	last	the next step
second	next	then	at this point	finally	

8 Understanding Chronology Look back at Paragraph H on pages 223–224. Quickly look for time words; mark them as you find them. Then use them to help you number these steps in order from first to last.

1. _____ People take the coffin to the cemetery.

2. _____ Friends and family gather for music and the comfort of each other's company.

3. _____ Family members encourage the person to think religious thoughts.

4. _____ People light the funeral pyre, and the body is cremated.

5. _____ Relatives begin to wail loudly.

UNDERSTANDING SYMBOLS

In certain fields, such as anthropology, psychology, and literature, academic readings frequently include *symbols*. Symbols are actual, tangible objects; in other words, they are something that you can touch. They represent either a different object or—more often—an *idea*. For example, a flag is a symbol of a country; a road is symbolic of a person's life. Sometimes the reading interprets the symbols, but sometimes you, the reader, must make inferences and figure out what the symbols mean.

Here are some words that indicate the inclusion of a symbol:

symbolizes   is symbolic of   is associated with   represents   stands for

9 **Understanding Symbols** Read the questions below. Turn back to the reading selection to find the answers. Look for words that indicate symbols.

1. In a vision quest, what does the smoke from the pipe symbolize?

2. In a Korean home, what are some things that people might do as a pregnant woman nears the time of delivery? List them. What do these actions symbolize?

3. In Bedouin culture, what does the henna symbolize?

10 **Checking Your Understanding** Turn back to Activity 2 on page 220 and answer the questions that you wrote.

11 **Applying the Reading** Choose one rite of passage from your culture (but not one that was included in the reading selection). You will tell a group of classmates about this rite. To prepare for this, think about what happens in the rite and fill in information in the graphic organizer below.

The Rite of Passage: _____

Previous Status	Transition	New Status

Steps (Details)

Are there symbols? _____

If so, what are they? _____

New Days, New Ways: Changing Rites of Passage

Before You Read

1 **Identifying the Main Idea and Writing a Summary** For each paragraph that follows, practice what you have learned about finding the main idea and summarizing paragraphs. First, read each paragraph without using a dictionary. Mark the information in any way that helps you to understand it. (For example, you could highlight the main idea with one color and the supporting details with another.) Then write the main idea in one sentence. To summarize the paragraph write the main idea and add the important details in as few words as possible. (You might need to write more than one sentence.) Paragraph A is done as an example.

New Days, New Ways: Changing Rites of Passage

Vision Quests for Everyone

A   For centuries, Native Americans have gone through vision quests in hopes of gaining guidance and direction. Several companies and organizations are now offering a similar experience for non-Indians. For a fee, anyone who is looking for a new direction in life can go to certain wilderness areas in Canada or the United States and go through such a   5
ritual. The details may vary from one organization to another, but in most cases, experts in psychology or Native American culture help to prepare the person in advance. This preparation usually lasts for several days and includes meditation, natural vegetarian food, lessons in the meaning of a vision quest and perhaps dream groups, in which the seeker of the vision   10
discusses his or her dreams with psychological analysts. As on a traditional vision quest, people on this new-age quest spend one to four days alone in the wilderness. However, a difference is that they might choose to sleep in a tent and to bring drinking water. Some Native Americans are angry that non-Indians are doing this. They see it as a fad and say that the quest is   15
meaningless to a person outside the culture, tradition, and religion.

Main idea: _Anyone can now experience a Native American vision quest, for a fee._

Summary: _Although some Native Americans do not approve, several companies and organizations are offering non-Indians the opportunity (for a fee) to experience a vision quest that is similar to the traditional one._

A New Emirati Wedding

B   In the United Arab Emirates, on the Arabian Peninsula, the traditional wedding seems to be changing, at least for some people. A typical Emirati wedding is extremely lavish—elegant, expensive, and huge. There might be 1,000 guests at the three-day celebration for the bride and groom. The groom has to pay these bills, and after such a wedding, the couple begins their marriage in terrible debt. Each wedding seems to be bigger than the one before it. Several years ago, the government decided that things were getting out of hand—out of control—so they started a Marriage Fund. This is money for young Emirati men who agree to marry Emirati women, not foreigners. Many of these men agree to have a group celebration. At one such group celebration, at which the UAE president was the guest of honor, there were several of the components of a traditional wedding: a lavish feast of exquisite food and entertainment by Bedouin dancers waving their swords. The difference? There were 650 grooms. It was, one person pointed out, "a symbol of a new spirit of economy."

▲ Grooms at a mass wedding in the United Arab Emirates

Main idea: _____

_____

Summary: _____

_____

_____

Getting Married—Japanese Style?

C   In Japan, too, weddings are different these days. A popular wedding is a *seiyaku*, which means "sincere vow or promise." Although less than one percent of all Japanese are Christian, 80 percent choose this Western-style Christian wedding. It certainly *looks* like a Western wedding; the bride wears a white gown, for example, and the groom wears a tuxedo. It also closely follows all the steps in a Christian wedding: there is the processional (in which the bride walks down the center aisle of the church to join the groom at the front), hymns (religious songs), readings of Christian scriptures, the exchange of vows, and of course the wedding kiss. In fact, some people say that this new Japanese Christian wedding is more traditional than most Christian weddings in the West, except for the fact that the couple is usually careful to choose a "lucky day" for the ceremony. So why do so many Japanese choose this style of wedding when the Japanese culture already has rich, beautiful marriage traditions? One answer may be that this is a trend, and the Japanese are somewhat famous for following new trends. Another reason may be that traditional Japanese weddings are even more expensive than those in the Western style.

▲ A Japanese *seiyaku:* more traditional than a Western wedding?

Main idea: _____

_____

Summary: _____

_____

_____

Weddings Anywhere, Any Way

D   While most Japanese weddings these days are in a traditional Western style, many couples in Western countries are looking for a *non*-Western wedding experience that expresses something of their personal interests. It is now possible to get married in a helicopter, on a ski slope, in the ocean (with dolphins, in Florida), in a hot-air balloon, or in a drive-through in Las Vegas (in which the couple stays in their car for the ceremony). For couples who want both to travel and have a traditional wedding (just not perhaps *their* tradition), it is possible to have a Hindu wedding in Goa, India. The groom wears an Indian *kurta*, and the bride wears a red sari and traditional Indian jewelry, with her hands decorated in henna. They walk

▲ A wedding that literally flies—in a hot-air balloon

around a pyre seven times and repeat their seven promises of love. The ⁷⁵ ceremony is conducted by a Hindu priest, either at a temple or on a beach.

Main idea: _____

_____

Summary: _____

_____

_____

Unique Ways of "Moving On"

E   People are also designing unusual funerals. Several years ago, after the death of an American man who created a popular TV series, his body was cremated, and the ashes from this cremation were sent into space to spend eternity among the stars. In Britain, there are special funerals for people ⁸⁰ who love motorcycles; one company offers "slow, fast, and very fast funerals." In Malaysia, a group called "33 Taiping Music Band" plays music at funerals. They perform at Buddhist, Christian, or Hindu funerals. The lead singer, Chan Yoke Cheong, speaks fluent English, Cantonese, and Mandarin, so it is not surprising that he also sings in these languages. But ⁸⁵ what might be surprising is that he also perfectly sings hymns in Tamil—an Indian language he does not speak—at Hindu funerals. The band wears white shirts, black pants, ties, and large leather cowboy hats. Maybe the strangest recent funeral, however, was held in Pennsylvania, in the United States. James Henry Smith had been a huge fan of an American football ⁹⁰ team, the Pittsburgh Steelers. At his funeral, the guests walked into the funeral home to find Mr. Smith's body not in a coffin but instead in his favorite chair. The deceased was sitting there, wearing the colors of the Steelers. On a small table next to the chair were a pack of cigarettes and a can of beer. In front of him, through the funeral, a TV played a tape of a ⁹⁵ Steelers game. His friends and family knew that he would approve.

Main idea: _____

_____

Summary: _____

_____

_____

Strategy

Identifying Opinions

It's important to be able to recognize the difference between facts and opinions. A fact can be checked and proven, even if you aren't sure if it is true or not. An opinion is an idea that people might disagree about. An opinion expresses a belief, idea, or feeling. One way to distinguish the two is to be aware of words that indicate *opinion*. Some of these words are modals (*should, shouldn't, ought to*), but most are adjectives or adverbs.

Examples

bad (-ly)	exquisite	good (well)	surprising
beautiful	favorite	horrible	too
brilliant	fun	interesting	wonderful (-ly)

Alternatively, instead of looking for specific words when you are trying to recognize opinions, you might try asking yourself, "Would some people disagree with this?" If your answer is *yes*, then it might be an opinion.

2 **Distinguishing Facts from Opinions** On the lines, write *fact* or *opinion*, according to what is stated or implied in the sentence.

1. _____ Non-Indians can go through a rite of passage similar to the vision quest of Native Americans.

2. _____ People who go through a new vision quest are not respectful of Native American culture.

3. _____ The government of the United Arab Emirates is trying to encourage unmarried Emirati men to marry Emirati women.

4. _____ Traditional Emirati weddings are too lavish.

5. _____ Traditional Japanese weddings are more beautiful than the new Western-style ones.

6. _____ A majority of Japanese couples choose a Western-style wedding.

7. _____ Many couples in Western countries are looking for a nontraditional wedding experience.

8. _____ It's very strange to get married in the ocean.

9. _____ Chan Yoke Cheong sings in perfect Tamil.

10. _____ People who don't approve of unusual funerals are too rigid.

3 **Discussing the Reading: Conducting a Survey** You are going to interview the students in your class and ask for their opinions on weddings. Then record their answers on another piece of paper.

1. Before you begin, think about your own answers to the questions and write them in the chart below.

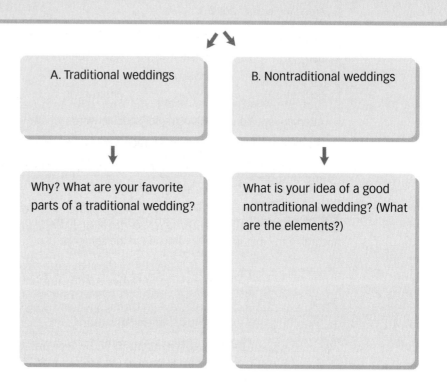

Which do you prefer? (Choose *one*. Then follow the arrow to the next question.)

A. Traditional weddings

B. Nontraditional weddings

Why? What are your favorite parts of a traditional wedding?

What is your idea of a good nontraditional wedding? (What are the elements?)

2. After you have decided on your own answers, pick up your notebook and a pencil. Move around the room. Interview as many people as possible in the time that you have.

- Record how many people answer "traditional" and how many answer "nontraditional." (卌 = 5, for example)
- For students who answer "traditional," ask them the question under A. Record their answers in note form.
- For students who answer "nontraditional," ask them the question under B. Record their answers in note form.

3. When you finish, come together as a class and discuss your results. Do more people prefer traditional or nontraditional weddings? Did any answers surprise you?

Responding in Writing

SUMMARIZING A WHOLE READING

So far in this book, you've written summaries of single paragraphs. Here are some suggestions for summarizing a longer piece.

- Begin by highlighting key parts of the original piece. Mark the main ideas with one color and important details with another.

- Make sure that you truly understand the original article. It's not possible to write a good summary of something that you don't understand.

- Choose the main idea of each section or paragraph to include in your summary. Also choose a few of the most important details.

- Group some ideas from several sections or paragraphs together in one sentence.

- Remember that *summarizing is not translation*. It's usually easier to write a good summary if you put the original aside and not look at it as you write.

- In writing a summary, use your own words. Do not simply copy from the original. To use your own words, follow these steps:

  - Change sentence structure whenever possible. For example, change the active voice to the passive voice or the passive voice to the active.

  - Use synonyms whenever possible.

  - Do not try to find synonyms for technical terms or for words for which there is no synonym.

4 **Practice** Choose one of the two reading selections from this chapter: "Rites of Passage" (pages 221–224) or "New Days, New Ways: Changing Rites of Passage" (pages 227–230). Summarize it in one paragraph. When you finish, compare your summary to that of another student who has summarized the same selection.

5 **Writing Your Own Ideas** Choose one of these topics to write about.

- a traditional rite of passage in your culture
- a new or changing rite of passage in your culture
- your reaction to one of the rituals that you have read about
- your opinion of one of the nontraditional rituals that you have read about
- your idea of the perfect wedding (or funeral)

Write a one-paragraph letter to your teacher in which you explore your topic.

What is the main idea of your paragraph? _____

1 **Determining Categories** Circle the words that typically belong in each underlined category.

1. actions at funerals

      praying   chanting   wailing   grinning

2. people in religion

      priests   colleagues   monks   merchants

3. words that are associated with death

      trousseau   coffin   cremation   deceased

4. groups of people

      organization   tribe   community   society

5. expressions of emotion

      hug   wail   suppress   shout

6. rites of passage

      proposal   wedding   indigenous   coming-of-age

ANALYZING WORD ROOTS AND PREFIXES

Here are some more word roots and prefixes and their meanings.

Prefix	Meaning
im-	in; not
pro-	before; forward

Word Root	Meaning
corp	body
dox	opinion, belief
gam	marriage
mort	death
ortho	straight; correct
scribe; script	writing
spir	breathe

2 **Analyzing Word Roots and Prefixes** Without using a dictionary, guess the meaning of each underlined word. Use the list of word roots and prefixes on the previous page and look back at the list in Chapter 9, page 213, for additional help.

1. The mortality rate is very high in that village.
   - (A) birth
   - (B) employment
   - (C) marriage
   - (D) divorce
   - (E) death

2. He's in the hospital on a respirator.
   - (A) strict diet
   - (B) machine that pumps blood (as the heart does)
   - (C) machine to help him breathe
   - (D) special bed to help his back problems
   - (E) machine that checks his temperature regularly

3. The physician studied the corpse.
   - (A) dead body
   - (B) new medical instrument
   - (C) ceremony
   - (D) medical text
   - (E) evidence

4. People in that society believe in polygamy.
   - (A) many gods
   - (B) marriage
   - (C) marriage to more than one person
   - (D) the necessity of marrying someone from a different village
   - (E) the economic benefits of globalization

5. Without the wedding ring, the ceremony couldn't proceed.
   - (A) end
   - (B) begin
   - (C) go forward; continue
   - (D) occur
   - (E) be legal and official

6. It was an unorthodox ceremony.
   - (A) not interesting or worth attention
   - (B) not religious
   - (C) not in a church
   - (D) not straight
   - (E) not according to accepted opinion

7. Their love was immortal.
   - (A) never dying
   - (B) beautiful
   - (C) pure
   - (D) inside marriage
   - (E) not accepted by society

8. The ceremony was transcribed.
   - (A) postponed
   - (B) concluded
   - (C) moved to another place
   - (D) cancelled
   - (E) written down

3 **Focusing on Words from the Academic Word List** Fill in the blanks with words from the Academic Word List in the box. When you finish, turn back to page 221, Paragraph B, and check your answers.

community	physically	status	vision
incorporation	previous	transition	

Anthropologists use the term *rite of passage* for a ceremony or ritual of _____ that marks a person's change from one _____ or social position to another. Although such rites differ in details, they share certain characteristics. All rites of passage include three stages: separation, transition, and _____ of the person back into the society. In the first stage, the person is separated from his or her _____ status. Sometimes in this stage, as in a _____ quest, the person is *literally* and _____ separated from the _____ . In the transition stage, the person is in between—not in either status. In the last stage, the person re-joins the society, now with the new status.

4 **Searching the Internet** Choose one of these rites of passage to research, or select your own. Search the Internet for sites that tell about nontraditional ways to conduct it. Tell your group about either the strangest or the most interesting way that you found.

- a wedding
- a funeral
- an engagement
- a vision quest
- other: _____

TOEFL® iBT

TOPIC-SENTENCE PATTERNS ON THE TOEFL® INTERNET-BASED TEST (iBT)

The reading "Rites of Passage" (pages 221–224) shows several interesting main-idea patterns. You can see that the main idea is not always stated in the first sentence of a paragraph.

For example, the main idea of Paragraph A in "Rites of Passage" is expressed at the end. Also, two sentences, not just one, form the main idea. Paragraph B has its main idea in a sentence in a familiar position, at the beginning. The main idea for Paragraph C can be found in the first two sentences of the paragraph.

1 Practice Read the following passage, paying special attention to the main idea of each paragraph. Then do the exercise that follows.

Learning to Drive: An American Rite of Passage

A   Every society has rites of passage that fit its culture. In hunter-gatherer societies, passing into adulthood often means going out to a hunting ground to prove one's strength and courage. In societies that value group cooperation over individual glory, the rite of passage may involve joining an organization like the army or a large company and adopting its discipline. American society is perfectly reflected in the rituals of learning to drive and getting one's license.

B   This observation is not just a joke, a way of laughing at America's car culture. Examine driving in relation to other well-known rites of passage. For one thing, most Americans learn how to drive at 15 or 16, about the age for ritually entering adulthood in other cultures. For another, objects that are significant in the culture, such as paperwork and money, are a crucial part of the rite. Other cultures might ritually use rice, water, or clothing instead. Also the values of American culture—such as mobility, independence, and individual responsibility—can be pursued through this rite. The values of other cultures (group loyalty, physical endurance, religious devotion, etc.) are supported by their own rites of passage.

C   Although a few Americans never learn to drive or learn how only in their later years, the vast majority learn in their mid-teens. The timing of the ritual has great significance. Most young Americans have, by this time, gone through puberty (the changes in their body chemistry that make them adults). Most 15-year-olds are tall enough to see clearly from the driver's seat and strong enough to turn a steering wheel. They also typically have coordination good enough to operate windshield wipers, headlights, turn signals, and a car radio while safely steering. At earlier ages, they might not have been physically able to handle such tasks.

D Also at this time, they are ready to move slowly from their homes and schools toward the wider world. Both family and school prepare teenagers for this transition. Many American parents take their children to an empty parking lot at the age of 12 to 15 in order to let them safely get used to the layout and handling of a car. The parent sits in the passenger seat and tries not to show fear as the child learns how to work the accelerator pedal, the brakes, and other basic controls. The child is then put into the school's hands. Public high schools usually offer "driver's ed" classes to 15-year-olds. The familiar school environment comforts them as they learn about the world beyond and its very serious, impersonal driving requirements.

E The ultimate goal for each driving student involves certification from the state that one is qualified to drive. This comes in the form of a temporary driver's permit, then a full driver's license, issued by the state in which the student lives. American society treasures such state-issued permits and reveres the processes for obtaining them. Almost any profession, from hair-dressing to hotel operation to medicine, involves them. Learning to drive is the perfect introduction to this paperwork-oriented society. Insurance applications, approval slips, score sheets for driving tests—all are good preparation for a lifetime of petitioning the state and large companies for permission or fair treatment.

F America's cultural preoccupation with money is also addressed in the ritual. For perhaps the first time in his or her life, a student faces significant short- and long-term expenses. Most middle-class Americans require a teenager to pay at least part of the cost of driving a car. Parents may help pay for the car itself, or the insurance, but teenagers usually have to buy their own gas and pay their own tickets if they have an encounter with the police. Teenagers who may have thought of money as a toy now see it as a necessary thing. Indeed, a teenager may be motivated to get his or her first part-time job in order to pay the costs of driving a car.

G A diverse place like the United States has several systems of values operating alongside each other. It is fair to say, however, that some values are almost universal among Americans. One of these is mobility, the freedom to go where you want, when you want. Another is independence, the freedom to act as you see fit without needing help from any authority. Still another is personal responsibility, the sense that you take the credit or blame for your own successes or your own mistakes. Being a driver brings each of these deep-seated values into play.

H Nothing promotes mobility like having a car and the fuel to run it. Teenagers who were used to staying within a mile or two of home gain the ability to explore an entire city. They usually want to do so without having to explain themselves to their parents, so they independently learn directions, practice safe-driving techniques, and budget their money for travel. Failure to do so will require them to ask their parents for help, which they do not want to do. And driving is serious, literally a matter of life and death. Even though teenagers are often not as careful as they ought to be, they usually recognize that they are responsible for the lives and safety of themselves and others while they are on the road. This represents a true passage from the world of a child into that of an adult.

2 **Identifying the Main Idea** For each paragraph, write the main idea on the lines below. If a paragraph does not have its own topic sentence, write the main idea in your own words. Then compare your answers with those of one or two other students. There may be some disagreements about answers because different students will analyze the reading in different ways.

1. Paragraph A _____

_____

2. Paragraph B _____

_____

3. Paragraph C _____

_____

4. Paragraph D _____

_____

5. Paragraph E _____

_____

6. Paragraph F _____

_____

7. Paragraph G _____

_____

8. Paragraph H _____

_____

Self-Assessment Log

Read the lists below. Check (✓) the strategies and vocabulary that you learned in this chapter. Look through the chapter or ask your instructor about the strategies and words that you do not understand.

Reading and Vocabulary-Building Strategies

- ❑ Getting the main ideas
- ❑ Making inferences
- ❑ Understanding chronology
- ❑ Understanding symbols

- ❑ Applying the reading
- ❑ Distinguishing facts from opinions
- ❑ Summarizing: review and extension
- ❑ Analyzing word roots and affixes

Target Vocabulary

Nouns

- ❑ coffin
- ❑ community*
- ❑ cremation
- ❑ deceased
- ❑ funerals

- ❑ incorporation*
- ❑ monks
- ❑ rite of passage
- ❑ status*
- ❑ transition*

- ❑ trousseau
- ❑ vision*

Verbs

- ❑ chant
- ❑ wail

Adjectives

- ❑ indigenous
- ❑ previous*

Adverb

- ❑ physically*

* These words are from the Academic Word List. For more information on this list, see www.vuw.ac.nz/lals/research/awl.

Vocabulary Index

*These words are from the Academic Word List. For more information on this list, see
http://www.vuw.ac.nz/lals/research/awl.

job hunting
job opening
job security
keep up with
leisure
livelihood
manufacturing jobs
old-fashioned
online
outsourcing
overwork
passionate
personnel office
posts
rigid*
secure*
self-confidence
technology* field
telecommuting
temporary*
ulcers
upgrade
varies (vary)*
workaholism
workforce
worldwide

Chapter 5

areas*
competitive edge
creative*
culture*
designers*
distinguish
economy*
enroll
enthusiastically
essence
experience
expert*
fads
invested*
irrational*
lifestyles
profit
slang
so*
spot

suddenly
survive*
trend*
trendspotting

Chapter 6

benefits*
created*
economic*
fuel
gap
get around
global*
goods
hands on
harbor
hold (someone) back
in the market for
infrastructure*
landlocked
nutrients
obstacle
on board
on your own
policies (policy)*
priority*
private eye
protectionist policies
pulled into
reduce
require*
rough it
runs
subsidy*
take (one's) time
technology*
tide
track down
whodunit

Chapter 7

acquire*
apparently*
brain
capacity*
chatter
claims

coin
communication*
context*
creatures
degree
emotions
evidence*
feeds
focusing*
gender*
gestures
glue
grin
head (of something)
head back
identical*
journal*
mammals
nature
nurture
organs
percent*
picked up
pod
prey
primates
realize
reassure
research*
respond*
shedding light on
situation
species
structures*
subjects
swagger
upright
verbal
vocalize
wagging

Chapter 8

arabesques
archaeologists
architecture
armor
called*
calligraphy

---

*These words are from the Academic Word List. For more information on this list, see
http://www.vuw.ac.nz/lals/research/awl.

cosmetics
culture*
depict
destination
documents*
experts*
flowered
founded*
mausoleums
merchants
mosques
oasis
over*
project*
region*
significant*
silk
statues
technology*
to this end
traditional*
under*

Chapter 9

adults*
colleagues*
evidence*
identity*
imply*
infant
insights*
institute*
intelligence*
involved*
logic*
maturation*
mature*
maturity*
memory
mental*
neuroscientists
personality
psychologist*
researchers*

Chapter 10

chant
coffin
community*
cremation
deceased
funerals
incorporation*
indigenous
monks
physically*
previous*
rite of passage
status*
transition*
trousseau
vision*
wail

---

*These words are from the Academic Word List. For more information on this list, see
http://www.vuw.ac.nz/lals/research/awl.

Skills Index

Photo and Text Credits

Photo Credits

Text Credits